PLAYING WITH DESIRE:
CHRISTOPHER MARLOWE AND THE ART OF TANTALIZATION

FRED B. TROMLY

Playing with Desire: Christopher Marlowe and the Art of Tantalization

UNIVERSITY OF TORONTO PRESS
Toronto Buffalo London

PR 2677 D47 T76 1998

Printed in Canada

ISBN 0-8020-4355-0

Printed on acid-free paper

Canadian Cataloguing in Publication Data

Tromly, Frederic B., 1943–
    Playing with desire : Christopher Marlowe and the art of tantalization

Includes bibliographical references and index.
ISBN 0-8020-4355-0

1. Marlowe, Christopher, 1564–1593 – Criticism, interpretation, etc.
2. Desire in literature. I. Title.

PR2677.D47T76 1998   822'.3   C98-931506-1

University of Toronto Press acknowledges the financial assistance to its
publishing program of the Canada Council for the Arts and the Ontario Arts
Council.

This book has been published with the help of a grant from the Humanities
and Social Sciences Federation of Canada, using funds provided by the Social
Sciences and Humanities Research Council of Canada.

For my mother and father –
Ruth and Fred Tromly –
with love and gratitude

Contents

Acknowledgments

This book has benefited from a generous amount of institutional support, most decisively a grant and year-long teaching-release stipend from what was then the Social Sciences and Humanities Research Council of Canada. Without the Council's support, I might not have undertaken this work, and certainly the outcome would have been a diminished thing. More recently, the award of a grant from the Aid to Scholarly Publications Programme of the Humanities and Social Sciences Federation of Canada made the publication possible. The Marlowe Society of America and its then-president Constance Kuriyama provided a useful forum for testing ideas at the Third International Marlowe Conference (Corpus Christi College, Cambridge, 1993).

Without exception, the staff at the University of Toronto Press has been a pleasure to work with. In overseeing the production, Barb Porter remained amiable, even after I made some late changes; and at every stage the support of Suzanne Rancourt has been, in every sense of the word, decisive. Judy Williams has been an ideal copy editor, tactful but unsparing. I am also beholden to the anonymous scholar who wrote an excellent reader's report for the Press. Before the Press saw it, Didi Pollock formatted and greatly improved the consistency of the text.

This book has Trent University, my academic home for almost three decades, written all over it. The University's support has been various, including a timely seed-grant early on, years of stellar assistance from the Interlibrary Loans staff, and a sympathetic Dean of Arts and Sciences, Robert Campbell. I have been especially fortunate in the students and colleagues who have shared – or humoured me by pretending to share – my interest in Marlowe. Former students who have shown a sustained and sustaining interest in the book include David Boulding,

Christopher Jackson, Margaret Owens, Holly Potter, Linda Rozmovits, Anne Russell, and Gordon Teskey, and for helpful comments on the manuscript I want to thank two more students-turned-colleagues, Stephen Guy-Bray and Sharon Ragaz.

For their readiness to exchange ideas and to steal time from their own writing projects to improve mine, I am grateful to many colleagues in the Department of English Literature, especially Stephen Brown, Mary Polito, Beth Popham, and Michael Treadwell. I give special thanks to James Neufeld and Zailig Pollock, the former for his crucial support at the beginning and end of this adventure, and the latter for friendship and generosity which took the tangible form of trenchant comment on at least one version of every chapter.

The animating wit of Sheldon P. Zitner, my first and best teacher of Shakespeare, continues to be a source of inspiration, and I like to think that the late William A. Ringler, Jr, my kind mentor in graduate school, would have enjoyed this book.

The protracted gestation of *Playing with Desire* has allowed me to benefit from the timely appearance of a number of important works on Marlowe, most notably the last two volumes of the Revels edition of his plays. But an unforeseen development on the domestic front proved to be still more helpful: the coming of age of my fine sons, Luke and Ben, as critical, sometimes exceedingly critical, readers. Finally, I salute my dear wife, Annette – I could not have finished this project without her unflagging impatience.

A Note on Texts

Marlowe's plays and poems are quoted from the modern-spelling texts in the recently completed Revels Plays series:

Dido Queen of Carthage and *The Massacre at Paris*, ed. H.J. Oliver. London: Methuen, 1968
The Poems, ed. Millar Maclure. London: Methuen, 1968
The Jew of Malta, ed. N.W. Bawcutt. Manchester: Manchester University Press, 1978
Tamburlaine the Great, ed. J.S. Cunningham. Manchester: Manchester University Press, 1981
Doctor Faustus: A- and B-texts (1604, 1616), ed. David Bevington and Eric Rasmussen. Manchester: Manchester University Press, 1993
Edward the Second, ed. Charles R. Forker. Manchester: Manchester University Press, 1994

Quotations of Shakespeare are from *The Riverside Shakespeare*, ed. G. Blakemore Evans (Boston: Houghton Mifflin, 1974). Unless noted, the text for other Renaissance plays is *Drama of the English Renaissance*, ed. Russell A. Fraser and Norman Rabkin, 2 vols. (New York: Macmillan, 1976). For other Elizabethan writers, I have silently modernized spelling and punctuation so that they would not seem more distant than Marlowe.

PLAYING WITH DESIRE

I saw likewise stand,
Up to the chin amidst a liquid lake,
Tormented Tantalus, yet could not slake
His burning thirst. Oft as his scornful cup
Th'old man would taste, so oft 'twas swallowed up,
And all the black earth to his feet descried;
Divine power (plaguing him) the lake still dried.
About his head, on high trees clustering, hung
Pears, Apples, Granets, Olives, ever young,
Delicious Figs, and many fruit trees more
Of other burthen, whose alluring store
When th'old Soul strived to pluck, the winds from sight
In gloomy vapours made them vanish quite.

Homer, *The Odyssey*, translated by George Chapman (11:794–806)

... unhappy in thine end,
Marley, the Muses' darling for thy verse;
Fit to write passions for the souls below,
If any wretched souls in passion speak.

George Peele, 'The Honour of the Garter' (1593)

Introduction

This book is about a distinctive but unremarked preoccupation of Christopher Marlowe's writing: games of tantalization in which enticing objects and ideas are offered and then withdrawn before they can be grasped. These teasing games so thoroughly pervade Marlowe's work as to be a virtual *sine qua non* of his engaged imagination, and they occur often enough to provide a framework for studying almost his entire body of work. The pages which follow trace the changing representation of tantalizing games in all seven of Marlowe's plays. This focus on tantalization is particularly fruitful in that it provides a means of bridging a gap rarely crossed in Marlowe studies, the gap that separates his plays from his poems. Thus, in addition to illuminating the plays, it enables a close consideration of Marlowe's most important achievements in verse: his erotic narrative *Hero and Leander*, his translation of Ovid's *Amores* (*All Ovid's Elegies*), and his lyric 'The Passionate Shepherd to His Love.' Altogether, *Playing with Desire* takes a more comprehensive look at Marlowe's body of work than any study since the posthumous publication of Clifford Leech's essays.[1]

With the exception of the relatively brief treatments of *The Massacre at Paris* and 'The Passionate Shepherd to His Love,' the discussion of individual works follows their probable sequence of composition: *All Ovid's Elegies*, *Dido Queen of Carthage*, Parts One and Two of *Tamburlaine*, *The Jew of Malta*, *Edward II*, *Doctor Faustus*, and *Hero and Leander*.[2] While it is necessarily speculative in places, this sequence is consonant with the accepted facts, and it has long been familiar in Marlowe scholarship.[3] At the present time, there is very little controversy about the dating, or at least the sequencing, of Marlowe's works. The only work whose date is the subject of ongoing debate is *Doctor Faustus*, some arguing that it follows immediately after the *Tamburlaine* plays and others that it is one of his last plays. The latter placing seems to me the more likely, but, in any event, the interpretation of individual works in *Playing with Desire* does not depend on this ordering.

What emerges from this tentative reconstruction of Marlowe's writing career is a trajectory in which the motif of teasing begins as an erotic, Ovidian game and then becomes increasingly politicized and violent, even when it remains sexual. Instead of being a mutually satisfying form of love-play, as it usually is in Ovid, tantalization is transformed into a sadistic mockery of desire. Already in Marlowe's probably early translation of *All Ovid's Elegies* the mainly high-spirited sexual sport begins to darken near the end of the sequence, as the figure of Tantalus in the underworld comes into focus. In *Dido Queen of Carthage*, almost certainly Marlowe's first play, the motif of sexual teasing is transformed at the ending into a cruel, un-Ovidian representation of Dido's emotional vulnerability. In the two parts of *Tamburlaine*, the protagonist's insatiable desires are mirrored in the sadistic games he plays with others, most notably in his tantalizing with food and drink the caged emperor, Bajazeth. A similar withholding of alluring objects of desire becomes a fundamental expression of power in the worlds of *The Jew of Malta, Edward II*, and *Doctor Faustus*. In all of these plays the protagonist both tantalizes others and is himself tantalized. Moreover, Barabas, Edward, and Faustus share a common fate in that they are punished in ways which create stage-pictures calling to mind representations of the torment of Tantalus. The subject of the final chapter, the narrative poem *Hero and Leander*, returns to the sexual games of the Ovid translations, but it disconcertingly superimposes on this erotic teasing the derisive violence which tantalization has acquired in the tragedies.

Marlowe's deep interest in tantalization is apparent not only in the interaction of his characters but also in the action of his plays upon their audiences. For audiences, like characters, what is promised is usually denied. In the course of his work, Marlowe learns to construct his plays – and *Hero and Leander* as well – in such a way as to arouse and then to frustrate his audience's expectations. The manipulations of desire that his characters practise on each other, then, closely parallel the strategies he uses to engage and frustrate his viewers. With growing acerbity, I will argue, Marlowe's works situate the audience in the place of their painfully tantalized protagonists, a strategy which in the past has been mistaken for 'ambiguity.'[4] An examination of his propensity to play teasing games with his audiences reveals that Marlowe is a more disturbing, and more deliberately disturbing, writer than he is usually acknowledged to be.

The pervasive presence of tantalization in Marlowe's work provides strong evidence, if evidence be needed, that his death as an author has been greatly exaggerated in the recent past.[5] Over the last two decades, many influential critics of Renaissance drama have disparaged 'the anachronistic emphasis on the author,' usually arguing that playwrights were merely one strand in a vast web of cultural discourse which produced the plays.[6] This criticism has immersed Marlowe's works in, and often submerged them under, various discursive practices of the age, including politics, imperialism, sodomy, espionage, militarism, treason, heresy, and courtly surveillance.[7] While these discussions are often illuminating, the light they cast is invariably focused on various aspects of cultural theory and Elizabethan culture rather than on Marlowe's works, which are usually reduced to highly selective, decontextualized bits. Indeed, these studies leave one with the impression that Marlowe's works are collections of fragments that can be related meaningfully to just about everything in Elizabethan England except his other works. *Playing with Desire* is an attempt to re-member Marlowe's scattered corpus by reinvoking the central concept of authorial intention and by examining a recurrent, resonant expression of that intention.[8]

Fortunately, studies of Renaissance drama are increasingly voicing the sensible conviction that 'It is time to stop beating a dead author,' where 'author' in the lower case signals a return to individuals and actual practices.[9] Despite this recuperation, two arguments of de-authoring, anti-intentionalist criticism still enjoy an unwarranted currency. The more easily challenged claim asserts that the supposedly pervasive 'textual instability' of Renaissance playtexts precludes the attempt to discover the hand of a specific author or any signs of intention.[10] But, as G. Thomas Tanselle's masterly review of recent discussions of 'textual instability' argues, the laudable project of studying the complex historicity of texts need not, and should not, entail rejecting the idea of authorial intention. Moreover, the evidence of the playtexts themselves suggests that the actual degree of instability is considerably less than has been posited. In an even-handed study, R.A. Foakes has noted that in fact Renaissance texts contain far fewer signs of playhouse 'collaboration,' and thus less cause for invoking the spectre of 'textual instability,' than some critics have claimed.[11] Though Foakes does not discuss the texts of Marlowe's plays, they strongly corroborate his observations, for even though most were not published until after his death – and some long after it – they contain little material which modern editors have resisted attributing to him.

This is not to say, of course, that there are no problems in the texts of the plays (and poems) traditionally assigned to Marlowe. In fact, two of the seven plays present difficulties which may be insuperable. The text of *The Massacre at Paris*, as editors have long remarked, is extremely short and is probably a memorial reconstruction of a performance. The other problem is considerably more vexing, for it concerns *Doctor Faustus*, one of Marlowe's central works. Versions of *Doctor Faustus* exist in two significantly different and perhaps extensively revised playtexts, the so-called A text of 1604 and B text of 1616. While the relative authority of these texts *vis-à-vis* Marlowe's intentions is exceedingly difficult to ascertain, one should be wary of the radically sceptical desire to throw out the author with the clouded bibliographical bathwater.[12] In my view, the difficulties posed by the extant Marlowe texts, including those of *Doctor Faustus*, do not justify placing scare quotes around the playwright's name, let along stressing what Leah Marcus calls 'the absent authorial presence we call Marlowe.' And attempts to dismiss patterns of repeated motifs in these texts as merely 'the Marlowe effect' should be resisted, since these patterns may well be crucial signs of vibrant authorial presence.[13]

The other anti-authorial argument that needs to be answered involves the imprecise, semi-metaphorical usage of 'collaboration.' In addition to its traditional meaning (the swatting up of a script by a team of playwrights),[14] the term recently has been applied to many works never associated with a literal co-author. In a stunningly inclusive application, we learn that 'most literature in the period, and virtually all theatrical literature, must be seen as basically collaborative in nature.'[15] Since theatre is in many ways a collaborative activity, it is an easy step to deduce that the creation of the playscript must itself be an act of collaboration. Thus, a materialist critic suggests (vaguely) that 'the actual modes of human creativity that first generated the theatrical scripts of *Hamlet*, *King Lear*, or *The Tempest* were in all likelihood collaborative and improvisatory.'[16] While it is true that every *performance* of a Renaissance play was necessarily collaborative, it scarcely follows that the *composition* of that play must have been a shared activity. Authorial behaviour was, I believe, more various – and sometimes considerably less collegial – than many critics would care to allow.

In Christopher Marlowe we see perhaps the clearest example of a Renaissance dramatist's avoidance of collaboration, in both the restricted and generalized senses of the term. Though it would of course be misleading to represent him, or any Elizabethan playwright, as a solitary genius, the evidence indicates that Marlowe was less inclined than his colleagues to enter into working partnerships. While virtually every other important playwright (including Shakespeare, Jonson, and all of Marlowe's fellow 'University Wits') collaborated on occasion, and some on many occasions, there is no compelling evidence to indicate that Marlowe ever undertook to write a play with another person. The best-known evidence for Marlowe as a collaborator is the title-page of the posthumously published quarto of *Dido Queen of Carthage*, which states that the play was written by him and (in less prominent type) Thomas Nashe. Most commentators, however, believe Nashe's participation did not extend beyond preparing Marlowe's manuscript for the press, and a recent editor flatly declares that 'it has never been seriously entertained that he [Nashe] was a collaborator in this play.'[17] Early in the twentieth century, commentators had claimed to detect collaborative hands in many other Marlowe plays, but *Doctor Faustus* is the only work for which multiple authorship is still mooted. Another dramatist's hand has not been conclusively identified in *Doctor Faustus*, though numerous arguments for collaboration and a cohort of putative co-authors (Nashe, most frequently) have been put forward.[18] Like the textual debate over *Faustus*, with which it is intimately related, the question of collaboration in the play is likely never to be resolved of all ambiguity.

Even in its recent, more inclusive usage, 'collaboration' is not an activity particularly applicable to Marlowe. Though he must have known a good deal about the playhouses, actors, and audiences for whom he wrote so effectively, there is no evidence that he ever acted in plays (again, unlike many of his fellow dramatists). Nor, despite the title of a recent book, is there good reason to think he maintained a close relationship with Edward Alleyn, who played the lead in *Doctor Faustus, The Jew of Malta*, and the *Tamburlaine* plays, or indeed with any group of actors.[19] In this respect he could not have been more different from Shakespeare, who for almost two decades was involved with the same troupe as actor, principal writer, and shareholder. Given the well-documented history of his volatile temperament and fractious behaviour, and given what appears to be his devious activity as a double agent, Marlowe seems singularly ill equipped for the reciprocities of successful collaborative work.[20] The most likely product of a Marlovian collaboration is the counterfeit shilling for which he and Richard Baines were arrested in Flushing, and for which they promptly blamed each other.[21]

Though it resists the tendency to de-author Marlowe's work, *Playing with Desire* is not a biographical study. Apart from the equivocal witness of the works themselves, so little is known of Marlowe's inner life that a biographical interpretation would be forced to assume exactly what needs to be proven. We will never know, for instance, whether the boy Christopher played at teasing games like 'bob cherry' and 'snatch apple' with uncommon avidity.[22] Nor are we likely to know the nature of the games that as an adult he played in his bedchamber, let alone with whom. Though we must reconcile ourselves to learned ignorance of his personal life, it is nevertheless both possible and useful to locate Marlowe in his historical moment, and so my introductory chapter begins with Elizabethan attitudes to Tantalus and proceeds to suggest that Marlowe's passionate concern with games of teasing and withholding may represent a response to social and economic frustrations felt by many of his contemporaries. Ultimately, however, broad historical contextualizations are likely to prove more suggestive than explanatory, for Tantalus and tantalization figure much more prominently in Marlowe than in any other writer of his time.

1

Marlowe and the Torment of Tantalus

In his continuation of Marlowe's *Hero and Leander*, George Chapman employs a curious image to invoke his dead predecessor. He describes Marlowe as a poet 'whose living subject stood / Up to the chin in the Pierian flood, / And drunk to me half this Musaean story ...'[1] While drinking of the Muses' Pierian spring is a common trope for poetic inspiration, the odd detail of actually standing in the sacred water (and up to the chin) appears to be Chapman's invention. There is, however, one mythological figure who stands immersed in water in the posture which Chapman attributes to Marlowe. That figure is Tantalus. When, some years later, Chapman translates Homer's *ur*-description of Tantalus tormented in the waters of Hades (quoted as one of my epigraphs), he repeats the identical phrase from his Marlowe tribute: both figures are 'up to the chin' in water. The allusion to Tantalus complicates the tribute to Marlowe immensely, for this tormented sinner in Hades is hardly a conventional figure of inspiration, and the whole point of his standing in water is punitive: to increase his frustration at *not* being able to drink it. Chapman's lines conflate the heavenly waters of reward (the Pierian spring is usually located on Mount Olympus) and the hellish waters of denial and punishment. It is small wonder that this shadow-image of Tantalus has not come to the notice of commentators, for such a dark figure has no business appearing in a passage traditionally characterized as a 'commendation unmarred by suggestion of reproach.'[2]

Upon reflection, however, Chapman's implicit likening of Marlowe to Tantalus is not so startling. Recent scholarship has demonstrated that Chapman's attitude toward Marlowe's *Hero and Leander* was ambivalent, as he was dazzled by its beauty and offended by its violations of decorum. Hence, despite his title-page's claim that he 'finished' Marlowe's narrative, Chapman actually tames and contains the dead poet's transgressive spirit.[3] (On the subject of transgression, an action for which Tantalus was noted, one wonders if Chapman's Muses would necessarily welcome Marlowe wading in their sacred spring.) Perhaps Chapman sensed a connection between Marlowe's poetic powers and Tantalus' frustration, as if the agony of a punishing thirst and hunger were central to the master poet's inspiration. This association of Marlowe's imaginative power with the torments of Hades was not new with Chapman. Only a few weeks after Marlowe's death, his fellow playwright George Peele invoked him in lines which also link the Muses with the damned, and inspiration with punishment:

> unhappy in thine end,
> Marley, the Muses' darling for thy verse;
> Fit to write passions for the souls below,
> If any wretched souls in passion speak.[4]

Here the switch from 'the Muses' darling' (the 'musarum delicia' of countless academic eulogies) to the ambivalence of 'Fit to write passions for the souls below' is breathtaking. C.F. Tucker Brooke's gloss on the passage is useful: 'The idea ... is not that Marlowe has gone to Christian hell, but that in the next world his dark genius would be able to render articulate the woes of Pluto's wretched souls. He is fit to write "passions" for Tantalus and Sisyphus such as he has written for Faustus and Barabas.'[5]

Marlowe's writing provides the most telling evidence for identifying him with Tantalus, and the work which shows that evidence most explicitly is in fact *Hero and Leander*. As he sat down to continue (and surreptitiously transform) Marlowe's poem, Chapman would have remembered that it often insists on the link between desire and frustration, and that imagery associating Leander with Tantalus appears throughout. Near the end of Leander's first visit to Hero's tower, Marlowe's identification of him with Tantalus is unmistakable. As Leander begins to 'scorch and glow,' we learn of Hero's evasive action:

> She, with a kind of granting, put him by it,
> And ever as he thought himself most nigh it,
> Like to the tree of Tantalus she fled,
> And, seeming lavish, sav'd her maidenhead.   557–60

This is Marlowe's only passage (apart from the translations) which explicitly names Tantalus. Like many Renaissance writers, including Chapman in his tribute, Marlowe frequently evokes classical myths without actually naming them, and in many cases his most significant myths are only implicit in patterns of images.[6] In the plays especially, there is no need for Tantalus to be named, for we *see* versions of him in the stage-pictures Marlowe creates through props and the postures of actors. When, as often happens in Marlowe, a character invests an object with value and then withholds it from another character, or is himself/ herself prevented from obtaining it, the myth is re-enacted before our eyes. On a more abstract level, the play of tantalization is evoked when characters' emotional and intellectual expectations are raised and then frustrated. Though Marlowe was not unique in his interest in Tantalus, no other Renaissance writer or artist expresses a comparable fascination with this figure and with the psychology which he epitomizes.

The Myth and the Age

Like many other figures of classical mythology, Tantalus enjoyed a rebirth of interest in Renaissance Europe.[7] Though mythographers culled so many lineages, deeds, and attributes of Tantalus from ancient sources that they wondered if 'multiple Tantali' had lived, sixteenth-century art and literature reveal little interest in these scholarly details and recherché stories.[8] With surprisingly few exceptions, a single picture dominates early modern Europe's imagining of Tantalus: the scene of his punishment in the underworld.[9] Probably the earliest and certainly the most authoritative depiction of this scene occurs in Homer's account of the great sinners whom Odysseus meets on his tour of hell. Suffering from the extremities of hunger and thirst, Tantalus is punished in a most ingenious fashion. Boughs of luscious fruit tempt him with their savour, but as he grasps at them they fly just beyond his reach. Correspondingly, Tantalus' thirst is provoked by the waters in which he stands, but, when he bends to drink, the water disappears into the earth. With variations on some details (e.g., how deeply in the water Tantalus stands and whether he attempts to seize the fruit with his outstretched hands or his gaping mouth), this scene is repeated again and again. In these depictions, Tantalus represents the epitome of frustration and of desire which is literally fruitless. In his invariably open mouth and strained gestures, we see appetite in its most desperately abject and embarrassing form.

Vivid as these visual representations are, there is one dimension of Tantalus' punishment which they cannot convey: its endless, humiliating repetitiveness. Tantalus lunges for the elusive fruit and water not once or twice, but for all eternity. In essence, his punishment is a game played on his uncontrollable appetites, and, since he never learns the futility of his actions, his torment is mechanical and compulsive. Though his fellow sufferers in Hades (most notably Sisyphus, Ixion, and Tityus) also undergo endlessly repeated torments and are rendered impotent as punishment for their exorbitant desires, the frustration of Tantalus is by far the most demeaning.[10] Sisyphus resembles Tantalus, but the former's futile act (repeatedly rolling the same boulder up a steep hill) requires a degree of resolve which is ennobling. Camus can depict Sisyphus as an existential hero because 'There is no fate that cannot be surmounted by scorn.'[11] Tantalus, however, is pre-eminently an object of scorn, and from Lucian to Goya and Daumier it is to lovers of satire and caricature that he most appeals.[12]

The best depiction of Tantalus' endless, compulsive participation in the perverse game being played upon him occurs in Seneca's grotesque tragedy *Thyestes*, an influential play in the Renaissance and one which Marlowe knew well.[13] The idea of repetition pervades *Thyestes*, as the ghost of Tantalus rises from Hades to deliver the Prologue, and in the body of the play his grandsons Atreus and Thyestes proceed to re-enact his unnatural crimes. In the play's first Chorus, a long passage ('the most elaborate extant description of Tantalus in the underworld')[14] emphasizes the derisory game-like quality of his punishment. After describing how the boughs offer their fruit 'In playful mockery of his empty mouthings,' Seneca ridicules Tantalus' vain attempt to restrain his appetite:

> Time and again deluded, now the sufferer,
> Famished and desperate with his long torture,
> Will not attempt to touch them, turns his head down,
> Clenches his teeth and swallows down his hunger –
> Only to see the riches of the orchard
> Lowered to meet him, juicy apples dancing
> On bending branches, goading again his hunger
> Till he must shoot out hands to clutch ... but useless –[15]

As if this is not adequately humiliating, Tantalus soon lunges also for the water at his lips, and yet again is fooled. It is no wonder that the

Seneca who imagined this scene so vividly was also a Stoic philosopher, for his Tantalus is the antithesis of the ideal of centred self-sufficiency. Seneca's Tantalus represents man reduced to the reflex action of appetite and emptied out by frustrated desire.[16] In this punishment, desire becomes essentially mechanical, an uncontrollable response to an enticing stimulus, a compulsion which imprisons.

As the primal scene with fruit and water indicates, the Tantalus myth is above all a story about punishing desire, or desire becoming its own punishment. In the myth's historical development, the spectacular punishment of Tantalus overshadows the specification of his crimes. Thus, Homer's account, which is one of the earliest extant, vividly describes Tantalus' punishment but makes no reference to the crime (though the preceding lines mention the crime as well as the punishment of Tityus). For mythographers and moralists, the task has always been to invent a crime which accords with and justifies this diabolically clever punishment.[17]

In the classical tradition the crime of Tantalus takes two canonical forms, both of which appropriately involve food. According to the more repulsive and probably older version of the myth, Tantalus kills his son Pelops, dismembers and cooks him, and then serves him to the gods.[18] After Ceres eats a mouthful, the gods realize their error, revivify Pelops, and replace the missing bite (from his shoulder) with an ivory prosthesis. Tantalus' motive for this monstrous sacrifice is obscure, most mythographers attributing it to his proud, curious desire to test the omniscience (and hence the divinity) of the gods.[19] The alternative form of the myth mitigates the horrors of child murder and cannibalism by inventing a desecrated feast with the gods involving a less disgusting food-crime. In this more decorous version, the gods give Tantalus the great honour of supping with them, but he betrays their trust by divulging their secrets to his mortal companions, even sharing with them the gods' nectar and ambrosia.[20] In both versions, tantalization is a symmetrical punishment for exorbitant appetite and the unnatural violation of a feast. Thus, Tantalus is a figure about whom it is virtually impossible to say something positive, and when Sir Philip Sidney discussed the power of poetry to create pure examples of virtue and vice, he illustrated the latter by instancing Tantalus and his grandson Atreus, who represent 'nothing that is not to be shunned.'[21]

The mythographical tradition did not always attribute the suffering of Tantalus directly to the gods. When the myth was subjected to moral and allegorical interpretation, Tantalus often became an emblem for a pain which is self-originating and self-inflicted, as if his desire is by its very nature its own punishment. This view emphasizes the contradictory, ironic nature of Tantalus' attributes. On the one hand, he is associated with abundance, since he is a king, the son of Zeus, and also proverbially wealthy.[22] On the other hand, with his gaping mouth and empty hands, he is the epitome of deficiency and impoverishment. In a venerable interpretation first advanced by Horace and Petronius, Tantalus represents the sterile avarice of the rich miser who starves himself amidst plenty.[23] Thus, Erasmus advises rhetoricians-in-training that 'if one should propose that the avaricious man does not so much have what he has, as that which he does not have, he would use the fable of Tantalus with a preface.'[24] Geffrey Whitney's emblem (fig. 2), which like its original in Alciatus is titled 'Avaritia,' falls squarely into this tradition, and the poem accompanying it declares that the covetous man is a Tantalus because 'He doth abound, yet starves and nothing spends,/ But keeps his gold, as if it were not his.'[25] Since Tantalus is pathetically incapable of enjoying what he has, he is thus essentially self-punished. In Whitney's paradox, 'he doth his hunger feed.'

Whether divinely ordained or self-inflicted, the torments of Tantalus come to express a central perception of early modern Europe: that desire is by its very nature unappeasable because it cannot be satisfied with the objects which it pursues, even when it possesses them. What Stephen Greenblatt has called the 'problem of elusiveness' in Renaissance thought – that desired ends always recede beyond one's grasp – could evoke emotions ranging from pious exhilaration to paranoid anxiety.[26] On the one hand, humankind's innate desire for the unreachable could be taken as evidence of God's solicitude, and John Donne could declare that 'God hath imprinted in every *natural man* ... an endless, and undeterminable desire of more, than this life can minister unto him. Still *God* leaves man in *expectation*.'[27] On the other hand, a speaker in a sixteenth-century philosophical dialogue characterizes 'the very indisposition of our souls toward contentment' as a curse:

it is the cursed nature of our soul ever to long for the very thing it lacks ... The man who owns a field itches to join another to it, just as he who owns one kingdom seeks a second. Alexander the Great, we read, cried because he had no more worlds to conquer. Our desires are, in themselves, infinite, and to own much effects nothing except to redouble our desire.[28]

In a meditation on the true ends of desire, Marsilio Ficino hovers between these extremes when he applies the suffering of humankind to that of Tantalus. He exclaims that 'we are all Tantali,' for 'we all thirst for the good and the true, yet all drink dreams.' This state of delusion is tantalizing, he says, for humans can barely sense 'the shadowy faint trace of nectar and ambrosia, lapping our uppermost lip,' and hence 'a panting thirst continuously burns up the wretched Tantali.'[29] Whether these intimations of immortality are a saving grace or a teasing curse, Ficino does not say.

Tantalus, Icarus, and Marlowe

Marlowe knew his mythology and mythography well,[30] and traces of the traditional interpretations of Tantalus are present, as we shall see, throughout his work. But what is most important about his use of the Tantalus myth is his own invention, for he repeatedly links it with a counter-myth: the story of Icarus. Marlowe's joining of Tantalus with Icarus is particularly interesting because Renaissance writers and artists rarely paired them.[31]

Unlike Tantalus, Icarus is a familiar figure in Marlowe criticism, and every student knows the outline of the myth: Daedalus gives to his son Icarus wings of wax and exhorts him not to fly too high or too low; but the boy, enthralled by the joy of flight, ignores his father's advice, flies too close to the sun, and falls to his death when his waxen wings melt. Beginning with Una Ellis-Fermor's monograph, which printed Philippe Desportes' sonnet 'Icare' as an epigraph, critics have stressed the importance of Icarus for Marlowe.[32] The fullest application of the Icarus myth to Marlowe and his work was undertaken by Harry Levin in his classic study *The Overreacher* (1952), which featured Geffrey Whitney's woodcut of Icarus on its title-page (fig. 1). In his first chapter Levin deftly linked Icarus with the rhetorical figure of hyperbole, which an Elizabethan treatise on poetry had termed 'the over reacher.' For Marlowe, Levin declared, the hyperbolic style is an instrument for expressing desire, as it 'presupposes a state of mind to which all things are possible, for which limitations exist to be overcome.' In his last chapter, Levin moves from the style to the man, attributing to Marlowe an 'Icarus complex' and identifying 'the Icarian desire for flight' as the animating impulse of both the poet and his protagonists. For two decades and more, the authority of *The Overreacher* was so great that reading Marlowe and spotting Icarus figures became practically synonymous activities.[33]

By repeatedly transforming this poster-boy figure of the daring Icarus

28 *In Aſtrologos.*

HEARE, ICARVS with mountinge vp alofte,
Came headlonge downe, and fell into the Sea:
His waxed winges, the ſonne did make ſo ſofte,
They melted ſtraighte, and feathers fell awaie:
So, whilſte he flewe, and of no dowbte did care,
He mooude his armes, but loe, the ſame were bare.

Let ſuche beware, which paſte theire reache doe mounte,
Whoe ſeeke the thinges, to mortall men deny'de,
And ſearche the Heauens, and all the ſtarres accoumpte,
And tell therebie, what after ſhall betyde:
With bluſſhinge nowe, theire weakeneſſe rightlie weye,
Leaſt as they clime, they fall to theire decaye.

Martial. 1. *Illud quod medium eſt, atque inter vtrumque, probamus.*

Ouid. Triſt. 2. *Dum petit infirmis nimium ſublimia pennis*
Icarus, Icariis nomina fecit aquis.
Vitaret cælum Phaëton, ſi viueret, & quos
Optauit ſtultè tangere, nollet equos.

Amor

Figure 1: Icarus, from Geffrey Whitney's *A Choice of Emblems* (Leiden, 1586), 28

7.4   *Auaritia.*

.Ouid. Metam.
lib..4.

Heare Tantalvs, as Poëttes doe deuine,
This guerdon hathe, for his offence in hell:
The pleasante fruite, dothe to his lippe decline,
A riuer faire vnto his chinne doth swell:
  Yet, twixt these two, for foode the wretche dothe sterue,
  For bothe doe flee, when they his neede shoulde serue.

The couetons man, this fable reprehendes,
For chaunge his name, and Tantalvs hee is,
Hee dothe abounde, yet sterues and nothing spendes,
But keepes his goulde, as if it weare not his:
  With slender fare, he doth his hunger feede,
  And dare not touche his store, when hee doth neede.

Horat. serm. r,
.Sat. r.

Tantalus à labris sitiens fugientia captat
Flumina, quid rides? mutato nomine de te
Fabula narratur, congestis vndique saccis
Indormis inhians: & tanquam parcere sacris
Congeris &c. ——   ——

O vita,

Figure 2: Tantalus, from Geffrey Whitney's *A Choice of Emblems* (Leiden, 1586),
74

into Tantalus, the least elevated and dignified sinner in Hades, Marlowe creates a composite myth of his own. The differences between the two figures are caught in popular representations that Marlowe knew, two woodcuts from an English book of emblems that appeared in the year he graduated from Cambridge. Throughout Marlowe's work we meet a recurrent metamorphosis in which Icarian aspiration falls heavily downward to become Tantalian frustration. The audacious desire of Icarus to fly toward the sun is transposed into Tantalus' pathetic attempts to grasp apples which fly from his reach. It is as if, after having fallen into the sea, Icarus does not drown but lives to suffer the humiliation of being endlessly teased and frustrated.[34] The overreacher is reduced to an underreacher. Marlowe's protagonists invariably announce their desires in Icarian hyperbole but eventually become victims of a Tantalian game, rendered powerless by the forces that manipulate their desires. One of Marlowe's pervasive ironies is that it is through the experience of desire that his protagonists derive a feeling of power, but it is also through their desires that they are most easily played with and rendered helpless. For Marlowe tantalization is the act in which desire and impotence meet and become inseparable.

In the metamorphosis of Icarus into Tantalus, Marlowe created a myth which spoke to the experience of many of his contemporaries. While the phenomenon of great promise giving way to great disappointment is common enough at all times, it had a special pathos in late Elizabethan England. Indeed, a historian has argued that Marlowe's generation is notable for the quasi-religious fervour with which it glorified 'the aspiring mind' and invented grand imaginative projects which proved impossible to realize.[35] Apart from the delusively grandiose schemes of dreamers like Essex, Raleigh, and Bacon, social and political forces created a bottle-neck through which even modest ambitions could not rise. A prominent problem for intellectuals was that Oxford and Cambridge had multiplied their admission of students to meet a demand for clergymen and administrators that by Marlowe's time had fallen off, and hence the humanist dream of serving the state by dint of prowess at liberal studies was becoming anachronistic.[36] Marlowe and his fellow University Wits, according to Ian Watt, were troubled by 'the disparity between the vast expectations that the academy aroused and the meager opportunities of realizing them that society afforded.'[37] Indeed, so much imaginative writing was done by men whose ambitions had been blocked that G.K. Hunter has declared that 'The literature of the 'eighties and 'nineties is, in fact, largely a product of frustration.'[38]

It is tempting to speculate that Marlowe's penchant for transforming Icarus into Tantalus derives directly from his own experience as well as from his contemporaries'. When he took up his scholarship to Cambridge, the sixteen-year-old Marlowe may well have sensed something like the 'frolic courage' which Icarus felt as he ignored his father's warnings and soared high into the sky.[39] Escaping from a home in which his improvident father's Bible was the only book, this highly imaginative young man likely fantasized that not only Cambridge but all the world was before him.[40] After his graduation, it also seems plausible to assume that, despite his remarkable literary accomplishments, Marlowe finally shared the frustration which afflicted so many underemployed university men of his time. Given the dismal economics (for playwrights) of play-writing, Marlowe could not have lived well on the sale of his plays alone, and it is interesting that the search for patronage is a prominent motif in his late work.[41] There is also a good deal of evidence to indicate that, as one would expect, Marlowe was himself searching for the support of a patron. In this connection, it should be noted that Elizabethan commentators sometimes associated the picture of Tantalus in Hades with the humiliating frustrations of a courtier's subservience.[42] In so far as Marlowe saw himself as dependent for sustenance on the whims of the mighty, he might well have identified with Tantalus. But such speculation about Marlowe's view of himself is at best hypothetical; at worst it invites critical and biographical solipsism.

Instead of trying to ascertain the relevance of Icarus and Tantalus to Marlowe's life, it is more useful to relate these figures to two prominent, antithetical conceptions of his work. Icarus, the sublime figure who dares too much and suffers a literal fall that is fatal, has long typified the view of Marlowe as a tragic writer. Thus, Harry Levin remarked that 'Since Icarus was the archetype of the overreacher, Marlowe was by temperament a tragedian.' Since the early 1960s, however, many critics have rejected the idea of Marlowe as a tragedian and instead emphasized his ironic detachment from his protagonists and his penchant for caricature and grotesque comedy.[43] This rejection of the exclusively tragic Marlowe opened the way for a new understanding of Marlovian desire. In place of the high-flying Icarian model, many critics emphasized that the protagonists' desires were in fact mechanical and compulsive, more an expression of hollowness than heroism.[44] Perhaps because their antagonism to the much-touted Icarus had induced a wariness about all mythological constructs, these post-*Overreacher* critics did not notice how remarkably germane Tantalus is to many of their concerns.

Among the contemporary resonances of the myth is its stress on desire that is futile and self-consuming, on suffering that becomes comic through repetition, and on apparent resolutions that prove to be inconclusive. (As well, the figure of Tantalus would appear to be particularly germane to critics deploying the Lacanian notion of desire as predicated on an enduring lack.)[45] In addition to its relevance to these commonly voiced issues, the figure of Tantalus illuminates an un-Icarian aspect of the works that has yet to come into critical focus: the pervasive element of manipulative play and sadistic games of withholding.

Marlowe's Duke of Guise and Fellow Tantali

Nowhere in Marlowe is the presence of Tantalian imagery more marked than in the three passages which critics invariably cite as touchstones of his Icarianism: the lines in the Prologue to *Doctor Faustus* which ominously refer to the melting of the protagonist's 'waxen wings'; Dido's fantasy at the end of *Dido Queen of Carthage* in which she hopes to 'frame me wings of wax like Icarus' to pursue the fleeing Aeneas; and the lines from *The Massacre at Paris* in which the Duke of Guise soliloquizes about his soaring ambition.[46] Commentators have not noticed, however, that in none of these passages is the Icarian allusion the speaker's final word. In each case the explicit allusion to Icarus is quickly followed by verbal and stage images which invert it and tacitly point to Tantalus. For Marlowe's protagonists, the dream of becoming Icarus is ultimately revealed to be a delusion of Tantalus.

The passage which enacts most fully the transformation of Icarian into Tantalian images is the Duke of Guise's soliloquy in the second scene of *The Massacre at Paris*. As Marlowe's longest soliloquy and thus his most extended exploration of a mind in motion, these seventy-five lines have considerable interest. Virtually all the commentary on the speech, however, has been confined to a brief passage in its Icarian beginning, which has long been the proof-text for the idea of heroic desire in Marlowe:[47]

> Now, Guise, begins those deep-engender'd thoughts
> To burst abroad those never-dying flames
> Which cannot be extinguish'd but by blood.
> Oft have I levell'd, and at last have learn'd,
> That peril is the chiefest way to happiness,
> And resolution honour's fairest aim.

What glory is there in a common good
That hangs for every peasant to achieve?
That like I best that flies beyond my reach.
Set me to scale the high Pyramides,
And thereon set the diadem of France,
I'll either rend it with my nails to naught
Or mount the top with my aspiring wings,
Although my downfall be the deepest hell.   2.31–44

Icarus is evoked not only by the Guise's desire to 'mount the top with my aspiring wings' but also by his glorification of peril throughout the passage. In these fourteen lines, the Guise celebrates himself in the same terms with which continental poets like Sannazaro, Tansillo, and Desportes praise Icarus: as a glorious figure who inspires emulation because he disdains the base safety of the earth.[48] But the Guise's Icarian 'credo of the aspiring mind' harbours at its centre three lines which invert the idea of heroic flight:

What glory is there in a common good
That hangs for every peasant to achieve?
That like I best that flies beyond my reach.

The first two lines suggest that the passage will be merely an amplification of the Guise's paean to achieving what is difficult, but the third line veers off in a new direction. What we might expect is the paraphrase which appears in *Locrine*, a contemporary tragedy full of Marlovian pastiche: 'That likes me best that is not got with ease.'[49] But the Guise's 'That like I best that flies beyond my reach' suggests that he desires what is not got at all. That is, when he contrasts base success to the superior attractiveness of that which 'flies beyond my reach,' his emphasis falls on the evasiveness of the object rather than the strenuousness of the pursuit. What 'flies' is not the Guise soaring upward on Icarian wings but rather the desired object eluding his grasp.

That Marlowe associates the Guise specifically with Tantalus in these lines is clear from several details of imagery. The editor of the Revels edition of the play was on the right track in his gloss on the common good that 'hangs' for every peasant to achieve: 'The metaphor is presumably from fruit hanging on a tree, to be picked or plucked as easily by one man as another.'[50] If one carries the suggestion of hanging fruit into the next lines, then the reference to that which 'flies beyond my reach' is unmistakable. The only fruit traditionally characterized as 'flying' beyond reach is that which enticingly hangs over the head of Tantalus in the underworld. Indeed, the Guise's phrasing echoes a description of Tantalus in Marlowe's earlier work; in his verse translation of Ovid's *Amores* Marlowe describes Tantalus as one who seeks 'fruit flying touch' (2.2.44).[51] In the midst of a portrait of himself as a daredevil overreacher, the Guise evokes the miserable image of the archetypal underreacher. His language moves from the classical up-and-down dynamic of tragedy to the to-and-fro motion of enticement and evasion.

The remainder of the Guise's speech, which is far too long to quote in full, is in fact a colossal anticlimax, the bathetic musings of a fallen Icarus who can only fantasize about power. Immediately after the Guise refers to his downfall, his language is marked by an un-Icarian obsessiveness and heaviness:

> For this, I wake, when others think I sleep;
> For this, I wait, that scorns attendance else;
> For this, my quenchless thirst whereon I build
> Hath often pleaded kindred to the King;
> ...
> For this, hath heaven engend'rd me of earth;
> For this, this earth sustains my body's weight,
> And with this weight I'll counterpoise a crown
> Or with seditions weary all the world;   2.45–8, 53–6

The 'quenchless thirst whereon I build' clearly alludes to the punishment of Tantalus,[52] and the rhetoric of the passage is a brilliant translation of Tantalus' repeated physical gestures into verbal terms. Thus, the patterns of repetition suggest an obsessive impulse, and the Guise's fivefold reiteration of the phrase 'For this' sounds increasingly like Tantalus' compulsive attempts to snatch the elusive fruit. Of course the irony is that the more often the Guise repeats 'For this,' the farther the meaning of 'this' flies beyond his (and our) reach. In the remainder of the speech, the Guise indirectly acknowledges his emptiness by launching into a manic inventory of the means by which he says he will 'supply my wants and necessity.' And when he declares his wish '[t]o bring the will of our desires to end,' his curious phrasing suggests his alienation from his own desires, as if they have a will of their own.[53] Finally, his exhausted speech ends with the Tantalian fantasy that his is a hand that 'with a grasp may gripe the world.' As if to tease the Guise, three people will wear the crown in the course of the play, but he will never touch it. The shift from Icarian resolve to Tantalian frustration in the Guise's single speech is developed in Marlowe's other plays throughout the entire course of the action. If we treat the two parts of *Tamburlaine* as a single play, then a clear pattern emerges: in the opening scenes the protagonist imagines himself or herself to be wielding exalted powers, but in the closing scenes we see that he or she is in fact impotent, and the stage spectacle suggests a version of the torment of Tantalus. At the end of *Dido Queen of Carthage*, the abandoned Dido is so thoroughly self-deluded that, when she attempts to embrace Aeneas, she grasps – Tantalus-like – thin air. Late in the first part of *Tamburlaine* we see the mockery of the caged Emperor Bajazeth, who is tantalized by the withholding of food and drink at Tamburlaine's feast. The second *Tamburlaine* play ends with Tamburlaine in Bajazeth's position, as the most powerful of Marlowe's protagonists is paralysed and teased on his deathbed by the map which reminds him of the worlds he has not conquered. In *The Jew of Malta* Barabas undergoes a Tantalian dispossession of goods and power, and he winds up in a kettle of boiling water, begging his enemies for succour. The situation of the deposed and imprisoned king in *Edward II* is more literally Tantalus-like, as he stands in a cesspool and is elaborately teased by his murderer. Similarly, the Doctor Faustus who is likened to Icarus in the Prologue is reduced to the posture of a spiritually parched Tantalus at the close, as he strains for a drop of Christ's blood which flies beyond his reach. The unforgettable intensity with which Marlowe stages these scenes – and there are corresponding moments in his poems – darkly intimates that it is Tantalus, not Icarus, who represents the protagonists' true identity and inevitable fate.

Theatrical Tantalization: Marlowe and the Audience

A key difference between the Icarus and Tantalus myths is their sharply contrasting relevance to the stage, for the former lends itself much less readily to theatrical representation than does the latter. In physical terms, the story of Icarus' flight and fall cannot be mimed without inviting hilarity, and thus Marlowe's allusions to Icarus are exclusively verbal. But the punishment of Tantalus can be dramatized quite easily, and the appearance of 'Tantalus' tree' in Philip Henslowe's inventory of stage props indicates that in at least one Elizabethan play the archetypi-

cal tantalization was actually staged.[54] Marlowe associates his characters with Tantalus through a recurrent stage-picture in which they
desperately reach for an enticing object that eludes their grasp. In addition to lending itself to dramatic representation, the punishment of Tantalus is inherently theatrical because the full effect of its humiliation
depends on the presence of spectators. In pictures of Tantalus, the
implied but invisible audience is the gods who watch the trick they are
playing on him.[55] Similarly, in Marlowe's plays there is often an on-
stage audience which watches and enjoys the protagonist's Tantalian
torment.[56] The audience in the theatre, then, views not only the suffering protagonist but also the protagonist being watched. By being
detached, like the tormentors on stage, the audience is invited to participate in the sportive mockery. A recurrent note in reviews of modern
Marlowe productions is the reference to audiences who find themselves
laughing at the victims of appalling cruelty.

But Marlowe never allows his audience the complacent privilege of
complete detachment. For Marlowe the theatre is a 'playhouse' in more
ways than one. The same impulse which turns his protagonist into a
Tantalus also shapes his manipulation of his audience, for he develops a
dramaturgy in which the dynamic of tantalization engages the viewer.
Thus, Marlowe's audience frequently finds itself in the situation of his
protagonists: provoked by expectation and frustrated of satisfaction.
The tantalization which is represented on stage replicates itself in the
action of the play on the audience. For Marlowe, the playhouse becomes
a theatre of power where he demonstrates his control over his audience
by playing with its responses, and especially by arousing desires which
he refuses to fulfil. The audience, too, becomes an Icarus tantalized.[57]

The myth of Tantalus, unlike that of Icarus, has parallels with the
dynamics of theatrical response, for a playwright can easily frustrate the
expectations which his art has created. On the bare, illusionistic Elizabethan stage, where the audience actively responds to poetic suggestion
and co-operates with the playwright (and actors) to imagine a world it
cannot see, the possibilities for playing with an audience's responses are
legion. As his writing career unfolds, Marlowe increasingly assumes for
himself the privileges and powers of the supreme game-player; the coer-
cive rhythms of tantalization – the enticing promise and then the sudden denial of satisfaction – become the dominant rhythms of his art. In
Alexander Leggatt's fine observation, 'It is part of the paradox of Marlowe that the times when he appears to be making his most ringing
statements are the times when he is really most elusive.'[58] This is to say

that the dramatic form of Marlowe's plays is not the up-and-down of Icarian tragedy, with its strong sense of closure, but rather the open-ended to-and-fro of Tantalian comedy, replete with anticlimaxes and false endings.

Marlowe's teasing dramaturgy stands in sharp contrast to that of the earnest, deferential playwrights of the previous generation. To illustrate Marlowe's method by its opposite, one need look no farther than the Elizabethan morality play which carries the un-Marlovian title *Enough Is as Good as a Feast*. In the Prologue, the playwright (W. Wager) shows great solicitude for his 'worshipful audience' and wishes that he were as inspired as Orpheus, whose music brought such calm to all the restless sufferers in Hades that 'Tantalus forgot his hunger and thirst.' With painful sincerity ('I desire with all my heart'), the playwright hopes that his play will prove to be so 'pleasant in every part, / That those which come for recreation / May not be void of their expectation.'[59] This concern of the author not to frustrate his audience dovetails with his subject matter, which is the centrality of Contentation (contentedness) to the moral life. By contrast, Marlowe's relationship to his audience is rarely respectful and never straightforward. Marlowe will not employ prologues to disambiguate his plays, as the authors of moralities do, but rather to raise false expectations about what is to follow. And it need hardly be said that contentedness fails to engage Marlowe's imagination.

Marlowe criticism has been slow to consider the possibility that tantalization may be a central strategy of his dramatic method, even though the words 'tantalizing' and 'teasing' frequently appear in discussions of particular moments in the plays.[60] The closest that critics have come is Judith Weil's observation that 'Marlowe seems to have been a rhetorical provocateur, as well as, quite possibly, a political one. He could tantalize and manipulate the imaginations of an audience in a masterful fashion. Rarely does he disappoint our expectations without first over-inflating them.' But she proceeds to argue that these manipulations are harnessed to an ethical project; Marlowe's teasing of his audience contributes to a pervasive Erasmian irony through which 'Marlowe mocks his heroes in a remarkably subtle style.'[61] Unfortunately, this thesis about Marlowe's humanistic intent scarcely allows his habitual 'disappoint[ment of] our expectations' to have the obvious effect: to mock not only his heroes but also his audience. As Douglas Duncan noted in a brief but incisive discussion of Marlowe and 'teasing drama' of the Renaissance, 'Whether we look forward to Jonson or back to Erasmus, we find in the more deeply-rooted humanists an educative concern which it is hard to feel that Marlowe shared.'[62] I would go farther and say that a contempt for 'educative concern' is one of the defining marks of Marlowe's work; he no more intends to inculcate a moral lesson in his audience than the gods torment Tantalus in order to educate and reform him.

To argue that Marlowe intended his plays to entice and to frustrate playgoers involves venturing into the growing but still problematic enterprise of studying the 'audience response' to Elizabethan drama.[63] This approach to the plays is inherently slippery, for theatre historians do not agree about even such fundamental matters as the social and gender composition of Elizabethan audiences. And very little factual evidence exists to document how Elizabethan audiences actually responded to specific moments in given plays. As Andrew Gurr tersely remarked, 'Evidence about the mindsets of Shakespearean audiences is appallingly meagre.'[64] And for the drama of the 1580s, the formative context of Marlowe's plays, the lack of evidence is still more acute.[65] Since facts are so few, any construction of how an audience would have responded to a play may be in fact merely the critic's sense of how that largely hypothetical audience *should* have responded. Invariably, the 'Model Spectator' postulated by some forms of reception theory begins to take on an uncanny resemblance to the theorist.

My response to the problem is to focus on the form of Marlowe's plays and poems, defining form in Kenneth Burke's apposite psychological terms as 'the creation of an appetite in the mind of the auditor, and the adequate satisfying of that appetite.'[66] Or, in Marlowe's case, the deliberately *inadequate* satisfying of that appetite. Thus, while it cannot be proven (or for that matter disproven) that Elizabethans actually responded in the ways I hypothesize, I find the recurrent formal patterns in which expectations are generated and then frustrated to be compelling evidence for Marlowe's intention to play with his audiences. This view is supported by a fact stressed in the discussions to follow: that these patterns are usually not present in Marlowe's sources, and, when they are, he markedly extends their significance.

In the most frequently cited of all classical references to Tantalus, Horace lampoons the degrading pursuit of wealth among Romans, identifying this covetousness with the torment of Tantalus. In a line which is the source of the proverbial phrase 'de te fabula narratur' ('the story is about you'), Horace suddenly warns his reader not to pretend to be superior to Tantalus:

The thirsting Tantalus doth catch at streams that from him flee.
Why laughest thou? the name but chang'd, the tale is told of thee.[67]

Marlowe compulsively insists on Horace's point, for in work after work he expresses the disconcerting impulse to turn his readers and spectators into Tantali.

2

Translation as Template: *All Ovid's Elegies*

Even though it is an imposing piece of work consisting of forty-eight poems and some 2400 lines, Marlowe's translation of Ovid's *Amores* has received short shrift in accounts of his imaginative development. Emphasizing its probable composition during Marlowe's student years at Cambridge, critics have elected to read *All Ovid's Elegies* with red pencil in hand, dismissing it as if it were an academic exercise of no real consequence – an assignment duly submitted and forgotten. (A recurrent and revealing feature of commentaries on the *Elegies* has been the donnish catalogue of Marlowe's Latin-to-English howlers.)[1] In the first comprehensive study of Marlowe's entire oeuvre, Una Ellis-Fermor removed the *Elegies* from serious attention by declaring the collection to be 'rather a prelude to his independent work than an integral part of it.'[2] Subsequent studies have endorsed this marginal status, conceding at the most that 'In all this mediocrity, we occasionally catch a glimpse of things to come.'[3] The great exception to this disesteem has been J.B. Steane's ground-breaking appreciation that the *Elegies* are 'a work as essentially Marlovian as any.'[4] Unfortunately, Steane does not adequately specify what the 'essentially Marlovian' nature of the collection is, nor has the issue been explored in the thirty years since the appearance of his book. It can be demonstrated, however, that Marlowe's translation of Ovid anticipates and illuminates his work to come in two decisive ways: through its pervasive relation of sexual desire to game-playing and through the narrative pattern in which this relation is presented – a pattern in which a masterful protagonist plays games in order to stimulate his desire but finally becomes the victim of games which frustrate and humiliate him.

Marlowe was of course not unique among young Elizabethans in being attracted to Ovid's *Amores*. Among the so-called University Wits of the 1580s, there was a good deal of interest in these witty and often wanton poems, partly because they were known to be the expression of Ovid's youthful muse. Thomas Nashe's lively prose, for instance, is studded with quotations from the *Amores* (including several from Marlowe's translation), and when John Lyly's repentant Euphues renounces his dissolute literary interests for the study of divinity, one of the books he bids farewell to is 'the pleasant Elegies of Ovid.'[5] Part of the attraction of the *Amores* must have been its ambiguous place in the traditional construction of the Ovidian canon. Unlike the *Metamorphoses* and even Ovid's other works of love-poetry such as the *Ars Amatoria* and the *Heroides*, the *Amores* had never been accepted by educational and religious authorities as a legitimate subject of study, and what a modern scholar has called an 'official code of silence' surrounded it.[6] Thus, the *Amores* was never set as a school text, never accorded the legitimizing sanction of a separate printed edition,[7] and, most important, never translated in its entirety before Marlowe.[8] (This resistance to translating the *Amores* persisted into the twentieth century; the editor of the 1914 Loeb Classical Library edition declined to translate an entire poem [3.7] as well as several juicy passages from others.) That Marlowe chose to translate these poems certainly bespeaks his uncommon literary ambition, and, since the *Amores* was Ovid's first work, perhaps even a thought of modelling his career on the Roman's.[9]

Because the *Elegies* are for the most part line-for-line and even word-for-word translations of Ovid, it is not difficult to identify moments when Marlowe's enthusiasms lead him to embellish his original. Foremost among these enthusiasms is Marlowe's frequent insertion of ludic words such as 'play,' 'game,' 'sport,' 'pranks,' and 'toying' into passages where the original Latin does not contain an equivalent term.[10] This game-playing terminology appears so frequently in Marlowe's best translations that it serves as a marker of his imaginative engagement. It is important to note that, far from being un-Ovidian, Marlowe's sportive terms elaborate an element which is so prominent in the *Amores* that a recent translator has referred to Ovid as '*homo ludens* in person.'[11] With a very light touch, Ovid treats love as a social game with rules which can be either followed or violated, but without serious consequence in either event. Moreover, the *Amores* contains many poems in which Ovid's persona of the poet-lover engages in playing games of deception on others (mistresses and rivals) and sometimes on himself. If love becomes inseparable from gamesmanship in the *Amores*, so does the activity of writing love-poems. Throughout the poems Ovid toys with the highly codified (and therefore predictable) conventions of Roman love-elegy, often springing on his reader carefully prepared surprises. Ovid proves to be a master of reader psychology, as he engages in what has been characterized as a 'constant play on his reader's expectations.'[12] This is to say that Ovid often manipulates his readers in the same deceptive manner as, within the dramatic fiction of the poems, he manipulates mistresses and rivals.

Marlowe's eager responsiveness to the ludic element in Ovid is apparent in a pair of his engaging translations (2.7 and 2.8). In the first poem, which is addressed to his mistress Corinna, Ovid vehemently denies her charge that he has had sex with her serving maiden. Spoken in an injured tone (why must she always so jealously misread his behaviour?), the entire poem consists of a vigorous and convincing protestation of innocence. In the following poem, however, Ovid addresses the serving woman in question, and we quickly hear of the 'secret pleasures' which he brags of having shared with her. As he slyly tells her (in Marlowe's words), she has been 'Apt to thy mistress, but more apt to me' (2.8.4). In the first poem, we only now realize, Ovid has placed his reader in the same unprivileged situation as the mistress he was addressing. In his translations of *Amores* 2.7 and 2.8 Marlowe clearly relishes Ovid's simultaneous playing with his mistress and his reader, and his poems make the idea of play even more prominent than it is in the original Latin. Marlowe's attraction to sex as play is evident in the first of the paired poems, where he translates the phrase 'Veneris conubia,' which suggests civil marriage, as 'Venus' game' (21). In his handling of the second poem, Marlowe makes the idea of play still more emphatic in his rendering of Ovid's words to the serving maiden:

> Whence knows Corinna that with thee I play'd?
> Yet blush'd I not, nor us'd I any saying
> That might be urg'd to witness our false playing.   2.8.6–8

Marlowe's 'with thee I play'd' translates 'concubitus,' meaning intercourse; here, as throughout the *Elegies*, he regards sex as synonymous with sport. Marlowe's 'false playing,' another phrase without an Ovidian equivalent, is especially suggestive, as it points to the furtive sexual play with the servant, to the verbal deception of his mistress, and by extension to the trick the poet has played on his reader.

In addition to stimulating Marlowe's interest in sexual and literary game-playing, Ovid's *Amores* supplied for the young writer a template for organizing these motifs into a particular narrative structure. This story could be called 'the teaser teased,' as the *Amores* begins with the poet-lover vaunting his game-playing cleverness (book 1), then shows him being used as a pawn in games which he had earlier taught his mistresses (book 2), and finally reveals that his peace of mind depends on his ability to deceive himself (book 3). The most pervasive irony takes the shape of a role-reversal in which the active, game-playing poet becomes the passive object of other people's games. We can trace the outline of Marlowe's engagement with the shifting dynamics of Ovidian teasing by concentrating on one outstanding translation from each of the three books of the *Elegies* (1.5, 2.19, 3.6) as well as the final poem of the collection (3.13).[13] (It should be noted that in modern editions of Ovid, the originals of Marlowe's 3.6 and 3.13 are numbered 3.7 and 3.14.) Taken together, these poems suggest an ironic curvature in the treatment of play and desire: first a celebration of sexual conquest and fulfilment, next an exploration of the ambiguous frustration and pleasure in sexual denial, then an episode of impotence in which frustration is merely humiliating, and finally the reduction of the poet to the desperate exigency of playing games with his own mind.

Showing and Hiding Bodies

The most frequently discussed of Marlowe's *Elegies* is the poem (1.5) recounting the visit to the poet's chamber one afternoon of the scantily clad Corinna. Since in many commentaries it is the *only* elegy which is discussed, and since it is always lifted out of its context in the whole sequence, it has come to stand as a synecdoche for Marlowe's *Elegies*. Unfortunately, the poem has often been misunderstood, and this misunderstanding, in turn, has been stamped on the entire collection of lyrics. It is short enough to quote in full:

> In summer's heat, and mid-time of the day,
> To rest my limbs upon a bed I lay;
> One window shut, the other open stood,
> Which gave such light as twinkles in a wood,
> Like twilight glimpse at setting of the sun,
> Or night being past, and yet not day begun.
> Such light to shamefast maidens must be shown,
> Where they may sport and seem to be unknown.

Then came Corinna in a long loose gown,
Her white neck hid with tresses hanging down,
Resembling fair Semiramis going to bed,
Or Lais of a thousand wooers sped.
I snatch'd her gown; being thin, the harm was small,
Yet striv'd she to be cover'd therewithal,
And striving thus as one that would be cast,
Betray'd herself, and yielded at the last.
Stark naked as she stood before mine eye,
Not one wen in her body could I spy.
What arms and shoulders did I touch and see,
How apt her breasts were to be press'd by me!
How smooth a belly under her waist saw I,
How large a leg, and what a lusty thigh!
To leave the rest, all lik'd me passing well;
I cling'd her naked body, down she fell.
Judge you the rest: being tir'd she bade me kiss;
Jove send me more such afternoons as this.

Responding to the way the phrase 'Stark naked' leaps out at the beginning of line 17, most of the commentary on the poem has taken the form
of paeans to naked bodies and sensuous fulfilment. But this emphasis is
very selective. What is missing from it is an awareness of how, like
Ovid's poem, Marlowe's translation plays with the idea of covering and
revealing, of offering and withholding. Since the poet is both inside and
outside the experience which he narrates, one needs to distinguish
between two different dimensions of teasing in the poem. For the poet
within the poem, there is the erotic teasing which is a part of its fantasy
of male sexual dominance. But the poet outside the poem is involved in
another, more mischievous kind of teasing. He toys with and ultimately
frustrates the aroused responses of the voyeuristic reader.

For the Ovid within the poem, desire is heightened and brought to a
climax by Corinna's coy offering and withholding of herself. That she
suddenly appears in the poet's chamber with her hair down and her
thin gown undone suggests that she is making herself easily available.
But the dream of sexual conquest (and the whole poem reads as if it is a
day-dream) depends on her not making herself *too* available. Accordingly, she denies the poet so as to arouse him, exerting just enough half-
hearted resistance to beget strife and to give him the pleasure of overcoming her without the onus of outright rape. In Marlowe, it should be

added, the stress on the physical overpowering of Corinna is stronger than in the original, as Ovid's words meaning 'I pressed her naked body to mine' become the more violent 'I cling'd her naked body, down she fell.' (When Marlowe reworks this scene in his narrative poem *Hero and Leander*, the violence will be still more pronounced and disconcertingly close to rape.) Marlowe's last line nicely captures the sleepy satisfaction of a man gratified with the performance of his virility: 'Jove send me more such afternoons as this.'

Unlike the poet inside the poem, who directly participates in the erotic 'sport' (8), the poet outside the poem manipulates and teases the response of the reader peeping in through the steamed window provided by the narrative. The difference is most marked in the double aspect of the much-imitated blazon of Corinna's body, which is at the centre of the poem.[14] What is triumphant scopophilia for the dramatized speaker quickly becomes frustrated voyeurism for the reader. For most of the blazon the reader can easily identify with the poet's possession of her body, which is now visual but soon (we are assured) to become physical. This blazon begins on high with her white neck (10), which is suggestively 'hid' by her long hair, and it moves progressively downward through her freshly uncovered arms and shoulders, enticing breasts, flat belly, and 'lusty thigh.' But the provocative description stops just short of its expected destination. While Ovid frustrates the reader by cleverly pretending to be worried about supplying too much detail ('why describe each feature?'), Marlowe more aggressively stresses the joke by emphasizing what the reader is not allowed to see: 'To leave the rest, all lik'd me passing well.'[15] Though Marlowe is less subtle than the Roman poet, like Ovid he 'deliberately frustrates the curiosity of his audience which he has just as deliberately aroused in the increasingly excited and intimate description of Corinna's charms.'[16]

This teasing of the reader's expectation of explicitness occurs again only two lines later. Immediately after the disappointment of not being allowed the final gaze, the reader's imagination is re-engaged by another graphic statement: 'I cling'd her naked body, down she fell.' But the first words of the next line close this newly opened curtain in the reader's face: 'Judge you the rest.' While both Ovid and Marlowe refuse to create details for the reader's fantasy to feed on, Ovid's disingenuous question ('cetera quis nescit' – 'who does not know the rest?') is more polite than Marlowe's direct challenge to the voyeuristic reader. Then, in a dazzling mid-line shift of time, the lovers are suddenly in the post-coital state of being 'tir'd.' After teasing the reader with the promise of sexual specificity, Ovid and Marlowe casually disclose that the love-making has already been consummated. It downplays the element of teasing to say that 'The technique is exactly that of the film, which enjoys a certain amount of nakedness and preliminary love-play but then cuts to the shot of the couple relaxed in bed after the action is over.'[17] Unlike the film convention, which usually provides for at least a brief transitional sequence (like a shot out the window) between show-ing the lovers undressing and the lovers smoking cigarettes, the effect in Ovid and especially in Marlowe is discontinuous and disconcerting – in a word, unconventional. Marlowe must have been pleased with what Ovid showed him about teasing the reader with extended foreplay and then suddenly declaring the love-making to be consummated, for his brilliant narrative technique in Hero and Leander will expand on the tan-talizing game which he plays in the Elegies.

In addition to teasing the reader with an uncompleted blazon and a too soon completed consummation, the poet plays a third trick on expectation in the final line: 'Jove send me more such afternoons as this!' The frustrated reader will hope, just as the satisfied poet within the poem hopes, for more such lubricious encounters in the poems/after-noons to come. But never again in the collection will the poet be rewarded with such an easy sexual conquest or the reader with such explicit images of female nakedness. Jove, alas, sends no more such afternoons. (The next poem [1.6] points to things to come by showing the lover haranguing the doorkeeper who refuses to allow him entrance to his mistress's lodgings.) It is only after the reader has finished all the poems (which readers of Marlowe's Elegies rarely do) that the extent of the misdirection created by 1.5 becomes clear. It is no coincidence that several of Marlowe's plays (most notably Dido Queen of Carthage and Edward II) similarly begin with titillating sexual material but also never return to this original degree of explicitness. Marlowe learned from Ovid how to engage, and tease, the erotic imagination.

While one should be wary of imposing neat patterns on such a richly varied group of poems as the Elegies, there is nevertheless a decisive movement in the sequence away from 'stark naked' sexuality to desire which is stimulated by the imagination and mediated through games of hiding and withholding. In terms of the collection as a whole, the most proleptic of the early Elegies proves not to be the bedding of Corinna but the poem (1.4) just before it, which explores how tantalization can frus-trate but also intensify desire. As opposed to the episode with Corinna at midday, the scenes in this poem take place not in the poet's chamber but in his mind as he imagines a banquet at which he will be separated from his mistress by the presence of her unsuspecting husband. The backdrop of the imagined banquet is important, for it suggests that the poet has become a Tantalus who can see but cannot touch: 'Shall I sit gazing as a bashful guest, / While others touch the damsel I love best?' (3–4). The most the poet can hope for is that, when the party has broken up, he and his mistress can use the crowd for cover and make some sort of fleeting contact. Marlowe's phrasing is poignant: 'There touch whatever thou canst touch of me' (58). Stimulated by thoughts of what he cannot have, the poet afflicts himself with the imagination of what will occur behind the couple's bedroom doors: 'Then will he kiss thee, and not only kiss / But force thee give him my stol'n honey bliss' (63–4). As his transformation of a fairly colourless phrase ('quod mihi das furtim' – what you give me secretly') into 'stol'n honey bliss' indicates, Marlowe heightens the tantalized lover's imaginings of his rival's pleasures.[18]

Following Frustration, Fleeing Fulfilment

The middle book of the *Amores* is marked by Ovid's exploration of the psychology of erotic game-playing, especially games which involve the sharpening of desire through teasing and frustration. Unlike 1.5, where Corinna's brief struggle is sufficient to arouse him, in these later poems the poet seeks a stronger form of denial, either as a prelude to sex or, more problematically, as an end in itself. We see an internalizing of desire, a focus on the play of impulses within the poet's mind rather than on the desired object's charms. Ovid insists that he is attracted to women who are elusive, difficult of access, preferably even prohibited; in the words of a modern translator of the *Amores*, 'this love-poet thrives on frustration.'[19] Perhaps making a virtue of necessity, the poet eroticizes denial, claiming the superior enticements of love-objects which can be imagined but not possessed.

Ovid's simplest articulation of the idea that frustration enhances desire is a passage in the *Ars Amatoria* in which he advises Roman matrons to play hard to get:

> it's their husbands' access to them,
> At will, that deprives so many wives of love.
> Let her put in a door, with a hard-faced porter to tell him
> 'Keep out', and he'll soon be touched with desire
> Through frustration.   3.585–9[20]

In the *Amores*, this abstract advice is embodied in many dramatized situations involving the delay or outright denial of the poet's access to a desired woman. In these poems, Ovid identifies himself with the conventional figure in Roman love-elegy of the *exclusus amator*, the shut-out lover who spends the cold night muttering outside his mistress' symbolic locked gates.[21] But Ovid expands the resonance of the stock figure, as he multiplies not only physical obstacles blocking satisfaction but also, more interestingly, psychological ones. So, in addition to barred doors, hostile gatekeepers, and a river in flood, there is something within Ovid himself which militates against fulfilment. No less than in Ovid's poems, in Marlowe's translations desire becomes literally unthinkable without some form of teasing and delay.

Ovid's most complex and interesting exploration of the psychology of erotic denial appears in the final poem of book 2 (2.19). In the Renaissance this poem was the *locus classicus* for discussions of delay and desire; Montaigne's essay 'That Our Desires Are Increased By Difficulties' quotes more frequently from it than from any other text.[22] Ovid's ambivalent attitude toward denial in 2.19 elicits from Marlowe a vigorous translation. In Marlowe as in Ovid, the poem modulates between two reasons for valuing erotic frustration: (1) it transforms the woman into forbidden fruit and thus increases the eventual satisfaction (an idea Freud was to dilate upon)[23] and (2) it is intrinsically enjoyable, since pain itself can bring masochistic pleasure.[24] These two views could be designated as, respectively, Icarian and Tantalian; the first depicts frustration as a stimulus to desire which results in the overcoming of obstacles, while the second depicts it as a static condition which leads only to endless repetition. The Icarian view is the more prominent and thematically signposted, perhaps because it involves in Peter Green's phrase a 'characteristically masculine notion of rejecting too easy a conquest.'[25] But Green does not note that after every expression of this forceful view the poet-lover immediately slides into the less 'masculine,' Tantalian attitude.

In one of Ovid's trademark reversals of expectation, the poem begins by turning upside down the poet-lover's earlier plea to Corinna's doorkeeper (1.6) to let him in. Now, instead of trying to gain access to his mistress, the witty poet urges her husband to do him a favour by guarding her more carefully. Marlowe's translation begins with a Donne-like explosion of sharp contempt:

Fool, if to keep thy wife thou hast no need,
Keep her for me, my more desire to breed.
We scorn things lawful, stol'n sweets we affect ...

Marlowe intensifies the note of defiance in Ovid, as in the third line he increases both the scorn for the lawful and the desire for the forbidden.[26] But the tone immediately modulates away from this swashbuckling pose, and only three lines later the poet exclaims: 'What should I do with fortune that ne'er fails me? / Nothing I love that at all times avails me' (7–8). Though Marlowe's couplet lessens the masochism of Ovid's lines, there is nevertheless a suggestion that the pain of failure can be pleasurable.[27]

The poet's ambivalence about frustration returns when he contrasts his past relationship with Corinna to his present one with a new, unnamed mistress. Corinna used to tease him by pretending to have headaches when he was eager, thereby creating an amorous delay which heightened the joy of eventual consummation: 'So having vex'd she nourish'd my warm fire, / And was again most apt to my desire' (15–16). When he turns to address his new mistress, however, he exhorts her to increase his suffering and makes no mention of sexual fulfilment:

> Thou also, that late took'st mine eyes away,
> Oft cozen me, oft being woo'd, say nay;
> And on thy threshold let me lie dispread,
> Suff'ring much cold by hoary night's frost bred.
> So shall my love continue many years;
> This doth delight me, this my courage cheers.   19–24

Beginning with the reference to her as one who '[took] mine eyes away,' the passage repeatedly images her in active and himself in passive terms. In the last line, the emphatic but imprecise repetition of 'This' can only refer to the years of enthusiastic suffering which the poet antici-pates. His delight stems not from having his 'warm fire' nourished but from the thought of 'Suff'ring much cold.'

This ambivalence about the pain and pleasure of erotic frustration is the focus of a rich passage at the heart of the poem and also at the heart of the *Elegies*. Once again, the progression is from images of active male desire to images of tantalized passivity:

> Fat love, and too much fulsome, me annoys,
> Even as sweet meat a glutted stomach cloys.
> In brazen tower had not Danae dwelt,
> A mother's joy by Jove she had not felt;
> While Juno Io keeps, when horns she wore,
> Jove lik'd her better then he did before.

> Who covets lawful things takes leaves from woods,
> And drinks stol'n waters in surrounding floods.
> Her lover let her mock that long will reign,
> Aye me, let not my warnings cause my pain!
> Whatever haps, by suff'rance harm is done;
> What flies I follow, what follows me I shun.   25–36

After the opening rejection of a very unpleasant sexual surfeit, the poet argues that the attempts to prevent Jove from approaching Danae and Io served instead to stimulate the god's appetite and potency. He then dismisses the desire for women who are available, likening it to such pointless, undemanding activities as plucking leaves (instead of fruit?) from trees or drinking water while standing in a flood.[28] A shadowy allusion to the punishment of Tantalus hovers over these images of plucking at trees and drinking water while surrounded by the water, as an explicit allusion earlier in book 2 indicates: 'Water in waters, and fruit flying touch / Tantalus seeks, his long tongue's gain is such' (2.2.43–4). The idea of the lover's tantalization continues into the next lines, which place women in the role of kings or gods who rule men through their ability to 'mock' them. Even his anxiety about being punished for giving away to women the amatory secrets of men ('let not my warnings cause my pain') may recall Tantalus' crime of telling mortals the secrets of the gods.[29]

The passage reaches its climax in the elegant line which is one of the most psychologically rich in the *Amores*: 'What flies I follow, what follows me I shun' ('quod sequitur, fugio; quod fugit, ipse sequor'). Though the poet began the passage by likening himself to Jove as a heroic, overreaching seducer, he now announces his proclivity to desire women whom he cannot possess and to avoid those who are willing. The clever construction of the line implies the impulse of game-playing, but the game seems to be played *on* the poet as much as played *by* him. Despite the energetic fleeing and pursuing which it conjures up, the line conveys a distinct sense of powerlessness, as if the poet is caught up in a pattern of flight and pursuit which he cannot control. The phrase 'what flies I follow' expresses a desire which is provoked by teasing, and indeed it applies so appositely to Tantalus that it could be spoken by him. When Thomas Howell wrote a commonplace lyric explicitly likening his amatory suffering to the punishment of Tantalus ('Most dainty food I see, / yet starve for want of meat'), he gave his poem the Ovidian title 'I follow what flyeth from me.'[30]

Ovid's 'quod sequitur, fugio; quod fugit, ipse sequor,' and similar formulations of ambivalence,[31] must have engaged Marlowe's imagination, for the idea resonates throughout the rest of his works. It figures
prominently in his Ovidian narrative *Hero and Leander*, and, as my next
chapter demonstrates, it provides one of the central organizing ideas in
his tragedy *Dido Queen of Carthage*. It appears in less explicitly erotic
contexts as well, such as the Duke of Guise's exclamation, 'That like I
best that flies beyond my reach.' Like the passage from *Elegy* 2.19, the
Guise's soliloquy moves from a scornful reference to easily available
(and thus vulgar) pleasure to a desire for objects so elusive that no one
can grasp them. It is no coincidence that both of these characters who
are deluded by their own claims to heroism eventually become passive
figures cuckolded by rivals. The distance between the late *Elegies* and
Marlowe's tragedies is not as great as one might first imagine.

The Poet-Lover as Tantalus

In the third and final book of the *Amores*, the tenor of Ovid's poems
darkens; for the first time in the sequence, 'frustration and disillusion
are the predominant emotions expressed.'[32] Of course the note of failure
and frustration is not new to book 3. As a recent commentator has
noted, 'Depending on how one counts, at least half of the *Amores*
involve the poet's inability to convince an addressee to do what he
wants them to, or to carry out a course of action he had at the outset
decided was in his best interests.'[33] But in book 3 the emphasis on failure is pervasive and unmistakable. In the central poem of the book (3.6),
the poet suffers from an onset of sexual impotence (the only such incident in Roman love-elegy), and many poems reveal other forms of
powerlessness, ranging from being unable to cross a swollen stream
(3.5) to being unable to compete with the gifts of a rich rival (3.7). This
inability to act is the complement of another important motif which
reaches a crescendo in the final book of the *Amores*: the ironic discrepancy between the poet's facile ability to manipulate language and the
failure of that language to make an impact on the external world. It is
one of the poet's many futile addresses to an indifferent audience, the
elegy (1.13) beseeching the dawn goddess Aurora to delay the coming of
day, which contains the words that Faustus will quote in Latin in *his*
hapless attempt to arrest the passage of time: 'O lente, lente currite
noctis equi!'[34] Though early in the sequence the poet asserts that verse
has magical powers, including the power quite literally to open doors

for him (2.1), in book 3 (3.8) he finds himself lamenting the cruel death of Tibullus, a master poet who could be saved neither by his own words nor by those of the people who loved him.

Marlowe's most outstanding translations in book 3 are two poems (3.6 and 3.13) in which the idea of sexual play intersects with the motif of powerlessness. Just as he had magnified the element of play in Ovid's early poems of sexual fulfilment, so Marlowe exaggerates this same element in the late poems; he does so by inverting the motif as it appeared earlier, making the poet the passive object rather than the designing subject of the love-games. We can see this inverted sense of game-playing in Marlowe's engaged and engaging translation of 3.6, the poem about the incident of temporary impotence. That the poet-lover proves to be least capable when the woman is most willing takes to its logical conclusion the idea implicit in 'fleeing and following': that desire and the availability of the desired object are in inverse ratio.

As a commentator on Ovid has noted, the poet's humiliating impotence in 3.6 'looks rather like nemesis for the cockiness' he had expressed in earlier poems.[35] In book 2, for instance, the poet had bragged about his ability to keep two avid mistresses busy: 'Let one wench cloy me with sweet love's delight,/If one can do't, if not, two every night' (2.10.21–2). He even claims that increase of appetite grows by what it feeds on: 'Pleasure adds fuel to my lustful fire,/I pay them home with that they most desire' (2.10.25–6). Marlowe follows Ovid in emphasizing the reversal of the poet's fortunes by echoing ironically the early poem (1.5) in which Corinna visited his chamber in a spirit of playful submission. Like Corinna, the woman in 3.13 wears a 'loose gown,' and in both encounters a lusty thigh is revealed underneath. This rhetorical situation, in which the revelation of the protagonist's impotence is accompanied by ironic echoes of his earlier claims to power, will become a common motif in the final act of Marlowe's plays, most strikingly in *Doctor Faustus*.

With the same intensity he had earlier used to project himself into the lover's triumph over Corinna, Marlowe now imagines himself in the plight of the lover reduced to an object.[36] Nowhere is the poem more energetic than in its opening description of failed love-making:

Idly I lay with her, as if I lov'd not,
And like a burden griev'd the bed that mov'd not.
Though both of us perform'd our true intent,
Yet could I not cast anchor where I meant.

She on my neck her ivory arms did throw,
Her arms far whiter than the Scythian snow,
And eagerly she kiss'd me with her tongue,
And under mine her wanton thigh she flung.
Yea, and she sooth'd me up, and call'd me 'Sir,'
And us'd all speech that might provoke and stir.
Yet like as if cold hemlock I had drunk,
It mocked me, hung down the head, and sunk.   3–14

Just as in 1.5 Marlowe had revised Ovid by increasing the violence of
the poet against Corinna, now he turns the tables and increases that of
the woman against the poet. In a variation on the idea of fleeing provok-
ing following, his lassitude provokes her manic energy. Thus, Ovid's
discreet reference to an inability (in the Loeb translation) 'to use the
pleasurable part of my languid loins' becomes in Marlowe a vivid failure to 'cast anchor,' a failure which immediately galvanizes her entire
body. In a series of stressed verbs, the poet becomes an object around
whom she throws her arms, under whom she flings her thigh (versus
Ovid's decorous 'supposuit' – 'placed underneath'), and into whose
mouth she 'eagerly' inserts her tongue. She accompanies her physical
onslaught with vigorous verbal massage, as she tries to 'provoke and
stir' him through suggestive talk. The end result of all this activity is the
magnificent bathos of 'It mocked me, hung down the head, and sunk,'
where Marlowe's phrasing makes both the physiology and psychology
of impotence more graphic than does Ovid's 'propositum destituere
meum' ('my intention failed me'). In what has been called the Elizabethan 'pornography of male impotence,' this is a key text.[37]

In this poem erotic tantalization remains important, but in a new way.
It is no longer a game to make an eventual fulfilment more satisfying
but rather a state of humiliation. At the centre of the poem, the poet likens himself to Tantalus:

I wish'd to be receiv'd in, in I get me;
To kiss, I kiss: to lie with her she let me.
Why was I blest? why made king to refuse it?
Chuff-like had I not gold and could not use it?
So in a spring thirsts[38] he that told so much,
And looks upon the fruits he cannot touch.   47–52

Marlowe follows Ovid in not naming Tantalus as the 'he' who thirsts in a spring and looks upon fruit; modern translators, who cannot rely on their readers' grasp of mythology, usually insert his name into the text. Whether or not it is left implicit, this reference to Tantalus is powerful, as it caps with a note of cold finality the bustling repetitions and lively double rhymes of the preceding lines. This brief but telling glimpse of Tantalus in the underworld provides an image of enticement and game-playing emptied of human pleasure. Earlier in the sequence, to be tantalized was to be provoked to wit and desire, but here the clear reference to both the crime and punishment of Tantalus suggests how un-erotic and humiliating tantalization has become.

More is involved in the speaker's abject humiliation than his failure to perform sexually. He is forced to acknowledge that, instead of being the supreme erotic game-player he has fancied himself, he is in fact the plaything of others. Thus he fears that his body is wasting away because dark forces of witchcraft are at work. He may be the victim of potent Thessalian charms or perhaps someone has employed sympathetic magic and 'pierc'd my liver with sharp needles' points,' thus turning him into a human voodoo doll. Or perhaps he is one of the possessed: 'Why might not then my sinews be enchanted, / And I grow faint as with some spirit haunted?' Ironically, this idea of being possessed returns near the end of the poem, when – now that he is alone – his reluctant member suddenly springs to life:

> Now, when he should not jet, he bolts upright,
> And craves his task, and seeks to be at fight.
> Lie down with shame, and see thou stir no more,
> Seeing thou wouldst deceive me as before.
> Thou cozenest me: by thee surpris'd am I,
> And bide sore loss with endless infamy.   67–72

The poet expresses a distinct note of paranoia; his concern that 'thou wouldst deceive me as before' suggests that he fears his hopes, like those of Tantalus, are being toyed with again.

This poem, like many of the earlier *Elegies*, plays with the notion of fleeing and following desire, but now it translates the motif into exaggerated physical movements. For instance, it is the poet's failure to 'cast anchor' which provokes her vigorous overtures, and in turn it seems to be her athletic eagerness which robs him of his desire. Ironically, his desire is awakened only when neither she nor he wishes it to be. When she scornfully leaves him at the end of the poem, it is the sight of her naked feet which, finally, entices the poet: 'With that, her loose gown on, from me she cast her; / In skipping out her naked feet much grac'd her' (81–2). He is aroused, it would seem, not so much by pedal fetishism as by the teasing interplay between the concealment of her 'loose gown' and the sudden appearance of her 'naked feet.' It is only when she flees that his desire follows.

The final poem of the sequence (excepting a short envoi) emphasizes the entrapment of the poet in a situation which he had earlier mastered, and it is one of Marlowe's best translations. As usual in his liveliest translations, the idea of erotic sport crops up more frequently than in Ovid's original, where there is little or no warrant for such phrases as 'false playing' (1), 'night's pranks' (7), 'lascivious toyings' (17) (cf. 'lascivious toys' at 1.4.21), 'tricks' (18), and 'thousand sports' (24). This vocabulary, which is so reminiscent of the poet's amorous escapades early in the sequence, carries a surprise – for the poet conspicuously fails to participate in this vigorous erotic play. Or, rather, he now participates as an unwilling spectator, for his mistress continues to play *his* old games, but now with other men. The brisk opening couplet sums up the poem: 'Seeing thou art fair, I bar not thy false playing, / But let not me, poor soul, know of thy straying.' Marlowe's translation of these lines shows his care to create ironic echoes of phrases which he had used in earlier poems, when the speaker ruled the world of sport. In the opening line, for instance, the collocation of 'fair' and 'false playing' recalls the poet's earlier libertine observation that 'Fair women play, she's chaste whom none will have' (1.8.43). Also, the reference here to the woman's 'false playing' may remind us of the poet's pride in his own 'false playing' (2.8.8) when he deceived his mistress and slept with her handmaid. And Marlowe's use of the word 'bar,' which has no equivalent in Ovid, recalls the frequent motif of barred doors, but again with a difference. In 3.4 the poet had argued to the husband that locking up his wife would not work; now he seems to be sadly heeding his own advice. In this, the final metamorphosis of the *Elegies*, the poet has become virtually indistinguishable from the hapless husbands he had earlier mocked.

The poet's desperate tone stems from his awareness of his total lack of power, his inability to play. It is as if the various kinds of impotence which he recorded with shock in the previous poems have now become a fact of life no longer warranting mention. Though the poet does not participate in the erotic sport of the woman he addresses, it is not quite right to say that he does not play any games. In an ironic transformation of some of the earlier sexual triangles of the *Amores*, where his amorous play with his mistress involved the deception of a rival, the poet now enlists the aid of the woman to help him delude himself about her 'thousand sports' with his rivals. While she will play her games in 'The bed [that] is for lascivious toyings meet,' his must take place in his mind. Foremost among these mental games is the manoeuvre in which thinking and self-deception will become synonymous: 'Deceive all; let me err, and think I am right, / And like a wittol think thee void of slight' (29–30). But of course the game is futile, for (as the protagonists of the plays will also discover) no amount of repeating that one wants to be deceived can actually create the desired delusion.[39]

A good way to describe the poet's mental game is to say that he wants to dissociate what he knows from what he sees. But, ironically, each time that he asks to be deceived he proceeds to picture her infidelities more vividly. At the beginning he is content to tell her that her 'night's pranks' and 'hidden secrets' should not see the light of day. But, though he wishes her to 'seem as you were full of grace,' he cannot forget the evidence of his eyes, such as the bed 'by tumbling made uneven.' (There is not even a distant equivalent in Ovid for 'tumbling.') Finally, he turns from what he actually sees and, more luridly than in Ovid, he begins to imagine catching his mistress and her lover *in flagrante delicto*:

> Though while the deed be doing you be took,
> And I see when you ope the two-leav'd book,
> Swear I was blind, deny, if you be wise,
> And I will trust your words more than mine eyes.

Marlowe's vivid metaphor, again not present in Ovid, of the 'two-leav'd book' suggests that the poet will not easily be able to banish thoughts of her betrayal from his mind.[40] Thus, after all the clever, wishful talk of self-delusion, he ends by indicating that he is still not deluded. She will, he says, be 'justified' by her denial of wrongdoing, but in the poem's last words he reminds her that 'The cause acquits you not, but I that wink.' This poem, closing with a wink of the I/eye, is the expression of a person who can neither look on reality with open eye nor blind himself. For this teaser turned Tantalus, delusion has become the food of love.

The poet-lover's descent in the *Elegies* from transgressive desire to tantalized frustration marshals the way for the protagonists of Marlowe's plays. Figures as diverse as Dido, Tamburlaine, and Faustus are caught up in a similar pattern: early in the play each is presented as a person who exerts power through playing games with people, and at the end each suffers the torment of Tantalus, as he or she becomes the object of a humiliating game of withholding from which escape is not possible. There is, however, a crucial difference in tone between Ovid's and Marlowe's use of the teaser-teased motif. In the Roman poet, the effect remains humorous, as Ovid the author of the *Amores* invites the reader to smile at his hapless namesake, the poet figure within the poems. As a critic has noted, 'It is a favourite form of irony with Ovid to envisage the tables turned upon himself.'[41] Even in the unhappiest of the *Elegies*, Ovid never allows his reader to forget that love, and writing poems about love, remains essentially comical. In Marlowe's plays and in *Hero and Leander*, however, there is nothing light-hearted in the reversals of game-playing. The depictions of the protagonists' failures are so mercilessly objectivized that an audience's laughter at the game of tantalization cannot help but be cruel.

3

Playing with the Powerless: *Dido Queen of Carthage*

Marlowe's *Tragedy of Dido Queen of Carthage* is both more like and more unlike his translation of Ovid's *Amores* (*All Ovid's Elegies*) than commentators have indicated. For the most part, critics have been content to note general points of contact between the two works: that both are learned and that Marlowe probably wrote both when he was at Cambridge; that *Dido* is closer in spirit to Ovid than to Virgil's *Aeneid*, the source of its plot; that the poetry of *Dido* is in various ways 'Ovidian.'[1] The primary link, however, between the two works has not been noted. This is the play's emphasis on an Ovidian motif which Marlowe had eagerly responded to in his *Elegies*: erotic games involving enticement and teasing. In *Dido*, the curtain literally opens on the spectacle of sexual game-playing, as we see '*Jupiter dandling Ganymede upon his knee*' (s.d.) and cajoling the boy: 'Come, gentle Ganymede, and play with me: / I love thee well, say Juno what she will' (1.1.1–2). Ganymede interprets 'play with me' in a sense that Jupiter perhaps does not intend, for he proceeds to twist the king of gods around his peevish little finger. As in the *Elegies*, the lovers in *Dido* 'play with' each other more in terms of manipulation than mutuality. This lack of mutuality is apparent in the major form the play's love-games take, which is the Ovidian idea of love as obsessive pursuit and flight. In *Dido* as in the *Elegies*, people flee from the love which pursues them and pursue the love which flees them.

If Ovidian game-playing is what most intimately connects the two works, it is also the focus of some of their most significant differences. More precisely, what differentiates them is Marlowe's distinctive inflection of Ovidian game-playing in *Dido*: an emphasis on sadistic sport and (in a phrase from the play) smiling at tears. In Ovid, the poet-lover often plays games on others, and in the late poems he becomes the object of the games of his mistresses, whom he had earlier instructed. But Ovid's love-games are never hurtful, and the humour is for the most part quite genial. The poet takes no pleasure in inflicting physical or mental suffering on those with whom he plays, and indeed such pleasure as he finds in pain derives from his savouring of his own suffering. At the end of the *Elegies*, when the poet-lover is hoist with his own petard of erotic deception and frustrated by an episode of impotence, we may well be amused at his predicament. But we also feel that Ovid the poet is smiling at his namesake in the poems and that 'we are sharing the sense of humour of a man who can laugh at his own follies.'[2]

In *Dido Queen of Carthage*, however, sport always comes at someone's expense. It is here that for the first time we encounter what has been called Marlowe's 'humour of discomfiture.'[3] Powerlessness pervades this tragedy, beginning with storm-tossed ships and memories of a helpless city destroyed and ending with the suicide of the abandoned protagonist. *Dido* is full of cruel games played on people without power, games which are disconcertingly amusing precisely because they stress their victims' loss of control. Repeatedly, the audience watches characters being played with by forces they cannot resist, and often are not even aware of. Though all the mortals in the play are caught up in the games of the gods, it is ultimately Dido who exemplifies the state of impotence and who may provoke the audience's ambivalent amusement. At the end of the play, her situation is in many ways similar to that of the poet-lover at the close of the *Elegies*. Like him, Dido is an erstwhile controlling figure who is rendered helpless by frustrated desire, and in her intense yearning she assumes the posture on stage of the mythological figure to whom he was likened: the pathetic but laughably deluded Tantalus.

Following and Fleeing Love

In *Dido Queen of Carthage*, love is as much a motion as an emotion. It is through motion that desire is both manifested and begotten, as Marlowe transforms the epic linearity of the *Aeneid* into the to-and-fro interplay of lovers, a physical and psychological coming and going. As in the *Elegies*, desire is sharpened by what it cannot have; indeed, nothing excites love in this play so much as the active disregard of the love-object. In *Dido Queen of Carthage* Marlowe represents the motions of desire as an oscillating rhythm of flight and pursuit, enticement and escape, which pulses through the whole play.[4] The origin of this rhythm can be traced to the *Elegies*, and especially to the central line which Marlowe translated as 'What flies I follow, what follows me I shun' ('quod sequitur, fugio; quod fugit, ipse sequor' [2.19.36]).[5] Ovid's line is far more suggestive than its immediate context (the lover is urging the husband to guard his wife more assiduously) might indicate, for it seems to bespeak not so much the conquest of difficult circumstances as the impossibility of making any erotic contact at all. The speaker avoids the women who are available and pursues those who avoid him.

This Ovidian rhythm of flight and pursuit is most clearly – even diagrammatically – depicted in the subplot of *Dido*, which is entirely Marlowe's invention. At the centre of the subplot is Iarbas, the proud king of the neighbouring Getulians and suitor to Dido. In the *Aeneid* Iarbas is merely a shadowy figure who remains in his kingdom, but Marlowe places him in residence at Dido's court, thus making him an active rival to Aeneas.[6] In another departure from Virgil, Marlowe creates a second love triangle by having Dido's sister Anna suffer an unrequited love for Iarbas. The line 'What flies I follow, what follows me I shun' precisely describes Iarbas' situation, as he flees from Anna's blatant offering of herself and pursues the elusive Dido. The motif of flight and pursuit is most explicit in an interchange between Iarbas and Anna at the end of 4.2. When Iarbas tells her of his unrequited love for Dido, Anna offers herself to him: 'Away with Dido, Anna be thy song: / Anna that doth admire thee more than heaven!' (45–6). Iarbas' response to this declaration is a speedy exit. (Here, as he will in *Hero and Leander*, Marlowe humorously literalizes the psychological flight and pursuit.) Iarbas' parting words are a paranoiac expansion of Ovid's 'quod sequitur, fugio': 'For I will fly from these alluring eyes, / That do pursue my peace where'er it goes' (50–1). But of course his flight provokes her pursuit, and so she exits with a desperately masochistic elaboration of the 'quod fugit, ipse sequor' half of Ovid's line: 'I'll follow thee with outcries ne'er the less, / And strew thy walks with my dishevell'd hair' (55–6).

Clearly, the idea of fleeing and following which shapes the relationship of Iarbas and Anna derives from Ovid, but with a difference. In Ovid the poet-lover takes pleasure in the game, but it is neither a game nor enjoyable for Iarbas and Anna. Throughout the play the proud Getulian king voices his sexual frustration with an anger that we never hear in Ovid:

How long, fair Dido, shall I pine for thee?
'Tis not enough that thou dost grant me love,

But that I may enjoy what I desire;
That love is childish which consists in words.   3.1.7–10

When Dido dismisses him after he insists that he wants to 'enjoy what I desire,' his comment (in another Ovidian echo)[7] is revealing: 'I go to feed the humour of my love' (3.1.50). Just as Tantalus' appetite grows each time he snatches at the apples in vain, so Iarbas feeds on his frustration and makes himself all the hungrier. When he sees Dido and Aeneas leaving the cave after their love-making, his reference to 'these adulterers surfeited with sin' (4.1.20) reveals his tantalized hunger (and moral hypocrisy). In his overheated mind, his desire for consummation with Dido and revenge on Aeneas blend, as he fantasizes about drinking the 'dying blood' (3.3.28) of one and making 'love dronken with ... sweet desire' (3.3.75) with the other. But his thirst is never assuaged.

In the Neoplatonic philosophy of love, what Ficino calls 'the fruitful hunt' and 'successful chase' of lovers is a process of sublimation which provokes an ascent to God, the origin of love.[8] But Iarbas' pursuit of Dido and Anna's pursuit of Iarbas lead them downward to their deaths by suicide (another Marlovian invention) at the close of the play. After Dido dies, the stage direction – 'Enter Iarbas running' – comically literalizes Iarbas' frenzied but futile pursuit, and the last phrase of his dying words registers his awareness that his suicide is in vain: 'Dido, I come to thee: ay me, Aeneas!' (5.1.318). Even in death the chase does not end, for Anna pursues the fleeing Iarbas into the afterworld. Her final line, which is also the final line of the play, expresses her obsessiveness. First she says 'Now, sweet Iarbas, stay,' which poignantly repeats what she had said the previous time he fled from her ('Iarbas, stay, loving Iarbas, stay' [4.2.52]). Her life and the play culminate with a crashing irony, as her last words to Iarbas repeat precisely his last words to Dido: 'I come to thee!'[9] In the world of shades to which they descend, nothing will change; Iarbas will continue to pursue Dido in vain, while Anna will forever plead with him to 'stay.'

This pattern of unending pursuit and flight – of pursuit which engenders flight and flight which in turn entices pursuit – is also central to the interplay between Dido and Aeneas, and in some ways Anna and Iarbas serve as a subplot model for their relationship. With Dido and Aeneas, as with Anna and Iarbas, the traditional roles of the sexual hunt are reversed, as each sister actively pursues an elusive man. Through adept juxtapositions of scenes, Marlowe is careful to emphasize the parallels in the two relationships. Immediately after Iarbas flees from Anna in act 4, for example, Aeneas enters and announces his decision to leave Dido: 'Carthage, my friendly host, adieu' (4.3.1). Similarly, when Iarbas dismisses Anna's wooing of him because it 'intercepts the course of my desire' (4.2.48), his words precisely suggest how Dido has intercepted Aeneas' course to the prophesied land of Italy. And Anna's pathetic cry to the departing Iarbas that 'I have honey to present thee with' (4.2.53) anticipates the catalogue of sybaritic pleasures which Dido will promise to the restive Aeneas and his men.

Unlike Anna and Iarbas, who are depicted with broad strokes, Dido and Aeneas are complex figures, and the dynamic of pursuit and flight in their relationship is accordingly more involved. In order to understand Aeneas' evasive response to Dido's pursuit of him, we need to recall that for him the events at Carthage take place under the long shadow cast by the fall of Troy. Indeed, for Aeneas Carthage threatens to become a second Troy. When Aeneas recounts the fall of Troy to Dido, he places a lurid emphasis (far greater than in the corresponding passage in the *Aeneid*) on the wild ferocity of the Greeks and the helplessness of the Trojan population. In his account the Trojans' bodies are tossed about and violated at the whim of the Greeks:

> Headless carcases piled up in heaps,
> Virgins half-dead dragg'd by their golden hair
> And with main force flung on a ring of pikes,
> Old men with swords thrust through their aged sides,
> Kneeling for mercy to a Greekish lad,
> Who with steel pole-axes dash'd out their brains.   2.1.194–9

The only possible response to this abject vulnerability is the desire to escape. Both at Troy and later at Carthage, the impulse to flee defines Aeneas' world of action. After he has left her, Dido fastens on his predilection for flight in a scornful question: 'And must I rave thus for a runagate?' (5.1.265). The term 'runagate,' which has no equivalent in the corresponding speech in Virgil, means 'deserter, fugitive, runaway' (*OED* 2); it reminds us that, all along, Marlowe's Aeneas has been more engaged in fleeing from danger than in pursuing the prophesied kingdom in Latium.

If he is to survive Troy's destruction, Aeneas must heed the terse command which Hector's mangled ghost delivers to him: 'Aeneas, fly!' When Aeneas descends into the maelstrom of burning Troy, twice he finds himself in situations where he heeds Hector's advice and flees for his life. First, in a scene which has no counterpart in Virgil, Aeneas is engulfed by bloody Pyrrhus and his Myrmidons, who carry 'balls of wildfire in their murdering paws' (2.1.217). In a climax which has the vividness of nightmare, Aeneas recalls how these savage figures 'hemm'd me about, crying, "This is he!"' When Dido interjects 'Ah, how could poor Aeneas scape their hands?' she makes him sound like a help-less child, an association which is strengthened by his ultimate means of escape:

> My mother Venus, jealous of my health,
> Convey'd me from their crooked nets and bands;
> So I escap'd the furious Pyrrhus' wrath ...   2.1.221–3

Aeneas is as passive ('convey'd') during his escape as he would have been if the Greeks had caught him in their 'crooked nets,' and this image points to what has been called 'the almost pathological quality of his passiveness' in the rest of the play.[10]

This terror of entanglement threatens Aeneas a second time as he leads his family from the conflagration of Troy. Unlike the earlier one, this episode has its origin in Virgil, but Marlowe emphasizes the ele-ment of a menacing encirclement: 'we were round-environ'd with the Greeks' (2.1.269). Aeneas fights his way free from this encirclement but realizes how limited his power is:

> O, there I lost my wife! and had not we
> Fought manfully, I had not told this tale.
> Yet manhood would not serve; of force we fled ...   2.1.270–2

Aeneas' experience of helplessness – and a corresponding desire to flee from it – has been seared into his mind. We should not be surprised to find that his amorous experience at Carthage becomes a re-enactment of his military experience at Troy, resulting a second time in his taking flight from a power which threatens to entrap him and render him help-less. At Carthage, as at Troy, Aeneas discovers that 'manhood would not serve.'

There is, then, a dark aura of ironic comedy surrounding what Tho-mas Nashe might have referred to as Dido's 'venereal machiavellism,'[11] for her strategies to entice Aeneas are all hopelessly counter-productive. For instance, Dido shows Aeneas her gallery of kingly suitors' pictures, thinking in Ovidian terms that competition stimulates desire among rivals. For good measure, she suggestively emphasizes how these suitors made strenuous efforts to 'compass' her: 'Yet none obtain'd me, I am free from all; And yet, God knows, entangled unto one' (3.1.152–3). Dido intends her remark about being 'entangled unto one' to be seductive, but Aeneas is now free because he escaped a fatal entanglement at Troy, where the Myrmidons tried to 'compass' him. The attempt to seduce backfires, and so Dido is forced to become the blatant suitor of Aeneas. She has tried to present herself to him as enticingly forbidden fruit, but he has not read Ovid, and so she desperately adopts the traditionally male, aggressive role. This reversal of sexual roles is acted out on stage when Dido pursues the elusive Aeneas by taking him on a deer-hunt. In the rich literary tradition of the love-hunt, usually the hunter represents the predatory male and the elusive quarry the coy maiden.[12] At the beginning of the Ars Amatoria, Ovid reminds men who want a woman that 'A hunter's skilled where to spread his nets for the stag.'[13] Ovid's advice on love venery is echoed by Dido's suggestive instructions to her huntsmen: 'why pitch you not your toils apace, / And rouse the light-foot deer from forth their lair?' (3.3.30–1). Like the 'light-foot deer,' the elusive Aeneas needs to be roused from hiding, but her reference to the 'toils' (hunting nets) eerily recalls the 'crooked nets' of the Myrmidons.

Aeneas powerfully expresses his fear of becoming entangled with and overwhelmed by Dido soon after Hermes appears to him in a dream and commands him (as Hector's ghost had done at Troy) to flee once again. In one of his most imaginative, Dido-like speeches, Aeneas fears that he will not be able to escape because of his bondage to her allurements:

> Yet Dido casts her eyes, like anchors, out,
> To stay my fleet from loosing forth the bay.
> 'Come back, come back!' I hear her cry afar,
> 'And let me link thy body to my lips,
> That, tied together by the striving tongues,
> We may as one sail into Italy.'   4.3.25–30

The pressure of fear transforms the benign conceit of eyebeams as anchor-lines into the grotesque image which for Dido represents erotic ecstasy and for Aeneas torture by entanglement: being 'tied together by the striving tongues.'

As the play progresses, the focus of Dido's enticement of Aeneas and his ensuing fear of her centres on her encompassing arms. In a different way from the *Aeneid*, this is a story of arms and the man. The pun on 'arms' is central to the play, for it connects the dangers of Aeneas' military experience in Troy with those of his erotic experience in Carthage. Marlowe's use of the term involves a twist on a conceit which Ovid played with often in the *Amores*: that the roles of warrior and of lover involve similar activities.[14] In *Dido*, as he had done in his translation of the *Amores*, Marlowe connects these two realms with a pun on 'arms' that was not available in Latin.[15] Unlike Ovid's elegies, which argue that love and war are interchangeable and that thus with no strain 'Hector to arms went from his wife's embraces' (1.9.35), Marlowe's play stresses the incompatibility of these two worlds.[16] 'Brave men-at-arms' (1.2.32) must prevent themselves from becoming effeminate boys in arms.

When Aeneas first plans to leave Dido, he prudently decides to forego the courtesy of saying farewell to her, for fear that 'Her silver arms will coll me round about / And tears of pearl cry, "Stay, Aeneas, stay"' (4.3.51–2). It is no wonder that he singles out the danger of her arms, for Dido obsessively speaks of her desire to hold Aeneas:

Stout love, in mine arms make thy Italy.   3.4.56

Not all the world can take thee from mine arms: 4.4.61

Or that the Tyrrhene sea were in mine arms,
That he might suffer shipwrack on my breast ...   4.4.101–3

And let rich Carthage fleet upon the seas,
So I may have Aeneas in mine arms.   4.4.134–5

Wherein have I offended Jupiter
That he should take Aeneas from mine arms?   5.1.129–30

Finally, just before Aeneas' decisive breaking away, Dido articulates the two stark alternatives which define for her the possibilities of their relationship:

Why starest thou in my face? if thou wilt stay,
Leap in mine arms: mine arms are open wide.
If not, turn from me, and I'll turn from thee;   5.1.179–81

Ironically, she has invited him to remain with her in the very terms which are most likely to drive him away. For Aeneas, leaping into the open arms of Dido would be tantamount to losing his sense of self. He answers her invitation by boarding his ship and raising anchor. Unlike Virgil's hero, Marlowe's Aeneas is not especially *pius*, and his ensuing voyage is as much a flight from the arms of Dido as a pursuit of the prophesied land of Italy.

Smiling at Tears

The most vexed question in the commentary on *Dido Queen of Carthage* has been whether or not the play is humorous, and, if it is, whether or not the humour is intentional. The issues are not easy to resolve, partly because there is no performance history – Elizabethan or modern – of the play, and thus no record of how audiences have actually responded. This lack of evidence is compounded by the fact that, as the title-page indicates, *Dido* was 'played by the children of her Majesty's Chapel,' and it is hard to reconstruct from playtexts how Elizabethan audiences responded to children acting romantic plots.[17] It does seem clear, however, that Marlowe is playing in a self-reflexive way with his child actors, creating a continuous current of metadramatic play by reminding us that, in more ways than one, his gods and heroes alike are really boys. At any given moment in the play, we may simultaneously be watching a boy actor charmingly strike the pose of an adult and a less than heroic man try to play the heroic role in which history has cast him. Especially in the case of Marlowe's unprepossessing version of Aeneas, who is 'a far more humble and self-depreciating hero than he had ever been before,'[18] we cannot be sure whether we are watching a child actor playing the part of a hero, or a hero acting like a child.[19] Generally speaking, to imagine the play acted by children is to multiply the possibilities for comedy.

Until fairly recently, most criticism of *Dido Queen of Carthage* was predicated on the mistaken assumption that Marlowe was attempting to recreate not only Virgil's story of Dido but also the high seriousness with which the Roman poet told it. The inevitable conclusion was that Marlowe 'showed himself unequal to his august source.'[20] Moments in Marlowe's play which appeared to be humorous were dismissed as accidents, artistic lapses stemming from his theatrical inexperience or propensity for bombast. Since Clifford Leech's important discussion, most commentators are willing to grant a degree of comic intent to Marlowe, though the older stance is still voiced.[21] What remains for criticism to acknowledge is the very dark quality of the play's humour, and especially the troubling way it presents violence against the helpless as amusing, both for onlookers within the play and (often) for audiences in the theatre.

Like so much in the play, the motif of sadistic sport first appears in the brief opening exchange between Jupiter and Ganymede. Trying to impress the boy with his power over Juno, Jupiter vows 'To hang her meteor-like 'twixt heaven and earth, / And bind her hand and foot with golden cords' (1.1.13–14). Whereupon Ganymede chillingly responds:

> Might I but see that pretty sport a-foot,
> O, how would I with Helen's brother laugh,
> And bring the Gods to wonder at the game!   1.1.16–18

For the 'pretty sport' to be complete, there must be spectators to enjoy the humiliating incapacitation of the goddess. Since some critics have argued for the ethical superiority of the mortals to the gods in the play,[22] it is noteworthy that Ganymede (who is human) plans to share this cruel laughter with 'Helen's brother' as well as the gods. Jupiter quickly perceives and caters to Ganymede's penchant for amusement at the suffering of others, for a few lines later he promises the boy that the lame smith Vulcan 'shall dance to make thee laughing sport' (32). This emphasis on pretty young Ganymede's sadism is proleptic, for the three central scenes in which a person is toyed with and wounded (Pyrrhus and Priam, Cupid and Dido, Cupid and the Nurse) all involve a young boy teasing and wounding a man or woman who is figuratively identified as a parent.

The most savage expression of the humour of helplessness is Pyrrhus' murder of Priam, which forms the climax of the fall of Troy narration and is one of the primal acts of violence in Marlowe's entire canon.[23] Once again Marlowe deliberately and disquietingly alters the *Aeneid*. In Virgil, the aged king Priam nobly berates Pyrrhus for his degeneracy and feebly heaves his spear before the raging Greek drags him to the altar and kills him with a single stab (2.533–53). In Marlowe, however, Priam not only lacks righteous indignation but is totally craven. Trembling with fear, he flatters Pyrrhus and begs for his life (in yet another instance of an old man trying to woo a boy), but his helpless terror feeds the young Greek's cruelty:

Not mov'd at all, but smiling at his tears,
This butcher, whilst his hands were yet held up,
Treading upon his breast, struck off his hands.   2.1.240-2

The strong caesuras and piling up of dependent clauses create a teasing, dreamlike suspension of motion until the sudden release of violence in 'struck off his hands.' (This grotesque game-playing made an impression on Shakespeare, whose Hecuba 'saw Pyrrhus make malicious sport / In mincing with his sword her husband's limbs' [*Hamlet* 2.2.513–4].)[24] Aeneas then goes on to emphasize Priam's further helplessness in even more terribly comic terms. Priam tries to defend his wife Hecuba against Pyrrhus' attack but understandably fails by 'Forgetting both his want of strength and hands.' The comic bathos is an invitation for spectators in the theatre to join in the laughter and become an audience of Pyrrhuses. Marlowe has totally subverted the sympathy for the suffering Trojans which is memorably expressed in Virgil's 'sunt lacrimae rerum et mentem mortalia tangunt' (*Aeneid* 1.462).

In the scene immediately following the account of Priam's death, Marlowe creates another incident of 'sportful malice,' one which is more central to the plot and more inviting to the audience. Moved by Aeneas' story, Dido wishes to 'think upon some pleasing sport, / To rid me from these melancholy thoughts' (2.1.303–4). What she does not know, however, is that her very sadness will soon become 'pleasing sport,' but sport for the gods. As in the *Aeneid*, Venus disguises her own son Cupid as Aeneas' boy Ascanius and orders him to cause Dido to fall in love with Aeneas. But there is a key difference between Marlowe and his source. While Virgil's Cupid simply breathes the poison of love into Dido, Marlowe's is instructed by his mother to play a game with his victim:

go to Dido, who, instead of him [Ascanius]
Will set thee on her lap and play with thee;
Then touch her white breast with this arrow head,
That she may dote upon Aeneas' love ...   2.1.324-7

Like Jupiter at the beginning of the play, who sits Ganymede on his knee and invites him to 'play with me,' Dido may think that she is toying with the child, but the reverse proves to be true.

Cupid's enthusiastic response to the command is reminiscent of the callow sadism with which Ganymede hoped to see Juno punished. Preparing us to see a game of pain, Cupid says 'I will ... so play my part / As every touch shall wound Queen Dido's heart' (2.1.332–3). There is an arch pun in 'every touch,' which primarily refers to Cupid's wielding of the arrow but also suggests the artistic flourishes with which he will play his sadistic 'part.' It is a commonplace of Renaissance love poetry that the 'imperious boy' Cupid unjustly punishes faithful lovers, as in Spenser's accusation that 'thou tyrant Love doest laugh and scorn / At their complaints, making their pain thy play.'[25] Spenser's lament assumes the sympathy of the reader at this manifest injustice. Marlowe, however, constructs his scene so that the audience is induced to share the laughter at Dido's pain. Ironically, Cupid comes to infatuate Dido as she is soberly telling her long-suffering suitor Iarbas that 'the Gods do know no wanton thought / Had ever residence in Dido's breast' (3.1.16–17). Full of wanton thoughts of his own, Cupid intervenes as he first 'plays with [her] garments' to attract her attention and then proceeds to toy with her. In good Ovidian fashion, he entices her by denying her: 'No, Dido will not take me in her arms; / I shall not be her son, she loves me not' (3.1.22–3). Soon Cupid is sitting on her lap, and she is calling him (as Jupiter had earlier called Ganymede) 'wag' and inviting his kisses, much to the consternation of the child-cuckolded Iarbas. Unlike Virgil's scene, which beautifully evokes the fateful awakening of Dido's 'unused heart' ('desuetaque corda' [1.722]), Marlowe reduces the widowed queen to a set of opposed emotions which see-saw with comic rapidity.

The interplay among the three becomes broadly comic as the same sequence repeats itself: each time that Iarbas threatens to leave, Dido expresses pity for him and calls him back, but then Cupid jabs her with the arrow and she abruptly sends the confused king away:

> *Iarbas*. Come, Dido, leave Ascanius; let us walk. [*jab*]
> *Dido*. Go thou away; Ascanius shall stay.
> *Iarbas*. Ungentle Queen, is this thy love to me?
> *Dido*. O stay, Iarbas, and I'll go with thee.
> *Cupid*. And if my mother go, I'll follow her.[26] [*jab*]
> *Dido*. Why stay'st thou here? thou art no love of mine.
> *Iarbas*. Iarbas, die, seeing she abandons thee!
> *Dido*. No, live, Iarbas; what hast thou deserv'd,
> That I should say thou art no love of mine?
> Something thou hast deserv'd – [*jab*] Away, I say,
> Depart from Carthage, come not in my sight.   (3.1.34–44)[27]

These double-takes and sight gags create a chain reaction in which the manly warrior Iarbas becomes a puppet on a string manipulated by the woman Dido, who in turn dances on the string manipulated by the child Cupid. The staged effect of these sudden reversals can scarcely fail to be funny – the puppeteer's strings extend into the audience.

In the context of the whole play, however, this farcical scene has a darker side, indeed several darker sides. Since it immediately follows the horrific account of the fall of Troy, the wounding of Dido with the golden arrow may call to mind both Pyrrhus' sportive violence against Priam and the strong emphasis on the Greeks' violation of helpless women.[28] Numerous lines in the later scene take on a deeper resonance. For instance, the bombast of the line 'Iarbas, die, seeing she abandons thee' is severely qualified by the fact that in act 5 he will in fact die because Dido abandons him, and the same will happen to the abandoned Dido. Another joke which later turns serious is the teasing of Iarbas in the line 'Something thou hast deserv'd – [jab] Away, I say.' In the final act, the question of what love has deserved arises frequently as we see the loyalty of Dido, Anna, and Iarbas rewarded by death. It is with good reason that Dido questions 'Wherein have I offended Jupiter / That he should take Aeneas from mine arms?' (5.1.129). Of course, the farce of Dido's induced infatuation becomes still more troubling when one realizes that this comic dotage does in fact seal her fate; this inducement of an obsessive passion for Aeneas will finally drive Dido to her suicide.

The problematic mixing of tragedy and farce in *Dido* is illuminated by the far less troubling blending of tragedy and comedy in a play influenced by it, *A Midsummer Night's Dream*. Like *Dido*, Shakespeare's play has two linked pairs of lovers whose movements in the woods are dominated by quite physical rhythms of pursuit and flight.[29] Moreover, there is a clear parallel between the touches of Venus' golden arrow which cause Dido to 'dote upon Aeneas' love' and the herbal juice which Oberon uses to 'make man or woman madly dote / Upon the next live creature that it sees' (*MND* 2.1.171–2).[30] In both plays, the stimulus creates a response of instantaneous (and thus comic) dotage. And in both plays the scene raises serious questions about the irrationality of love. But Shakespeare's humour does not become as dark as Marlowe's. For it to be so, Puck's potion would have to bring about not only the humiliation of Titania but also her death by her own hand.

The third scene of humorous humiliation again involves a sexually charged relationship between a male child and a maternal figure. At the end of act 4, Dido's old Nurse dandles and plays with Cupid, who is once again disguised as Ascanius. Though the scene is largely irrelevant in terms of plotting, it resonates because of its emphasis on cruel erotic play. The Nurse begins by enticing Cupid with promises of an orchard full of fruit and honey, which parallels Jupiter's wooing of Ganymede and Dido's of Cupid. Cupid plays along with her by pretending to be interested, but the roles are quickly reversed and the seducer seduced as she falls under the boy-god's influence. Like Dido, she is a widow whose long-dormant sexuality is awakened by what appears to be a little boy, this time apparently without the benefit of the golden arrow:

> *Nurse.* That I might live to see this boy a man!
>   How prettily he laughs! Go, ye wag,
>   You'll be a twigger when you come to age.
>   Say Dido what she will, I am not old;
>   I'll be no more a widow, I am young;
>   I'll have a husband, or else a lover.
> *Cupid.* [*Aside*] A husband, and no teeth!   4.5.18–24

It would be scarcely possible for an audience not to laugh at Cupid's cruel wisecrack, even though he is mocking her for the passion which he has induced. And it is amusing when the Nurse slips into an internal dialogue in which one part of her being is deluded by passion while another part is knowingly detached: 'Foolish is love, a toy. O sacred love, / If there be any heaven in earth, 'tis love' (4.5.26–7). Here the parallel with Dido's conflicted dismissing and recalling of Iarbas is unmistakable and humorous. This little vignette invites the audience to view the Nurse's vulnerability and confusion with merciless objectivity, through the eyes of Cupid. Like the Nurse, Dido in the final scene is depicted as suffering from an abandonment to desire and delusion which makes her open to ridicule.

Teasing Dido's Passion

The motifs of fleeing and following and of smiling at weakness find climactic expression in the play's final scene, and their presence quite decisively sets Marlowe's treatment of Dido apart from its Virgilian model. Within the inimical epic structure stressing the founding of Rome, Virgil depicts the tragedy of Dido's abandonment and death quite sympathetically.[31] Marlowe's ending, however, presents Aeneas' decision to leave as weak and unattractive but also depicts Dido's passions in exaggerated terms which invite the audience's imaginative disengagement. Commentators have not noted that, after Aeneas leaves Dido at 5.1.183, her suffering is repeatedly imaged in terms of the punishment of Tantalus in the underworld. As Aeneas flees, she attempts to grasp him, and throughout the scene the actor playing Dido should take a cue from her earlier references to holding Aeneas within her arms and emphasize how empty these outstretched arms now are. In addition to having the physical posture of Tantalus, Dido is caught in the same mental situation in which she is teased by repetition. Marlowe reshapes Virgil to emphasize the to-and-fro of oscillating feelings and teasing expectations. Whereas in Virgil Aeneas leaves Dido in a single, decisive action, Marlowe's Aeneas attempts to sneak away a first time in act 4, is foiled, and then succeeds on the second attempt. Dido's response to his leaving in act 5 is shaped by the expectation that what worked earlier may do so again. When she dispatches Anna to the seashore in hopes of detaining Aeneas, Dido expresses her hope: 'Once didst thou go and he came back again: / Now bring him back and thou shalt be a queen' (5.1.196–7). But of course Anna's initial success serves only to heighten Dido's ultimate frustration and despair.

The teasing of Dido's desires is intensified in Anna's report when she returns to her sister empty-handed after her meeting with Aeneas. This scene is entirely Marlowe's; in the corresponding moment in Virgil, Anna's comments are not reported, and the narrator simply says that Aeneas cannot be moved (4.438–9). Marlowe's Anna, however, describes Aeneas' flight in terms which are shaped by the tantalizing rhythm of promise and denial. First she says that in response to her cries Aeneas began to 'wag his hand, which, yet held up, / Made me suppose he would have heard me speak' (5.1.229–30). But the hope which these lines teasingly provoke is immediately destroyed by her next line: 'Then gan they drive into the ocean.' Perhaps Aeneas momentarily had faltered in his resolve and then changed his mind. In any event, Anna's account oscillates back to a second tantalizing moment, as she describes to Dido how Aeneas' men intervened on her behalf and seemed to sway their leader:

They gan to move him to redress my ruth,
And stay a while to hear what I could say;
But he, clapp'd under hatches, sail'd away.   5.1.238–40[32]

Once again, there is a building up to a moment of hope, then a pause, then a sudden brutal snatching away of promise as Aeneas flees. (The movement of the lines recalls the earlier description of Pyrrhus' teasing hesitation before dismembering Priam.) Presumably without intending to do so, Anna has tantalized her sister.

From this point onward, the teasing which afflicts Dido comes not from others but from her own frantic imagination. Her frustrated desire leaps into desperate delusions, as it attempts to create the reality that has left her. Perhaps the most important words in this long scene are those which Dido speaks just before Aeneas silently leaves her: 'For though thou hast the heart to say farewell, / I have not power to stay thee' (5.1.182–3). This is a poignant acknowledgment for the proud queen who not long since had claimed to control the elements as well as every facet of her subjects' existence: 'their lands, their goods, their lives' (4.4.76).[33] It is Dido's deeply felt impotence which generates the Tantalian enticements and delusions of her final speeches. Unable to accept the finality of his leaving, Dido deludes herself by imagining his returning to her grasp. In Virgil's depiction of Dido's death, there is no evidence of the delusions which are an expression of powerlessness; for an analogue for Dido's situation we should turn, once again, to Ovid's *Amores*. Dido's delusions are an ecstatically painful intensification of the desire to be deceived by his lover which Ovid expresses in the final poem of the *Amores*.

Dido's first words after Aeneas' exit reveal the teasing oscillations of her mind, which recall those of the ridiculously love-smitten Nurse:

> Is he gone?
> Ay, but he'll come again, he cannot go,
> He loves me too too well to serve me so.
> Yet he that in my sight would not relent
> Will, being absent, be obdurate still.
> By this is he got to the water-side;
> And see, the sailers take him by the hand,
> But he shrinks back, and now, rememb'ring me,
> Returns amain: welcome, welcome, my love!
> But where's Aeneas? Ah, he's gone, he's gone!   5.1.184–92

Dido cannot decide whether Aeneas is coming or going, and the conflicting motions of her mind mime the to-and-fro of enticement and escape, following and fleeing, that has characterized passion throughout the play. On stage, these emphatic verbal repetitions suggest accompanying gestures, perhaps even a movement of her own to mime the 'shrink[ing] back' which she imagines so vividly. These gestures, coupled with the rapid play of delusions in her mind, may invite the audience's amusement.

Marlowe creates an effective stage-image to convey Dido's impotence by having her remain on stage as we hear of Aeneas' leaving and see numerous characters (Anna, the Nurse, Iarbas) enter and exit. The essential rhythm of love in the play is for flight to provoke pursuit, but Dido is unable to move. Upon hearing that Aeneas has 'sail'd away,' Dido immediately declares 'I will follow him!' (5.1.240–1), only to be deflated by Anna's matter-of-fact response: 'How can ye go when he hath all your fleet?' Dido's frustrated motion erupts in the form of a magnificent flight of fancy:

> I'll frame me wings of wax like Icarus,
> And o'er his ships will soar unto the sun
> That they may melt and I fall in his arms:
> Or else I'll make a prayer unto the waves
> That I may swim to him, like Triton's niece;
> O Anna, fetch Arion's harp,
> That I may tice a dolphin to the shore
> And ride upon his back unto my love!   5.1.243–50

For Dido, as for Faustus in a similar moment at his end, the hope that she is an Icarus proves to be a delusion, a function of the fact that she is really a Tantalus. In the rapid play of images, she becomes increasingly earth-bound and dependent on others, including the dolphin which she hopes (in a last, desperate seduction) to 'tice.'

At the end of this long speech, which began with herself as a soaring Icarus, Dido tacitly acknowledges her powerlessness by fantasizing the return of Aeneas. Once again, she plays Tantalus with herself by imagining a to-and-fro movement of the elusive love-object:

> Now is he come on shore safe, without hurt;
> But see, Achates wills him put to sea,
> And all the sailors merry make for joy;
> But he, rememb'ring me, shrinks back again;
> See where he comes; welcome, welcome, my love!
> *Anna.* Ah sister, leave these idle fantasies ...   5.1.257–62

Several of these lines are an almost verbatim repetition of lines (discussed earlier) which were spoken by Dido immediately after Aeneas' departure (5.1.188–91). Editors have speculated that the repetition is an oversight on Marlowe's part, perhaps the result of a revision not properly tidied up.[34] But since there are so many verbal repetitions throughout the play, and especially in this final scene, Dido's redundancy may be intentional on Marlowe's part; the effect would be to suggest a mind turned in on itself and returning to an obsessive self-delusion, much as Tantalus repeatedly thinks that the apples have finally come within his grasp.

One of the play's large structural ironies is that Dido's painful delusion, which is precipitated by Aeneas' leaving Carthage, is a close parallel to the delusion suffered by Aeneas himself when he arrives at Carthage.[35] Bowed down by the weight of his helpless suffering at Troy, Aeneas begins to lose his hold on reality when he sees a statue of his father Priam: 'Methinks that town there should be Troy, yon Ida's hill, / There Xanthus stream, because here's Priamus – / And when I know it is not, then I die' (2.1.7–9). Aeneas desperately needs to convince himself that Troy is not dead; after a telling allusion to Pygmalion, he strives to bring the statue to life in his mind:

> Achates, though mine eyes say this is stone,
> Yet thinks my mind that this is Priamus;
> And when my grieved heart sighs and says no,
> Then would it leap out to give Priam life.
> O, were I not at all, so thou mightst be!
> Achates, see, King Priam wags his hand;
> He is alive; Troy is not overcome!   2.1.24–30

Achates' assessment, like Anna's to Dido, is clinically accurate: 'Thy mind, Aeneas, that would have it so / Deludes thy eyesight: Priamus is dead.' Marlowe's scene is a grotesque transformation of lines in Virgil in which Aeneas sees a fresco of the Fall of Troy in Dido's palace and weeps for what he has lost (*Aeneid* 1.453–92). Though he is described as one who 'feeds his soul on what is nothing but a picture' ('animum pictura pascit inani' [1.464]), Virgil's Aeneas is never actually deluded and does not confuse mimetic art with life.[36] In Marlowe, however, the very extremity of Aeneas' frantic suffering, like Dido's to follow, borders on the comic.[37] When the citizens of Carthage draw near, it is with as much prudence as paranoia that Achates warns his leader to 'Leave to lament, lest they laugh at our fears' (2.1.38).

In Dido's final speeches, Marlowe has depicted her futility, panic, and self-delusion with an intensity which invites uneasy comedy. A comparison with Shakespeare's Cleopatra, who is in part modelled on the Didos of Virgil and Marlowe, is revealing.[38] Both Shakespeare's and Marlowe's powerless queens fantasize about their departed lovers before committing suicide, but Cleopatra's imaginings ennoble both Antony and herself, while Dido wonders why 'must I rave thus for a runagate.' And whereas Cleopatra wraps herself in artifice and creates a poised, timeless image of herself in death, Dido dies with athletic violence, apparently (there are no stage directions at this point in the quarto) leaping into the flames of the fire which had been ignited in the trap. If Dido dies by jumping into the fire, the gesture richly resonates with the world of the play. *Dido Queen of Carthage* is full of desperate, faintly comic, and finally hopeless leaps, in which characters lunge toward a love-object which they would grasp or redeem.[39] Instead of soaring up like Icarus into the sun, Dido plunges into the flames below.

Marlowe's crowning touch in the play is to assimilate Dido's tragic act to the comic paradigm of flight and pursuit which has organized so much of the action. Unlike Virgil's treatment, in which Dido's is the sole suicide, Marlowe has Iarbas and Anna follow Dido by taking their lives in very quick succession. In the absence of stage directions, we may surmise that Iarbas and Anna imitate the manner of Dido's death, jumping into the smoking trap in what Clifford Leech drily termed a 'rapid series of departures downwards.'[40] These three deaths by flaming suicide connect with other images of fire in *Dido* and derive from an image pattern in the *Aeneid* linking love and flames; from a tragic perspective they create an emblem of the self-destructiveness of excessive sexual passion. But these seriatim deaths also sustain the play's comic image of love as a mechanical game of following and fleeing. The tragic and the comic cannot be disentangled, nor can they be harmoniously blended.

In the final scene of *Dido Queen of Carthage*, as in those of the later tragedies, Marlowe's staging complicates and disconcerts the audience's response to the protagonist's suffering. Though Dido suffers the agonies of Tantalus, there is a discrepancy between the intensity of her pain and any crime she can be construed as having committed. Moreover, our response to Dido may be shaped by the fact that she has generously performed the offices of pity throughout the play. Not only did she succour the broken Aeneas and mourn the fall of Troy, but even after he abandons her she fears that his ships will smash on the rocks and thus exhorts to the gods to 'Save, save Aeneas' (5.1.256). Suggestively, in the play's final lines Anna prays 'That gods and men may pity this my death / And rue our ends' (5.1.326–7). But the gods are devoid of pity for mortals who do not happen to be their offspring. As Richard A. Martin observes, 'If a meddling universe inspires Dido's passion, an indifferent universe presides over her self-destruction; the gods do not acknowledge Dido's suffering and death.'[41] If pity is to be shown it must come from humanity, from the audience in the theatre. Marlowe, however, proceeds to make that response difficult. It is typical of his dramaturgy that, immediately after reminding the audience of the need for ruth, he ends the play with a line which encourages detached, Olympian amusement, as Anna cries out, 'Now, sweet Iarbas, stay, I come to thee.' We *ought* to feel the pity for Dido and the other doomed lovers which the gods so conspicuously lack, and yet what we see is the final repetition of a farcical pattern of flight and pursuit.

4

The Conqueror's and the Playwright's Games: *Tamburlaine the Great*, Part One and Part Two

In some obvious ways Part One and Part Two of *Tamburlaine* mark a new direction in Marlowe's writing, a clean break from the Ovid translation and *Dido Queen of Carthage*. While the earlier works derive from Latin verse read at school, *Tamburlaine* has the feel of a thoroughly contemporary engagement with the energies of an expansionist age.[1] There is also a jagged discontinuity in subject matter, as Marlowe abandons the wanton world of Ovidian sexual play to depict the Scythian warrior – with the imposing figure of Edward Alleyn in the role – 'Threat'ning the world with high astounding terms / And scourging kingdoms with his conquering sword' (1:Prologue). 'Mighty,' an epithet frequently applied to Tamburlaine both by characters in the play and Elizabethan audiences, does not appear a single time in the *Elegies* or *Dido*.[2] Marlowe's rhythms of expression change as well; the oscillation of enticement and flight is superseded in *Tamburlaine* by the drum-beat of heroic single-mindedness. In Seamus Heaney's phrase, Marlowe's 'reader or audience is in thrall to the poetic equivalent of a dynamo-hum, a kind of potent undermusic.'[3]

But these striking differences between *Tamburlaine* and Marlowe's earlier work mask an important continuity, his ongoing interest in game-playing, especially games of teasing and denial. In Part One of *Tamburlaine*, Marlowe intensifies a motif which was fitfully apparent in his translation of the *Amores* and then more emphatic in *Dido*: the investing of Ovid's mainly light-hearted and amorous play with the intent to hurt. In *Dido* the instances of sportive cruelty were often distanced by narration (as in the account of Pyrrhus' mocking dismemberment of Priam), but in *Tamburlaine* the sadistic games are enacted on stage and are central to the plot. Indeed Part One's most powerful scene (4.4) is dominated by the savage game of tantalization which Tamburlaine plays upon his chief adversary, Bajazeth the Emperor of the Turks. Significantly, the primary literary inspiration for this scene, and for related material in act 5, is not Ovid's genial game-playing but rather Seneca's extravagant cruelty. The play which most informs the ending of Part One of *Tamburlaine* is *Thyestes*, Seneca's tragedy about the compulsive and disgusting crimes of the Tantalids.

While the cruelty running through the *Tamburlaine* plays has often been noted by critics, its central manifestation as game-playing has not. Thus, Clifford Leech refers to the plays' 'reduction of the living human body to the status of a property,' and Constance B. Kuriyama borrows from Goethe the terms 'hammer' and 'anvil' to characterize what she sees as the stark alternatives offered up by the play: to conquer and control or to be passive and violated.[4] Though these formulations are quite relevant to some scenes (most notably the famous deployment of Bajazeth as a footstool), they are imprecise for many others in which the primary expression of power and cruelty is Tamburlaine's ability to turn the lives of others into games which he controls. In addition to hammer and anvil, we need to think of player and played-upon, tantalizer and tantalized.

As they were first acted in London in the late 1580s, the *Tamburlaine* plays apparently contained more comic material than the earliest printed edition indicates. In a prefatory note to the 1590 octavo, the text from which all others ultimately derive, the printer Richard Jones makes an intriguing statement 'To the Gentlemen Readers and others that take pleasure in reading Histories':

I have purposely omitted and left out some fond and frivolous jestures, digressing and, in my poor opinion, far unmeet for the matter, which I thought might seem more tedious unto the wise than any way else to be regarded – though, haply, they have been of some vain conceited fondlings greatly gaped at, what times they were showed upon the stage in their graced deformities. Nevertheless, now to be mixtured in print with such matter of worth, it would prove a great disgrace to so honourable and stately a history.

Jones is the first of many editors to find the 'mixtured' nature of Marlowe's work offensive and to attempt the removal of the comic as a means of stressing the 'stately.'[5] It is, of course, impossible to know how extensive this excised material was and whether Marlowe or actors were responsible for it. Interestingly, Jones does not blame the disgraceful 'jestures' on actors, as one might expect, and bibliographical analysis indicates that the manuscript from which he printed his text did not derive from the theatre. Despite his excisions, Jones's text of *Tamburlaine* still contains a good deal of humorous material (some of it broadly comic), and 'these varied provocations to laughter' are so integral to both parts that it is difficult to imagine the play's ever having existed without them.[6]

Sporting with Crowns

Tamburlaine's games of tantalization, which are not mentioned in the historical sources, are central to Marlowe's conception of his protagonist. It would be too simple to see them as merely one more expression of his impulse to mock and belittle others, though that is their outcome. These games are more revealing, for they have their origin in the workings of what Alexander Leggatt has called Tamburlaine's 'imaginative desire': 'since Tamburlaine's imaginative desire is always greater than the objects which it seizes, that desire must always remain unsatisfied, always seeking new objects.'[7] Again and again, we see that the crowns and kingdoms which Tamburlaine strives so mightily to possess become meaningless once he has obtained them. But these objects that Tamburlaine cannot enjoy for themselves do have a use: to tease the desire of others. Through games of tantalization Tamburlaine contrives to turn people who are under his control into caricatures of himself; his manipulation of their hopes and desires creates a fun-house mirror in which his own failure to find satisfaction is reflected.

Marlowe's depiction of Tamburlaine plays a variation on the emblem tradition which said that Tantalus' punishment symbolizes the avaricious man's sterile joylessness amidst plenty. As the epigram accompanying Alciatus' widely disseminated woodcut explained, the depiction of Tantalus 'could be applied to you, miser, who, as if you did not have it, do not enjoy what you possess.'[8] Though mythographers, like Alciatus, usually identified this Tantalian frustration with miserliness, some commentators realized that it is a state of mind that can be associated with a 'range of human pursuits outside the counting-house. That this discontent can issue in heroic risk-taking as well as financial covetousness is argued in Pierre de La Primaudaye's *The French Academie*, a treatise on ethics which appeared in English when Marlowe was working on his *Tamburlaine* plays. After making the conventional observation that the covetous man is 'a Tantalus in hell, who between water and meat dieth of hunger,' La Primaudaye immediately proceeds to discuss this discontent as a powerful force which

carrieth away the natural desire of necessary things, to a dissordinate appetite of such things as are full of danger, rare, and hard to be gotten. And which is worse, compelling the avaricious to procure them with great pain and travel, it forbiddeth him to enjoy them, and stirring up his desire, depriveth him of the pleasure.[9]

The protagonist's progress through both parts of *Tamburlaine* is marked by just such anticipation and frustration, as his 'dissordinate appetite' for what is most difficult inspires undertakings which are successful but never satisfying. Significantly, the only expression of satisfaction in the plays comes from one of Tamburlaine's victims; when the wounded king of Arabia meets Zenocrate, his former betrothed, he declares his willingness to 'die with full contented heart' (1:5.1.18), which he proceeds to do. For the victor, however, there can be no content.

Tamburlaine's games of teasing begin in his first appearance on stage (1.2), when he toys with the lords accompanying the freshly captured Zenocrate. Of course, his interception of her on her way to be married is itself a withholding of a desired object, and perhaps it should come as no surprise (given the emphasis in the *Elegies* and *Dido* on how difficulty heightens desire) that he begins to woo her only after – immediately after – he learns that she is betrothed (1.2.33). Tamburlaine's playing with Zenocrate's entourage becomes overtly tantalizing when one of his soldiers arrives with the news that a thousand Persian horsemen have arrived to free the captives. Tamburlaine, whose forces number only five hundred foot-soldiers, seems for a moment to concede defeat but then quickly mocks his captives' new hopes:

> How now, my Lords of Egypt and Zenocrate?
> Now must your jewels be restored again,
> And I that triumphed so be overcome?
> How say you lordings, is not this your hope?   1.2.113–16

For his prisoners, there can be no safe answer to Tamburlaine's insolent question. To agree would risk his wrath, but to disagree would surrender the claim to freedom. When a captive 'lording' cautiously responds that 'We hope yourself will willingly restore them,' Tamburlaine's riposte is coldly assured: 'Such hope, such fortune, have the thousand

horse.' By holding out the captured jewels and hope of freedom in order
to make his prisoners reach for them in vain, Tamburlaine forcefully
demonstrates his dominance. His pleasure in playing with his various
prisoners' hopes spans Part One, for in the final scene he similarly dares
the Turkish Emperor to wish for his freedom: 'And now, my footstool, if
I lose the field, / You hope of liberty and restitution' (5.1.209–10).

Throughout Part One, Tamburlaine's teasing games revolve around a
specific prop, a crown. At first glance this playing with crowns may
seem out of character, for Tamburlaine's great speech on 'aspiring
minds' and the restless will reaches its rhetorical climax with its arrival
at 'the ripest fruit of all / That perfect bliss and sole felicity, / The sweet
fruition of an earthly crown' (2.7.27–9). One might think that crowns
will not be taken lightly by Tamburlaine. But, though he momentarily
turns it into a fetish, the crown is not a goal to which Tamburlaine is
deeply committed or from which he can draw sustenance. In Clifford
Leech's phrase, 'we see Tamburlaine finding the crown an insufficient
embodiment of his dream.'[10] Such satisfaction as he can find in crowns
stems from his ability to take them away, or withhold them, from others. Immediately after donning the crown, he locates its value in terms
of other people's desire:

> Though Mars himself, the angry god of arms,
> And all the earthly potentates conspire
> To dispossess me of this diadem,
> Yet will I wear it in despite of them ...   2.7.58–61

The suggestion is that, like the lover in the *Elegies* (especially 2.19), Tamburlaine requires rivalry in order to find pleasure in possession. Precisely because he cannot enjoy the crown in and for itself, he *wants* Mars
and all the kings of the world to desire it.

That Tamburlaine subsequently plays with crowns should not come
as a complete surprise, for three scenes before declaiming on the 'sweet
fruition of an earthly crown,' he further devalues a crown that has
already been placed in the earth. In a scene (2.4) full of 'fond and frivolous jestures,' Tamburlaine physically tantalizes the foolish Persian king
Mycetes, whom he surprises in the act of hiding his crown in a 'simple
hole.' Though there are no stage directions in the 1590 (or modern) editions, the ensuing dialogue suggests that Tamburlaine picks up the
crown and holds it toward Mycetes:

Tamburlaine. Is this your crown?
Mycetes. Ay, didst thou ever see a fairer?
Tamburlaine. You will not sell it, will ye?
Mycetes. Such another word, and I will have thee executed.
   Come, give it me.
Tamburlaine. No, I took it prisoner.
Mycetes. You lie, I gave it you.
Tamburlaine. Then 'tis mine.
Mycetes. No, I mean, I let you keep it.
Tamburlaine. Well, I mean you shall have it again.
   Here, take it for a while, I lend it thee ...   2.4.28–38

The brusqueness of Mycetes' 'Come, give it me' indicates that he
reaches for the proffered crown, and the response of 'No' suggests that
Tamburlaine draws it back. When Tamburlaine extends the crown a
second time, saying, 'Here, take it for a while,' Mycetes must decide
whether to reach for the crown again and thereby risk another humiliation. (In *Richard II* Shakespeare retains the stage business but reverses
the roles, as it is the weak king who taunts the ascendant usurper to
'seize the crown' [4.4.181].) After Mycetes does take the crown, the
humiliating game continues, for Tamburlaine warns him that soon
'shalt thou see me pull it from thy head: / Thou art no match for mighty
Tamburlaine' (2.4.40–1).

   For Tamburlaine, crowns are essentially toys, objects with which to
tease the desires of others. After he has overthrown Mycetes and
crowned the fallen king's brother Cosroe, Tamburlaine's thoughts turn
to taking the crown for himself:

> I am strongly moved
> That if I should desire the Persian crown
> I could attain it with a wondrous ease.   2.5.75–7

As if this 'wondrous ease' is indeed too easy, Tamburlaine decides that
it would be sporting to warn Cosroe that he intends to take the crown
for himself. What Tamburlaine calls his 'pretty jest' is very reminiscent
of the poet's amorous strategies in *All Ovid's Elegies*, especially the poem
(2.19) in which he increases his own pleasure by warning his mistress'
husband to guard her more carefully. In terms that recall his recent
treatment of Mycetes, Tamburlaine vaunts that he will 'Make but a jest

to win the Persian crown' and that he 'only made him [Cosroe] king to make us sport' (2.5.98, 101).

The most revealing evidence for the satisfaction which Tamburlaine takes in teasing people with crowns is the fact that he derives it from tantalizing friends as well as enemies. Though critics have claimed that 'Tamburlaine and his lieutenants live in almost idyllic amity and loyalty,' the mighty Scythian is in fact careful to demonstrate his superiority to his subordinates.[11] To be sure, when he is winning over Theridamas from the Persians, Tamburlaine promises him that he will be allowed to 'sit with Tamburlaine in all his majesty' (1.2.208). But the promised job-sharing never materializes. Indeed, when Theridamas shows signs of developing too high an ambition, Tamburlaine puts him in his (inferior) place; as Theridamas becomes carried away by his celebration of 'kingly joys,' Tamburlaine with a frosty smile asks, 'Why, say, Theridamas, wilt thou be a king?' (2.5.65). Sensing danger, Theridamas prudently eats his words: 'Nay, though I praise it, I can live without it.'[12] In this little game Tamburlaine seems to be daring Theridamas to remind him of his earlier promise of a shared kingship.

Tamburlaine's teasing of his subordinates is most blatant and most cruel when he tantalizes them with crowns. In their first appearance on stage, Tamburlaine promises his three lieutenants that they 'shall never part from me / Before I crown you kings in Asia' (1.2.244–5). Later, he declares that, after he seizes the Persian kingdom for himself, he will reward them with the crowns of Parthia, Scythia, and Media (2.5.83). But, following his success, he neglects to mention these crowns again. Later, when Tamburlaine learns that contributory kings will accompany Bajazeth in the field, he reiterates his promise: 'Then fight courageously, their crowns are yours' (3.3.30). Even Theridamas, who earlier had been guarded in his ambitions, goes into battle hungry for a crown: 'I long to see those crowns won by our swords, / That we may reign as kings of Africa' (3.3.98–9). After the battle has been won, Theridamas, Techelles, and Usumcasane approach Tamburlaine with the promised crowns in their hands, proudly announcing 'We have their crowns, their bodies strow the field' (3.3.215). Tamburlaine's response is at first predictable, but it suddenly takes a twist calculated to frustrate his friends: 'Each man a crown? Why, kingly fought, i'faith. / Deliver them into my treasury' (3.3.216–17). These two lines create the very rhythm of promise and denial; 'kingly fought' implies that the lieutenants deserve to be and indeed *will* be crowned (before the battle he had promised 'Fight all courageously and be you kings' [3.3.101]), but 'Deliver them' suddenly snatches the crowns away. Peter Hall's National Theatre production was alert to the comic potential of the scene. When Techelles, Usumcasane, and Theridamas 'romped onstage with their crowns, obviously thinking they were now theirs for the wearing,' the three commanders were suddenly stunned by Tamburlaine's command to hand them over.[13]

Shortly before he finally does crown his subordinates, Tamburlaine avails himself of a second opportunity to play with the desire that he has awakened in them. Near the end of the savage banquet in act 4, scene 4, a stage direction indicates that serving-men enter with a *'second course of crowns,'* which is either pastries in the form of crowns or perhaps the three crowns carried on trenchers as if they were food.[14] In either case, the association of crowns with food has ironic overtones, and it is significant that (in lines I will discuss in a moment) Tamburlaine has just finished teasing the starving Bajazeth with food and drink.

As if he were dangling the fruit of Tantalus in front of them, Tamburlaine teases his commanders with the long-promised crowns: 'Theridamas, Techelles and Casane, here are the cates you desire to finger, are they not?' (4.4.109–10). With its vivid evocation of their yearning ('desire to *finger*'), the question is calculated to embarrass. If his lieutenants fail to say that they want the enticing crowns, then Tamburlaine could conceivably use the occasion to withdraw his offer. But if they do try to finger the crowns, Tamburlaine may punish them for overreaching. The situation is uncomfortably reminiscent of the way he had earlier taunted Mycetes with *his* crown. The three lieutenants, who now seem less like friends than flunkies, can express their desire only by the awkward expedient of insisting upon their unworthiness:

> *Theridamas.* Ay, my lord, but none save kings must feed with these.
> *Techelles.* 'Tis enough for us to see them, and for Tamburlaine only to enjoy them.

It is only after they kowtow to him and abjectly accept tantalization as their just deserts that Tamburlaine finally hands over the crowns. To say that 'Tamburlaine dispenses with regal largesse the rewards of valour' is to miss his mockery, something his three lieutenants could hardly have done.[15] In Peter Hall's alert production, this long-awaited coronation was appropriately anticlimactic; the 'sweet fruition of an earthly crown' is reduced to Tamburlaine's 'dropping a crown on to each head as the captains squatted.'[16] Early in Part Two, crowns have been so thoroughly devalued that a prisoner of Tamburlaine uses one to bribe his lowly jail-keeper.[17]

There is one incident, however, which may appear to break this pattern of sporting with and devaluing crowns. This is the coronation of Zenocrate as Queen of Persia by Tamburlaine and his lieutenants, which occurs in the final lines of the play and which has been characterized as its climax.[18] In context, however, this coronation amounts to considerably less than a crowning moment. To be sure, it may seem to bring a measure of closure because it fulfils a promise made earlier by Tamburlaine (4.4.142–3). But by the end of the play crowns have come to mean less to her than to anyone else. When Tamburlaine promises her a crown at the end of the banquet scene, she (unlike his commanders at the equivalent moment) does not express pleasure or desire and in fact makes no verbal response at all. Later, only a hundred and fifty lines before her coronation, Zenocrate is moved by the sight of Bajazeth's and Zabina's corpses to utter a long threnody on the vanity of fighting 'for sceptres and for slippery crowns' (5.1.357). During her coronation the bodies of Bajazeth and Zabina remain on stage, and when Tamburlaine declares his intention to make Zenocrate 'my Queen of Persia,' she well may steal a glance at Zabina's corpse. Unlike Tamburlaine, Zenocrate finds no value in taking a crown from another, and, for her, this coronation is anything but the sweet fruition he declares it to be.

Tantalizing Bajazeth

In terms of theatrical intensity, the climax of *Tamburlaine* Part One is not the hollow coronation of act 5 but rather an anti-ceremony, the savage banquet at the end of act 4. Unlike most Elizabethan stage banquets, which are acted emblems of communal festivity and creaturely satisfaction, this feast is marked by compulsive rage and unappeasable hunger. (In Elizabethan performances there would have been a sharp contrast between the ordered arrangement of the symbolic banqueting props, which stand on the stage before the characters enter, and the barbaric passions which erupt during the feast.)[19] Both literary and social decorums rupture, and in the ensuing 'mixture' of poetry and prose the horrific becomes indistinguishable from the humorous.[20] The scene reveals, for the first time in the play, a descent into animal appetites and unspeakable human cruelty. In Peter Hall's production of *Tamburlaine*, the banquet scene marked the moment when 'the dare-devil gaiety of

Part One darkened decisively.'[21] For the first time in Marlowe's oeuvre, we see a convincing representation of hell on earth.

There are two centres of interest in the scene. One is of course Tamburlaine, who for the first time in the play is dressed *'all in scarlet,'* and the other is Bajazeth, whose spectacular imprisonment in an iron cage is mentioned in many contemporary allusions to the play.[22] Tamburlaine and Bajazeth stand apart from the other banqueters in that Tamburlaine stages the feast and Bajazeth is excluded from it. From the outset Tamburlaine declares 'let us freely banquet and carouse / Full bowls of wine unto the god of war' (4.4.5–6), but it is not clear that he himself partakes of food and drink; the scene will be more powerful if, unlike his carousing lieutenants, he does not.[23] Instead of enjoying food and drink for themselves, he uses them to tease Bajazeth, and the banquet scene becomes the play's climactic instance of tantalization. In place of the crowns which are toyed with in earlier scenes, the objects of desire are those which figure in the primal teasing of Tantalus: food and drink. To see the imprisoned, starving emperor Bajazeth placed in the middle of a banquet is to see a re-enactment of the punishment of Tantalus, another king (he still wears his crown in Whitney's woodcut) who suffers starvation in the midst of plenty. Throughout the banquet, Bajazeth remains locked within his cage, and thus he is frozen in place like Tantalus in the underworld, who is himself a prisoner.[24]

The teasing begins almost as soon as the scene begins, as the hungry, caged Bajazeth watches Tamburlaine's retinue 'freely banquet and carouse.' But Tamburlaine is not content to leave matters at that. Turning to his captive after vaunting his own power, Tamburlaine abruptly asks 'And now, Bajazeth, hast thou any stomach?' (10). The question is a twofold taunt, calculated to remind Bajazeth of his hunger and also to imply that he is no longer a man, as he lacks the 'stomach' of pride and anger. After he has commanded Bajazeth to eat ('Fall to your victuals') and awakened his rage, Tamburlaine cleverly switches tactics and suddenly offers him food – but in the humiliating form of meat on his sword's point. Here Tamburlaine repeats the 'jestures' of the crown-game he played with Mycetes on the battlefield, as once again he mockingly offers up the object which he has been holding out of reach. Being prouder than Mycetes, Bajazeth stamps on the meat and then flings a proffered waterpail on the ground. Tamburlaine's response is bitterly civil: 'Fast and welcome, sir, while hunger make you eat' ('while' carrying the force of 'until'). After Bajazeth is urged by his wife Zabina to eat in order to sustain life, Tamburlaine seizes another opportunity to humiliate him:

> *Tamburlaine.* Here, Turk, wilt thou have a clean trencher?
> *Bajazeth.* Ay, tyrant, and more meat.
> *Tamburlaine.* Soft, sir, you must be dieted; too much eating will make you
>   surfeit.   4.4.103–6

The word 'here' indicates that Tamburlaine offers a trencher to Bajazeth, and the mock solicitude of 'Soft, sir' suggests that he suddenly snatches it from the Turk's grasp. In this ingenious re-enactment of Tantalus' torment, Tamburlaine has goaded Bajazeth into shunning nourishment when he could have had it and then into asking for it when he could not.

Although the germ of the banquet scene is present in many of his sources, Marlowe alone emphasizes the twinned elements of starvation and tantalization. Most accounts mention Bajazeth's lack of proper food only to make a homiletic point about the transitory nature of power. In the words of his primary English source, George Whetstone's *The English Myrror*, Bajazeth

was taken prisoner, and presented to Tamburlaine, who closed this great Emperor in an iron cage, and as a dog fed him only with the fragments that fell from his table ... a notable example of the incertainty of worldly fortunes: Bajazeth, that in the morning was the mightiest Emperor on the earth, at night, was driven to feed among the dogs ...[25]

Earlier in act 4, in Bajazeth's first appearance in his cage, Marlowe follows his sources by having Tamburlaine order Zabina to 'feed him with the scraps / My servitors shall bring thee from my board' (4.2.87–8). But Marlowe quickly deviates from the tradition in emphasizing that, in addition to being humiliated, Bajazeth is being starved by his diet of orts. Thus, when Tamburlaine first mentions feeding table-scraps to Bajazeth, he specifies that 'he that gives him other food than this / Shall sit by him and starve to death himself' (4.2.89–90). And two scenes later at the banquet, Bajazeth indicates that he has indeed been starved: 'unless I eat, I die' (4.4.100). It is this extreme hunger which makes Marlowe's other innovation – the tantalization – impossible for Bajazeth to resist.

Why does Tamburlaine tease Bajazeth in such a sustained, energetic fashion? A partial answer is that tantalization represents a paying back of Bajazeth in his own coin, for when we first see him he is besieging Constantinople and orders its supply of food and water to be cut off (3.1.58–62). Later, before their decisive battle, Tamburlaine tells Bajazeth that he will free

> Those Christian captives which you keep as slaves,
> Burdening their bodies with your heavy chains
> And feeding them with thin and slender fare ...   3.3.47–9

The punishment of Bajazeth, like that of Tantalus, is a re-enactment of his crime. In a reversal of roles familiar from the *Elegies* and *Dido Queen of Carthage*, the erstwhile tantalizer is tantalized.

At a deeper level, however, Tamburlaine's playing with Bajazeth reveals more about himself than his victim. Throughout the play, he has attempted to manifest his power by directing the gaze of onlookers to sights which he has constructed, and his intention in staging the spectacle of Bajazeth's incarceration and tantalization is clearly to reveal how superior he is to his captive.[26] Doubtless, he would have approved of the critic's observation that 'there is probably no other scene in Elizabethan drama that so astringently contrasts the rewards and facts of victory with the powerlessness and facts of defeat.'[27] But, in spite of Tamburlaine's carefully arranged and lurid contrasts between victor and victim, between banqueting table and iron cage, the two figures are not so different as he wishes. We may sense that 'Ultimately Tamburlaine, for all his itineraries of conquest and his call for maps, occupies a space as claustrophobic as Bajazeth, caged in the company of his neuroses.'[28] Moreover, through his tantalizing of Bajazeth, Tamburlaine inadvertently reveals the ground of similarity between the two of them. He is inflicting on Bajazeth the insatiable hunger and thirst which he has long felt within himself; in more ways than one, Bajazeth suffers the torment of Tamburlaine. In the Scythian's phrase, Bajazeth and his wife 'make a goodly show at a banquet' because he vainly hopes to find in the spectacle of their degrading tantalization a nourishment which food cannot provide him.

There are many suggestions in the banquet scene that Tamburlaine's figurative feeding on Bajazeth could become literal. Earlier in the play, Tamburlaine's appetites are associated with a sublimated desire for rule in phrases such as '[t]hirsting with sovereignty' (2.1.20), 'fiery thirster after sovereignty' (2.6.31), and 'thirst of reign' (2.7.12). But the banquet scene suggests that Tamburlaine's thirst has become an unnatural appetite, as carousing wine and spilling blood are conflated.[29] The banquet scene also contains a number of appallingly jocular references to cannibalism, usually to the eating of one's own flesh or that of a close family member. Thus Bajazeth speaks of eating Tamburlaine's 'blood-raw heart' and the Scythian counters by suggesting that the Turk feed himself and his wife with his own heart (12–14). Tamburlaine finds the idea of Bajazeth's consuming himself attractive, for in quick succession he asks 'Are you so daintily brought up you cannot eat your own flesh?' (36–7) and then vaunts that he will 'make thee slice the brawns of thy arms into carbonadoes, and eat them' (44–5). Finally he exhorts Bajazeth to butcher his wife Zabina (the flesh of his flesh) 'while she is fat, for if she live but a while longer, she will fall into a consumption with fretting, and then she will not be worth the eating' (49–52).

In its emphasis on cannibalism and tantalization, the banquet scene alludes to both the crime and the punishment of Tantalus. Throughout the scene Marlowe recalls Seneca's tragedy *Thyestes*, which begins with the appearance on earth of the ghost of Tantalus and concludes with the bloody banquet at which his grandchildren re-enact his crime: Atreus kills the children of his brother Thyestes and then feeds them to him. Thyestean banquets, in which people are served in pastries to unsuspecting family members, are all too common in Elizabethan drama.[30] The banquet scene in *Tamburlaine* reinvents the lurid Thyestean feast by evoking it through metaphor, a subtlety lost in a recent stage production's emphasis on quite literal acts of cannibalism.[31]

Seneca's *Thyestes*, which Antonin Artaud thought the best example of the Theatre of Cruelty, has an extreme power to disturb.[32] But the exquisite cruelty of *Thyestes* finds its match in the banquet scene of *Tamburlaine*, and the entire ending of Marlowe's play is more deeply Senecan than critics have noted.[33] Not only do motifs in *Tamburlaine*, such as the quenching of thirst by drinking blood and the consumption by fire of internal organs, first appear in *Thyestes* (102–3, 98–9), but also both works emphasize the deliberate and shocking transgression of moral boundaries.[34] Like Thyestes, Bajazeth and Zabina can express the enormity of their suffering only through the conceit that hell has irrupted into the everyday world, as if the earth's crust has suddenly broken open to reveal a passageway to the underworld (4.2.26–9; 5.1.217; 5.1.238). When he first learns of the horrible crime that Atreus has perpetrated, Thyestes declares that 'the gods are fled' (1021); similarly, the spectacle of Bajazeth's humiliation compels Zabina to ask 'is there left no Mahomet, no God ... ?' (5.1.239). But perhaps the deepest imprint of Seneca's play on Marlowe's can be seen in the way Tamburlaine plays Atreus to Bajazeth's Thyestes, shamelessly exulting in his triumph over his powerless victim. In both plays, however, there is a strong suggestion that the victor fails to find the satisfaction which he has expected and indeed that his desires are finally insatiable.[35] Like Atreus, Tamburlaine cannot escape the torment of Tantalus, and the banquet scene's imagery of cannibalism becomes sickeningly familiar in Part Two of *Tamburlaine*.[36]

Tamburlaine, Part Two: The Teaser Teased

Despite its repeated suggestion that Tamburlaine is a Tantalus, Part One of *Tamburlaine* can be seen as chronicling the triumph of his will. In external terms, at least, Tamburlaine does accomplish what he desires to accomplish. In Part Two, however, the world clearly proves impervious to all attempts – and especially Tamburlaine's attempts – to impose the will on it. An austere truth of Part Two, in Helen Gardner's formulation, is that 'The world is not the plaything of the ambitious mind.'[37] But the converse of this statement makes a still more incisive point about the play: the ambitious mind is the plaything of the world. Often in Part Two the world plays tricks on people who aspire to control or even understand it, such as the spectacular ruse through which Olympia provokes her unwanted suitor Theridamas into inadvertently stabbing her to death. But the most resonant games are those which the world plays upon Tamburlaine. In Part One, a distinguishing mark of the protagonist was his delight in games of mockery, especially games involving tantalization. Whether he is withholding the crowns he promised to his commanders or feasting in front of the starving Bajazeth, Tamburlaine revels in the power to entice and withhold. In Part Two, however, Tamburlaine no longer undertakes to play these games. In fact, just the opposite happens: Tamburlaine himself becomes the dupe of greater powers, as people and events escape from his grasp and take on an existence independent of his will. In a reversal of his favourite game, he becomes the object of play, the teased instead of the teaser.

Part Two's inversion of the earlier game-playing paradigm is most apparent in the relationship between Tamburlaine and Callapine, the son of Bajazeth. At first Part Two seems to begin where Part One left off, for Callapine is the prisoner of Tamburlaine, as his father had been. But the son easily escapes from Tamburlaine's control by means of the enticing rhetoric that his captor had monopolized in Part One, and throughout the rest of the play Callapine eludes Tamburlaine's persistent attempts to recapture him. (Callapine's flight and Tamburlaine's pursuit recall the Ovidian motif of 'fleeing and following' from the *Elegies* and *Dido Queen of Carthage*.) Thus, on the eve of their first battle, Tamburlaine threatens to imprison him again, vowing 'you shall not trouble me thus to come and fetch you' (3.5.100–2). But, even though Tamburlaine wins the field, Callapine eludes the Scythian's grasp in order to fight (and flee) another day. Tamburlaine's final attempt to 'come and fetch' Callapine occurs at the end of the play, and once again he defeats the young Turk but fails to capture him. In a pathetic vaunt Tamburlaine is reduced to declaring that 'could I but a while pursue the field, / That Callapine should be my slave again' (5.3.117–18). But within a hundred lines, Tamburlaine the Great is dead, while Callapine remains free to threaten Tamburlaine's sons, who according to Marlowe's sources were conquered by Bajazeth's children.

In addition to diminishing Tamburlaine's power to control the world, Part Two reduces his knowledge of the world. As a study of Marlowe's plots has observed, in Part Two 'The hero no longer occupies the epistemic center of the play, knowing everything and planning the events according to copious information.'[38] Tamburlaine's lack of knowledge, and thus his vulnerability to being teased, is poignantly obvious in his death scene, where the prospect of his own demise reduces him to the status of a hopeful, impotent spectator. In his interview with his doctor, Tamburlaine's powerlessness is apparent. When the conqueror demands the plain truth ('Tell me, what think you of my sickness now?' [5.3.81]), the physician responds with a highly technical analysis of Tamburlaine's urine. Not only is the 'hypostasis' 'thick and obscure,' but the 'humidum and calor' of his blood are spent, and besides 'this day is critical, / Dangerous to those whose crisis is as yours.'[39] Finally the doctor reaches the obscurely threatening conclusion

> that the soul,
> Wanting those organons by which it moves,
> Cannot endure, by argument of art.   5.3.95–7

Then, totally unexpectedly, he suddenly switches to plain English and replaces the death sentence with two lines of pure Pollyanna: 'Yet if your majesty may escape this day, / No doubt but you shall soon recover all.' The effect of this sudden redirection is disconcerting; it teases Tamburlaine (and the audience) with a glimmer of hope in a situation which had just been revealed to be definitively hopeless. The mighty conqueror's response is pathetic in its feeble self-solicitude: 'Then will I comfort all my vital parts / And live in spite of death above a day' (5.3.100–1). But the hope is delusory.

For Tamburlaine, Callapine's elusiveness and even his own fleeting mortality are merely troublesome compared to his agonizing failure to hold on to Zenocrate. More painfully than any other event in Part Two, Zenocrate's death makes Tamburlaine aware of the shocking limits of his power. Tamburlaine's rise in Part One had commenced with his seizure of Zenocrate, and his continued possession of her is a sign to him of his success. At her deathbed, he is reduced to the status of mere spectator for the first time in either play. Moroever, his language no longer seems able to affect the world. Movingly, Tamburlaine's glorification of Zenocrate in a long speech of expansive, celebratory lyricism concludes with a nervous query: 'Physicians, will no physic do her good?' The doctor's response is a model of professional evasion: 'My lord, your majesty shall soon perceive – / And if she pass this fit, the worst is past' (2.4.39–40). The effect is to tease Tamburlaine with a hope which will prove false.

The keynote of Tamburlaine's grief is sounded when, just before Zenocrate dies, he refers rather cryptically to 'the malice of the angry skies, / Whose jealousy admits no second mate' (2.4.11–12). Though the editor of the Revels *Tamburlaine* glosses the lines as 'a reference to the legendary jealousy of Juno,' it makes better sense to see the allusion pointing to Jupiter, who is jealous because he does not want to share Zenocrate with Tamburlaine, her 'second mate.'[40] When Zenocrate dies, Tamburlaine responds as if a precious object had been taken away from him by a rival. His first impulse is to berate the 'Fatal Sisters' for 'taking hence my fair Zenocrate,' but he quickly replaces these female figures with a male competitor, claiming that

> amorous Jove hath snatched my love from hence,
> Meaning to make her stately queen of heaven.
> What god soever holds thee in his arms,
> Giving thee nectar and ambrosia,
> Behold me here, divine Zenocrate,
> Raving, impatient, desperate and mad ...   2.4.107–12

An unmistakable irony plays around these lines if we recall that, at the beginning of Part One, Tamburlaine himself had snatched Zenocrate away from the King of Arabia in order to make her his own 'stately queen.' The irony is compounded by the fact that Tamburlaine has just been speaking of Rome's 'wanton poets' and in fact compared Zenocrate to Ovid's Corinna, for this passage also recalls the world of *All Ovid's Elegies*, especially the late poems in which the once masterful poet-lover loses his mistress to a rival.

The imagery pervading Zenocrate's death scene suggests that her departure creates in Tamburlaine a deprivation akin to being starved of vitality. In the opening lines of the scene, he had implicitly associated himself with the sun, which after the death of Zenocrate 'wants the fuel that inflamed his beams' (2.4.4). Immediately after her death, however, Tamburlaine eschews the cosmic metaphor and identifies himself as suffering from a fatal lack of sustenance. Poignantly, he pleads with Theridamas to refrain from saying that Zenocrate is dead: 'Though she be dead, yet let me think she lives, / And feed my mind that dies for want of her' (2.4.127–8). Tamburlaine's 'feed my mind' is a strange and revealing turn of phrase, suggesting that the food of self-delusion will fill the cavity of a starving mind. Like the speaker in the final poem of *All Ovid's Elegies*, who pleads with his mistress to betray him only behind closed doors so he can still pretend she is true, Tamburlaine tries desperately to deceive himself. His feast on illusion begins immediately, for he addresses Zenocrate's corpse and declares, 'Where'er her soul be, thou shalt stay with me' (2.4.129). Fiercely holding on to all that is left to grasp, he makes a fetish of her remains and constructs a mobile mausoleum to accompany him on his travels.

Of course, Tamburlaine's furious response to Zenocrate's death reveals his extraordinary indifference or insensitivity to her desires, for her last words to him were: 'But let me die, my love, yet let me die, / With love and patience let your true love die' (2.4.66–7). Moreover, her plea for Tamburlaine to release her to die may remind us that her very first words to him in Part One were a similar plea for freedom. Now, as before, he does not let her go. He carries her embalmed corpse with him in order to demonstrate that he still has the power to maintain her presence and to encompass her. Later (3.2) Tamburlaine will ascribe the magical potency of a talisman to his 'Sweet picture of divine Zenocrate' which 'will draw the gods from heaven' and pull the stars from the southern hemisphere to view it (3.2.26–8). Thus Tamburlaine proves to himself that he will be able to control the forces that snatched Zenocrate away. And the picture will re-embody the absent Zenocrate. Addressing the painting as he had earlier addressed her corpse, Tamburlaine declares, 'Thou shalt not beautify Larissa plains, / But keep within the circle of mine arms' (3.2.34–5). Like Queen Dido, he uses the image of encircling arms to deny an abandonment.

The subplot reflects Tamburlaine's attempt to prevent Zenocrate's departure in the episode of Theridamas' unsuccessful and brutally insensitive wooing of Olympia. When Theridamas first comes upon Olympia at the sack of Balsera, the moment is not very propitious for romance, for she is burning the bodies of her husband and the dear child she has freshly slain, and is hastening to kill herself. Like Zenocrate, Olympia desires only to cease living, but Theridamas is deaf to her pleas as he launches into paeans of grotesquely inappropriate enticement. The resemblance of Theridamas to Tamburlaine even extends to their shared fears, for Theridamas imagines himself competing with the gods for possession of the beloved. When once he failed to find Olympia in his tent, he tells her, he was enraged, 'Supposing amorous Jove had sent his son, / The winged Hermes, to convey thee hence' (4.2.18–19). More blatantly than Tamburlaine, Theridamas becomes the object of a game, for Olympia escapes his grasp by tricking him into stabbing her to death. Instead of acknowledging the contrary will of the woman to whom he says he is devoted, Theridamas fantasizes (as Tamburlaine had done) that he is being cuckolded by a god: 'Infernal Dis is courting of my love, / Inventing masks and stately shows for her' (4.2.93–4). Like his leader, Theridamas is left empty-handed.

The clearest expression of how completely satisfaction has eluded Tamburlaine occurs in the final scene, as he gives his last command:

> Give me a map, then let me see how much
> Is left for me to conquer all the world,
> That these my boys may finish all my wants. 3.123–5

In effect, Tamburlaine is tantalizing himself with all the prizes which he has not taken. In Part One he had provoked himself to overreach through images of inaccessible beauty and unparalleled sovereignty, but now his self-teasing can no longer serve as a stimulus to action. We hear a new poignancy when Tamburlaine's heroic design to 'conquer all the world' slides into the feeble hope that 'my boys may finish all my wants.' These 'wants,' like the 'want' of Zenocrate which he earlier feared would destroy his mind, signify not desire but rather need, absence, and incompletion. Tamburlaine proceeds to itemize his conquests, and his account is notably prosaic, like the inventories of conquered lands that his commanders had submitted to him early in the play (1.3.174–217). Tamburlaine's pedestrian catalogue ends in lines which both crown and undercut his list – the play's climactic anticlimax:

Then by the northern part of Africa
I came at last to Graecia, and from thence
To Asia, where I stay against my will ...   5.3.140–2

All of Tamburlaine's relentless striving has served to conduct him to a
place where he does not want to be but cannot leave, save through the
release of death.

Tamburlaine, Part Two: Tantalizing the Audience

Modern stage practice has served Part Two of *Tamburlaine* especially
poorly, for even the best productions have severely cut it and then conflated what remained with Part One.[41] This practice has erased one of
the most interesting experiments of Part Two, its new conception of dramatic structure. The plot of Part One is a steady march of incident in
which Tamburlaine's opponents rise against him one at a time and in
climactic order. In Part Two, however, the plot is extremely dispersed,
with the inclusion of a number of subplot actions which do not bear
directly on Tamburlaine himself. As Marlowe had used up most of his
source material in Part One, it may seem as if he were forced to pad out
his sequel with not very relevant material gleaned from his desultory
reading (Ariosto's *Orlando Furioso*, a manuscript treatise on fortification,
etc.). Not surprisingly, Marlowe's sequel has been censured as a jerry-
built play 'whose isolated episodic sections and sensations are merely
strung out in a linear relationship without consequential form.'[42] Nor
have misgivings about Part Two's structural coherence been limited to
literary critics. In rehearsal for his National Theatre production (1976) of
a conflated *Tamburlaine*, Peter Hall worried in his diary about 'the shape
of the second part,' sensing that 'either I have failed to grasp the structure, or the structure doesn't quite work.'[43] Attempting to repair this
apparently deficient architecture, Hall finally (and '[w]ith some trepida-
tion') did what virtually all modern productions of Part Two do: in
addition to cutting material he rearranged the order of many scenes,
thereby creating what he called 'a completely different rhythm.'[44]

Hall's intuition that 'the structure doesn't quite work' is, I think, both
right and wrong. Right in that the play's discontinuities are theatrically
ineffective, if an effective plot is one which raises and then satisfies the
audience's expectations. But wrong in that the curious structure *does* in a
sense work, but to frustrate rather than gratify expectation. As an alternative to approaching the play as merely an incompetent, ramshackle

version of Part One, we should entertain the possibility that Marlowe was inventively playing with unsettling an audience's assumptions through anticlimax and discontinuous form. Repeatedly, the play springs its central events upon an unprepared and unsuspecting audience, while elaborately preparing for events which do not come about. Often we find that problematic passages or even whole scenes which critics have adduced as evidence of Marlowe's imaginative disengagement and sloppy plotting can be better understood as attempts to create uncertainty in his audience. The criticism which disparages the plot for failing to be Aristotelian misses what is most interesting in the play and also most relevant to Marlowe's unfolding oeuvre. From Part Two of *Tamburlaine* onwards, Marlowe's most careful plotting will prove to be constructed with the end of frustrating expectation.

Marlowe did not of course discover the idea of misdirecting audiences while writing Part Two of *Tamburlaine*. In translating Ovid's *Amores* he had plenty of occasion to observe the games which an elusive writer can play with his readers' expectations, and in *Dido Queen of Carthage* he often alludes to (or even quotes from) Virgil's sombre epic narrative before quickly descending to the mock heroic and sexually subversive. But the best evidence for Marlowe's prior interest in frustrating what he has led audiences to anticipate is an event in Part One of *Tamburlaine* which does not happen: the downfall of the proud protagonist. For an Elizabethan audience weaned on Fall of Princes literature, such traditional devices as the prophetic curses of his enemies and Zenocrate's forebodings of his fate would signal the imminent fall of ambitious Tamburlaine.[45] Referring primarily to Part One, Stephen Greenblatt notes that '*Tamburlaine* repeatedly teases its audience with the *form* of the cautionary tale, only to violate the convention.'[46] Whereas the toying with expectation in Part One hinges on an event (Tamburlaine's come-uppance) that does not happen, in the sequel the play of misdirection is much more various and energetic (and will become still more so in Marlowe's next play, *The Jew of Malta*). In Part Two, for the first time in Marlowe's work, withholding what the audience has been led to expect becomes a central strategy of his plot construction.

Part Two's status as a sequel, a work that does not stand alone, provides Marlowe with ample opportunity for subverting what the audience anticipates. (It is interesting that the second part of Shakespeare's *Henry IV*, like the second part of *Tamburlaine*, is also a play about the mockery of expectation.)[47] The great majority of Elizabethan playgoers would have come to see Part Two of *Tamburlaine* with expectations derived from having attended, or at least having heard about, a recent production of its predecessor. In the revival of the *Tamburlaine* plays in 1594–5, the first productions for which there is documentary evidence, Part Two was invariably staged in tandem with Part One, following it by no more than a day or two.[48] But Part Two of *Tamburlaine* is less a continuation than a reversal of its predecessor: it is a sequel in which nothing follows quite as it should, a sequel full of non sequiturs, surprises, and anticlimaxes.

Marlowe's strategy of misdirection and surprise is already at work in the Prologue's characterization of Part Two as a play

> Where death cuts off the progress of his pomp
> And murd'rous Fates throws all his triumphs down.
> But what became of fair Zenocrate,
> And with how many cities' sacrifice
> He celebrated her sad funeral,
> Himself in presence shall unfold at large.

Even without contrasting these lines to the assured, powerful Prologue of Part One, one senses that Marlowe is either napping or being mischievous.[49] It does not seem to be coincidental that the climactic line is also the most untrustworthy line in the passage: 'And murd'rous Fates throws all his triumphs down.' Since the previous line clearly alludes to Tamburlaine's death, this statement suggests an additional, completely devastating ('*all* his triumphs') defeat, a disastrous humiliation such as Fall of Princes literature prescribes for proud tyrants and such as Tamburlaine visited upon Bajazeth. But no such 'murd'rous Fates' befall Tamburlaine, who continues to be victorious in battle until he falls suddenly ill and dies at the close of the play. And even then his triumphs are not thrown down. Since the Prologue is rather early for the dramatist to be napping, it seems likely that Marlowe intends a deliberate misdirection.[50] The hypothesis is supported by the Prologue's coy refusal to specify the number of cities Tamburlaine sacrificed to celebrate Zenocrate's death. Given the proliferation of hyperbole in Part One, the question 'how many' may entice an audience into expecting a multitude of burning cities. But the answer turns out to be – one.

In an amusing irony, this disjointed Prologue assures the audience that the events of the play will 'unfold at large.' The term 'unfold' carried considerably more resonance in Renaissance philosophy and art than it does today. The notion that meanings and events unfold (*explicare*) was central to the Neoplatonic conception of the sensible world as a temporal explication of the eternal, infolded unity of the intelligible world. What Ernst Cassirer called 'the fundamental antithesis of *complicatio* and *explicatio*' was the master trope of Nicholas of Cusa's philosophy, and it informed such central works of the Renaissance imagination as Botticelli's *Primavera* and Spenser's *Faerie Queene*.[51] Marlowe's Prologue, however, invokes expectations of a lucid rhythm of explication and unfolding in order to frustrate them. As happens several times in Shakespeare's plays, the gesture offering to 'unfold' is followed by a coy withholding.[52]

Instead of the promised unfolding, the movement of the play is characterized by the Prologue's verbs of violent action: cutting off and throwing down. Suddenness is all. Like the sneak attack which the Christians mount against the Turks, events in the play 'issue suddenly' (2.1.23, 60). The effect is to tease the audience by emphasizing the unpredictable, unknowable nature of the play's events. What matters is not a coherent process of explication but rather the supremely arbitrary power of the playwright. The plot moves not through a continuous unfolding but through 'fits,' the paroxysms which suddenly afflict Zenocrate and Tamburlaine.

The promise of a play which 'unfolds at large' is immediately belied by the gap between the statements of the Prologue and the actual events of the first act. Though the Prologue closes with the assurance that Tamburlaine 'in presence' will unfold the significance of the play, the protagonist is in fact physically absent from the first two scenes. In virtually all modern productions of Part Two, however, the directors have chosen to open the play with Marlowe's third scene (which is dominated by Tamburlaine), thus avoiding the anticlimax that Marlowe carefully constructed.[53] Instead of the announced protagonist, Part Two opens with a conflict between Turks and Christians, which in fact dominates the play until the death of Zenocrate (2.4). On the opening afternoon of the first performance, no one in the theatre could have expected to see this conflict, since it is based on a well-known battle (at Varna) fought some forty years after the historical Tamburlaine's death.[54] Surely Marlowe must have known that he was beginning his play on an unexpected note of complication, not explication. It is no coincidence, given the Prologue which misleads and effectively betrays the audience, that the conflict between Christian and Turk focuses on treachery and bad faith.

Of all Marlowe's experiments with plotting surprise in the play, perhaps the most striking is the scene (2.4) in which Zemocrate dies. As we have seen, Tamburlaine is not prepared for this moment, and neither is Marlowe's audience. Apart from the Prologue's brief anticipation of Zenocrate's 'sad funeral,' there is no preparation at all in the text for the sudden descent of mortal sickness upon her. In the theatre, the shock should be palpable when, at the beginning of 2.4, '*The arras is drawn, and Zenocrate lies in her bed of state … three Physicians about her bed, tempering potions*' (s.d.). The cliché about the unpredictability of death comes vividly alive.

Marlowe's teasing of the audience's as well as Tamburlaine's expectations continues throughout the scene. Most notably, Zenocrate does not die at the moment for which the dialogue prepares us. She speaks what appear to be her dying words (the chiasmus suggesting closure) when she says 'Yet let me kiss my lord before I die, / And let me die with kissing of my lord' (2.4.69–70). It would be appropriate at this point (there are no stage directions) for her and Tamburlaine to kiss and then for her to close her eyes. She unexpectedly recovers, however, saying 'But since my life is lengthened yet a while …' (2.4.71–2). After Marlowe mocks expectation by deferring Zenocrate's death, he then plays the opposite trick, allowing her to die before anyone notices. In a moment that says a good deal about their relationship, Zenocrate unobtrusively dies as Tamburlaine is spinning out an elaborate poetic fantasy about her, oblivious to her physical reality.[55] The effect is to catch the theatre audience up in at least some of the confusion that Tamburlaine feels.[56]

In Part Two of *Tamburlaine* Marlowe's toying with expectation is not confined to the surprise of events either happening or not happening. He also plays games with his audience on a more intellectual level by engaging the issue of *why* events happen. This teasing game has two stages. First, Marlowe deploys a series of traditional signals which appear to be leading to a conventional (usually theological) explanation of the event. But, as soon as the audience reaches Tantalus-like for the satisfying explanation, Marlowe suddenly withdraws it.

A notable case in point is Marlowe's ambiguous handling of the Turks' victory over the treaty-breaking Christians in 2.2 and 2.3. Immediately before the battle, the Turkish leader Orcanes calls upon Christ for aid with which to 'discomfort and confound / The trustless force of those false Christians' (2.2.61–2). His prayer would seem to have been briskly and unequivocally answered, for the next scene begins with the entrance of the mortally wounded king of the Christians, the devious

Sigismund. Moreover, Sigismund's dying words appear to confirm the efficacy of Orcanes' prayer, for he declares that 'God hath thundered vengeance from on high, / For my accursed and hateful perjury' (2.3.2–3). The audience's conviction that it has witnessed an act of divine retribution seems further confirmed by the entrance of Orcanes, who infers from the spectacle of Sigismund's corpse that 'Christ or Mahomet hath been my friend.' For an alert audience it would seem that 'the whole three-scene sequence draws toward its close as a vignette of divine retribution for violence against the godhead.'[57]

But, when Orcanes asks his colleague Gazellus to confirm that divine justice has been at work, what had seemed an ironclad demonstration suddenly collapses like a house of cards:

> *Orcanes.* What sayest thou yet, Gazellus, to his foil,
>   Which we referred to justice of his Christ
>   And to His power, which here appears as full
>   As rays of Cynthia to the clearest sight?
> *Gazellus.* 'Tis but the fortune of the wars, my lord,
>   Whose power is often proved a miracle.   2.3.27–32

Marlowe's timing is very deft, as Orcanes' comment about the total transparency of the event is immediately punctured by the force of Gazellus' laconic and sceptical aphorism. Both the audience and Orcanes have reason to be surprised by this response, for a few lines earlier Gazellus too had attributed Sigismund's downfall to the fact that he was a 'perjured traitor' (2.3.12). Thus, virtually every line in the unfolding sequence supports a lucid interpretation which Marlowe suddenly snatches beyond the reach of the audience. Of course Gazellus *may* be wrong and Orcanes *may* be right after all, but the audience has lost its grasp on what had seemed a certainty.

In both theme and dramaturgy, this early scene closely foreshadows the cryptic, infolded nature of the play's most striking and most elusive moment: Tamburlaine's sudden fit at the end of 5.1. Since it heralds his imminent death, this felling of Tamburlaine is crucial for any interpretation of the play; to determine the cause of the sickness would be to reveal the forces beyond Tamburlaine's will which govern the world. As with the parallel event of Sigismund's defeat, however, Marlowe toys with ambiguities of causation to create a moment which both invites and frustrates religious interpretation. Instead of exhibiting what has been called an 'indifference to fixing causality precisely,' Marlowe deliberately leaves his audience uncomfortably suspended between belief and disbelief.[58]

The calculated ambiguities of Tamburlaine's illness stem in large part from its problematic relationship to his burning of the Koran, which occurs on stage only moments earlier. In a powerful spectacle, Tamburlaine challenges the potency of 'Mahomet' by burning the Koran, and then (in Robert Greene's phrase) he 'dares God out of heaven':

> Now, Mahomet, if thou have any power,
> Come down thyself and work a miracle;
> Thou art not worthy to be worshipped
> That suffers flames of fire to burn the writ
> Wherein the sum of thy religion rests.
> Why sendest thou not a furious whirlwind down
> ...
> Or vengeance on the head of Tamburlaine ... ?   5.1.186–94

Given the pointed reference to 'vengeance on the head of Tamburlaine,' Elizabethan audiences could scarcely have failed to entertain the thought that Tamburlaine's ensuing illness embodies the retribution which he has so rashly invited. The scene suggests an emblematic *tableau vivant* in which the Proud Tyrant is struck down at the moment of impious exaltation. This interpretation is hinted at by Techelles' question immediately after Tamburlaine expresses his pain ('What is it dares distemper Tamburlaine?' [5.1.218]), where 'dares' may suggest that Tamburlaine's daring of 'Mahomet' is now being repaid.

Although Marlowe invites the surmise that the illness is divinely authored, he also creates a set of contextual circumstances which serve to make this interpretation considerably less than compelling. Most notably, he allows just enough time to elapse between the blasphemy and the fit – there are fifteen lines of dialogue between the end of Tamburlaine's vaunt and his first expression of pain – to make a causal connection problematic. The handling of the scene in Hall's National Theatre production bore out Alexander Leggatt's earlier observation that the illness '*may* be Mahomet's revenge, but in theatrical terms the lapse of time between the defiance and the seizure is just long enough to create doubt.'[59] If 'Mahomet' does indeed strike Tamburlaine down as a warning to atheists (an idea which in itself might be considered blasphemous by Tudor Christians),[60] why does he not do so as an immediate and thus unmistakable response to the Scythian's blasphemies?

A host of other elements serve to complicate an audience's response. Unlike most Tudor dramatists who depict divine retribution, Marlowe refuses to disambiguate the event through recourse to reliable (but often clumsy) choric commentary.[61] Also, the likelihood of 'Mahomet's' having intervened is lessened by the fact that in the following scene Callapine prays to 'sacred Mahomet' for victory over Tamburlaine, and is immediately defeated. And, finally, the plausibility of retribution further recedes when Tamburlaine's physician delivers a detailed analysis of his urine, thus accounting for the illness in entirely naturalistic terms (like the comment on Sigismund's defeat as 'but the fortune of the wars').[62] Of course, these factors do not simply invalidate the hypothesis of divine intervention, and countervailing arguments can be made against each of them.[63] But the fact remains that Marlowe presents the play's climactic event in such a way as both to invite a conventional interpretation and to snatch that interpretation from reach.

5

Playing with Avarice:
The Jew of Malta

Far more than the callow sons to whom he reluctantly hands the chariot-reins, Tamburlaine's true spiritual heir is Barabas, the endlessly egotistic and energetic protagonist of *The Jew of Malta*. To be sure, Barabas does not inherit all of Tamburlaine's characteristics; he is himself aware that he lacks the ambition of those who (in an image recalling Tamburlaine) 'thirst so much for principality' (1.1.134). Despite his more constrained theatre of action – Barabas is in effect an island on an island – he does share some of Tamburlaine's defining traits, most notably a constant oscillation between desire and discontent. Barabas, too, is driven by a restless spirit of dissatisfaction; he can speak of contentment only in the conditional ('O Abigail, that I had thee here too, / Then my desires were fully satisfied' [2.1.51–2]), and he dies while exhorting his tongue to 'curse thy fill' (5.5.88). Like Tamburlaine, Barabas realizes and quickly rejects one eagerly anticipated objective after another, declaring that what had once been his bliss is now meaningless trash.[1] Gold is to Barabas what crowns are to Tamburlaine; it possesses powerful symbolic and imaginative value but fails to remain a satisfying object of desire. Like his predecessor, Barabas can enjoy his possessions only by employing them to tease the desires of others.

In *The Jew of Malta*, as he had done in the *Tamburlaine* plays, Marlowe draws upon a traditional linkage of this state of discontent with the sin of avarice and the figure of Tantalus.[2] We see this tradition, to cite a single instance, in Humfrey Gifford's lyric 'In Praise of the Contented Mind,' which cautions against the bondage of the soul to 'worldly pelf' by declaring that 'greedy men like Tantalus do fare / In midst of wealth they needy are and bare.'[3] Since *The Jew of Malta* concerns itself quite centrally with the desire for riches, it treats this idea of avarice more literally and explicitly than do the *Tamburlaine* plays, and there are occasions in the play when Barabas is identified in terms of the covetous Tantalus. But Marlowe does not make this commonplace idea explicit simply in order to endorse it; rather, he plays with the expectations which it conveys. In *The Jew of Malta*, he initiates the subversive theatrical enterprise for which Brecht was to praise Shaw: the dislocation of stock associations.[4] Thus, he will turn the stereotypical linkage of covetousness with Jews to his own uses by revealing that the truly covetous figures in the play are the Christians rather than Barabas. And he will turn the idea of Tantalian covetousness against his audience by suggesting that its appetite for moral and theatrical stereotypes, which he toys with in the play, is itself a manifestation of avarice.

It should be emphasized that in Elizabethan England covetousness was not merely an abstraction to be discussed in ethical philosophy and illustrated in emblem books. Many people (and Londoners in particular) perceived avarice with dread as a dark force corroding the very core of civil society. As Lawrence Manley has shown, one common way of responding to the bewilderingly transformative powers of money in the new London economy was to invoke the biblical assertion that 'Radix malorum est cupiditas.'[5] An Elizabethan translation of Cornelius Agrippa reveals this moral understanding of economics when it uses the venerable definition of avarice to characterize the essence of trade: 'Merchandise is a very subtle searcher-out of privy gains, a very greedy gulf of manifest spoil: never content with enough, but always very miserable for the desire to get.'[6] Often this lethal covetousness was vested in the shadowy persons of resident foreigners, people who were perceived to be dangerous because they did not belong to the social networks which safeguarded English decency. In 1593, the Privy Council was outraged by a versified attack against 'The strangers that do inhabit in this land,' which had been attached to the Dutch Church in London.[7] This incendiary libel, which is subscribed 'per Tamberlaine' to emphasize its bloodthirstiness, unites all of London's aliens into an inclusive You:

Your Machiavellian merchant spoils the state,
Your usury doth leave us all for dead,
Your artifex, and craftsman works our fate,
And like the Jews, you eat us up as bread.   5–8

In its references to Jews, Machiavelli, usury, and ravenous appetites, this passage carries us directly into the far more complex world of Marlowe's provocative, dangerous, and funny play.[8]

Barabas and Riches

In *The Jew of Malta*, as in Marlowe's previous works, the dynamics of desire involve a teasing of appetite, but the enticement has a new source. Instead of being generated by sexual desire (*Elegies, Dido*) or the lust for power (*Tamburlaine*), desire is provoked by the glittering attraction of riches. Throughout the play, material wealth is a constant presence on stage and in the dialogue. Various forms of riches (gold, silver, diamonds, and many kinds of precious jewels) are on everyone's tongue, often appearing in climactic position at the end of a line or a sentence. And in many scenes we see coins being counted, bagged up, tossed from balconies, extorted, and stolen. Above all, money is exchanged for a wide range of commodities, including slaves, sex, and political rule. In Malta the cash nexus rules supreme.[9] As virtually every commentator has noted, the Turk's frank response to the Governor's disingenuous question has much of the weight of the play behind it:

> *Governor.* Welcome, great bashaw; how fares Calymath?
>   What wind drives you thus into Malta road?
> *Basso.* The wind that bloweth all the world besides,
>   Desire of gold.   3.5.1–4

From 'great bashaw' to slave, from holy friar to pimp and prostitute, from Jew to Christian and Turk, it is the touch of avarice that makes the whole world kin. At the symbolic centre of Malta is the slave market, where 'Every one's price is written on his back' (2.3.3).

The observation that 'all the world' is motivated by the desire for gold would be universally true in *The Jew of Malta* were it not for two people, Barabas and his daughter Abigail. She is the more obvious exception to Malta's golden rule, for she represents a selfless devotion to others that finds in money no attraction. In the case of Barabas, however, the 'desire of gold' becomes an inadequate motivation, for reasons which are less morally fine but considerably more interesting. Whereas Abigail renounces the things of this world because they trap the soul within a labyrinth, Barabas finds that they are simply unsatisfying. If Abigail transcends greed, Barabas grows bored with it. Stephen Greenblatt's statement that 'Barabas' own desire of gold ... is the glowing core of that passion which fires all the characters' is true for only the first scene or two, and even in them Barabas' flame does not burn in a consistently hard and gemlike fashion.[10]

In his long counting-house soliloquy which opens the play, Barabas expresses contradictory attitudes to his wealth, by turns apostrophizing and dismissing it. Stacking coins into piles, he begins by arriving at what seems a final reckoning:

> So that of thus much that return was made:
> And of the third part of the Persian ships,
> There was the venture summed and satisfied.   1.1.1–3

But, unlike his financial accounts, neither the desires of Barabas nor the energies of his language will submit to being tidily 'summed and satisfied.' The third line of the play becomes the first of its many false endings. Having finished counting his coin, Barabas feels a kind of revulsion at the pettiness of bagging up these 'paltry silverlings': 'Fie, what a trouble 'tis to count this trash!' (1.1.7). Then, reinvoking his desire on a more imaginative level, he chants a long catalogue of increasingly precious jewels, finally declaring that

> This is the ware wherein consists my wealth:
> And thus, methinks, should men of judgement frame
> Their means of traffic from the vulgar trade,
> And as their wealth increaseth, so enclose
> Infinite riches in a little room.   1.1.33–7

Coming after thirty-six lines of soliloquy, the elegant formulation of 'Infinite riches in a little room' would seem to an innocent audience to 'enclose' everything that has gone before and thus mark the final cadence of a speech that is fully 'summed and satisfied.'

But the apparent closure is illusory, another false ending. Almost invariably, critics have discussed the 'Infinite riches in a little room' line out of context and thus failed to note that it does not in fact end the speech.[11] After a moment's pause in which perhaps he senses the approach of boredom, Barabas suddenly scatters the riches which he has so carefully compacted:

> But now how stands the wind?
> Into what corner peers my halcyon's bill?
> Ha, to the east? Yes: see how stands the vanes!   1.1.38–40

The lyrical image of enclosed wealth is literally thrown to the winds, and Barabas' focus shifts from exotic jewels to the gyrating beak of a mummified bird. This unexpected switch is characteristic of a play which finds life in its sudden changes of direction (that the bill 'peers' into corners conveys a grotesque vitality) and which seems perversely eager to undercut its most eloquent moments. Lyrical as Barabas may wax about storing up jewel-box wealth, his restless energies are attuned to the world of motion and change. Like the Tantalus of emblem literature and the wanton poet in *All Ovid's Elegies*, he finds that possession does not conduce to happiness.

The shifts in this opening soliloquy are proleptic, for as the play unfolds Barabas will express a wide spectrum of attitudes toward wealth, with indifference gradually coming to predominate. At first he seems crushed by the Governor's brutal seizure of all of his riches, and he is so delighted by his procurement of his back-up riches that, according to the stage direction, he '*hugs his bags*' (2.1.54). But by the end of act 2 Barabas is already showing a lack of concern for his economic losses, at least compared to his primary goal of avenging himself on the Governor of Malta. In a passage recalling and contrasting with the counting-house soliloquy, Barabas declares that the 'account' which matters most to him is not economic but passional, the account to be settled with Lodowick, the Governor's son:

> The account is made, for Lodowick dies.
> My factor sends me word a merchant's fled
> That owes me for a hundred tun of wine.
> I weigh it thus much: I have wealth enough.   2.3.244–7

What Barabas will not be able to get enough of is hatred and the desire for revenge.

At the outset Barabas appears to be a conventional figure of covetousness from the moral discourse of the age, as he is introduced by the quintessentially immoral Machevil and then discovered in his counting-house surrounded by heaps of money. And, to enforce the stereotype still further, the Prologue identifies Barabas as 'a Jew,/Who smiles to see how full his bags are crammed' (30–1). For most Elizabethans, 'Jew' and 'usurer' were virtually synonymous terms – that there were many usurers and very few Jews in England (apparently none of them money-lenders) did little to deter the time-honoured association of the two groups.[12] Accordingly, Jews on the Elizabethan stage were almost invariably depicted as usurers, and at first Barabas appears to fit the type.[13] The reference to stuffed money-bags, a frequent emblem of covetousness and usury, would have whetted the audience's anticipation of a money-lending Jew, and the stereotype would have seemed confirmed by the sight which Machevil reveals when he pulls open the curtain: the Jewish usurer covetously counting his money. For an Elizabethan audience, the 'emblematic simplicity of the scene' could scarcely be improved on.[14]

But, as is often the case with Marlowe, a traditional and recognizable image quickly comes to serve a subversive end. As soon as the tableau comes to life, vertiginous surprises begin, for the audience discovers that Barabas is not the usurer it thought and that his bags of gold are not the spoils of usury. Instead of the miserly usurer whom the Prologue and prejudice have prepared them for, playgoers find themselves watching a powerful, respected merchant-prince. On several occasions Barabas does confess to, or even boast of, practising usury, but the dramatic context of these remarks always provides good reason to doubt him. In one of the play's finer ironies, Barabas manipulates for his own ends the stereotypical association of Jews with usury. When the friars threaten him by hinting at their knowledge (derived from the confessional) of his murders, Barabas tries to cover himself by volubly confessing to lesser misdemeanours, including usury: 'I must needs say that I have been a great usurer' (4.1.39). After the friars continue to hint at his real crimes, Barabas conjures up the full resonance of the Christian myth of the Jewish usurer:

> I have been zealous in the Jewish faith,
> Hard-hearted to the poor, a covetous wretch,
> That would for lucre's sake have sold my soul.
> A hundred for a hundred I have ta'en;
> And now for store of wealth may I compare
> With all the Jews in Malta; but what is wealth?
> I am a Jew, and therefore am I lost.   4.1.51–7

This outrageous confession, in which being 'zealous in the Jewish faith' entails charging one hundred percent interest on loans, is music to the ears of those truly 'covetous wretch[es],' the friars. Barabas is playing the stereotype of the Jew, and thus he 'simply pays the Christians with their own bad coin.'[15]

As the play progressively makes clear, Barabas cares less about his wealth than do Malta's Christians. As early as the second scene, the riches in which Barabas is already losing interest draw the unwanted attention of the Christian authorities, who claim them for themselves. In a scene with numerous historical antecedents (the blackmailing of Jewish communities) and contemporary English parallels (levies on resident foreigners), the Christian authorities of Malta use their struggle with the Turks as a pretext to extort as much money as possible from the local Jewish population.[16] The key lines spoken by Ferneze, the Governor of Malta, express the rankest hypocrisy: 'Excess of wealth is cause of covetousness: / And covetousness, O, 'tis a monstrous sin!' (1.2.124–5). Here Ferneze takes a leaf from the book of Chaucer's cynical Pardoner, who boasts that 'Of avarice and of swich cursedness / Is all my preaching, forto make them free / To yeven their pence, and namely unto me.'[17] Since covetousness is a 'monstrous sin' springing not from too little but from too much riches, it is in theory an act of kindness to relieve Barabas of this soul-destroying wealth. But Barabas refuses to be taken in. Without missing a beat, he counters Ferneze's 'O, 'tis a monstrous sin' with an incisive response: 'Ay, but theft is worse ...'

Barabas' revenge becomes possible when he realizes that the power of his wealth to attract Christians can be used as a weapon against them. He will play games with his enemies, using his gold to lure them into traps. Even before Barabas concocts his wild program of revenge, the pleasure which he takes in manipulating people's hopes is clear from his guarded, misleading speech. Often Barabas' clever asides unexpectedly contradict or reverse a statement he has been making. As the Revels editor noted, asides like 'Assure yourselves I'll look – *unto myself*' (1.1.172) 'form a neat verbal equivalent for Barabas's device of arousing expectations he has no intention of fulfilling.'[18] Some lines in his long credo of evil to Ithamore indicate how easy it is to convert this verbal trick into a more lethal form of teasing:

And now and then, to cherish Christian thieves,
I am content to lose some of my crowns;
That I may, walking in my gallery,
See 'em go pinioned along by my door.   2.3.179–82

In an ironic variation on an important Reformation theme, Barabas has learned how to use (even lose) his riches.

Nowhere does Barabas play the game of Tantalus with more gusto than when he literally dangles his wealth before Ithamore:

> O trusty Ithamore, no servant, but my friend!
> I here adopt thee for mine only heir,
> All that I have is thine when I am dead,
> And whilst I live use half; spend as myself;
> Here, take my keys – I'll give 'em thee anon.
> Go buy thee garments – but thou shalt not want;   3.4.42–7

These lines are calculated not only to tantalize Ithamore but also – in a manner reminiscent of Tamburlaine's teasing of Mycetes – to mock him. Thus the unqualified promise of 'All that I have is thine' is quickly distanced by 'when I am dead,' and the command to 'Go buy thee garments' vaporizes into the vague assurance 'but thou shalt not want.' In the line offering the keys, the verbal teasing is acted out. 'Here take my keys' suggests that Barabas extends his ring of keys to Ithamore, and the pause in the middle of the line is just long enough for the slave to reach for them and for his master to jerk them back ('I'll give 'em thee anon'). Sending Ithamore away on an errand, Barabas contemptuously dismisses him and his like: 'Thus every villain ambles after wealth,/ Although he ne'er be richer than in hope' (3.4.52–3).

One of the play's pervasive jokes is that, covetous as Barabas may be, most of the Christians turn out to be worse, being at least as greedy and far less intelligent. As usual, Marlowe's vitriol is ecumenical.[19] We may, for instance, smile at Barabas' conflation of the desire for gold and the love of a daughter when he catches the bags which Abigail tosses and exclaims 'O my girl,/My gold, my fortune, my felicity' (2.1.47–8) and 'O girl, O gold, O beauty, O my bliss!' (2.1.54). But only two scenes later we see a Christian identify Abigail with material wealth when Lodowick asks (without being prompted), 'Well, Barabas, canst help me to a diamond?' (2.3.49).[20] Barabas immediately responds in kind, enticing Lodowick's covetousness by burnishing his image – Abigail becomes a diamond which 'sparkles bright and fair' (2.3.59) and 'outshines Cynthia's rays' (2.3.63). The entire scene, which takes place in the middle of the slave market, makes an incisive comment on the commodification of women, Barabas prostituting his daughter as Lodowick attempts to buy her. (This motif extends into the following scene, which opens with the first appearance of the prostitute Bellamira, who complains of poor business.) Lodowick's competitive desire to possess Abigail is intensified by the presence in the background of his rival Mathias (who is shopping for slaves with his pious, anti-Semitic mother); with ridiculous ease, Barabas exploits this competition between erstwhile friends, arranging the fight in which these two fine young Maltese puppets strike each other dead.

In a sequence which resembles the destruction of the lovers but is considerably funnier, Barabas uses his wealth to tantalize the two friars, Jacomo and Bernardine, turning them against each other in murderous rivalry. Through a delicious irony, Barabas whets the covetousness of the friars by confessing himself 'a covetous wretch' and offering to divest himself of his riches:

> Cellars of wine, and sollars full of wheat,
> Warehouses stuffed with spices and with drugs,
> Whole chests of gold, in bullion and in coin,
> Besides I know not how much weight in pearl,
> Orient and round, have I within my house;   4.1.63–7

This is a reprise of the opening scene's 'Infinite riches in a little room,' but the desire which Barabas had earlier expressed in soliloquy is now turned outward as temptation. In response, each friar vies for the favour of the supposedly penitent Barabas by stressing the asceticism of the opposing order ('They wear no shirts, and they go barefoot too'). After stirring up the spirit of covetous competition, Barabas tops off the irony with a hypocritical injunction which he has learned from the Governor; he blandly beseeches the ravening friars to 'be content' (4.1.98).[21] Even more than the young suitors, the friars are blinded by their desire, and Barabas destroys them with amusing ease.

In many ways the play comes full circle when, in a parodic version of Ferneze's original grab of Barabas' wealth, Bellamira and her pimp Pilia Borza employ Ithamore to blackmail Barabas and thereby relieve him of his second fortune. Though conceived in the 'back lanes' (3.1.17) rather than the council chambers and involving long hooks rather than legal instruments, this thievery is as opportunistic as Ferneze's. Like him, these low-lifes use religion to justify their theft, as in Ithamore's chilling exit line, 'To undo a Jew is charity, and not sin' (4.4.80). These thieves are also like Ferneze in the escalation of their demands; but where the self-assured Governor moves in the twinkling of an eye from claiming half of Barabas' wealth to seizing all of it, his underworld counterparts express their avarice in more modest increments: from a 'hundred crowns' to 'two hundred at least,' and then to 'three hundred' (4.2.78–80), from which they arrive at 'five hundred more' (4.3.22). When in a third grab they reach 'a thousand crowns' (4.4.75), Barabas finally brings the spiralling inflation to a halt by poisoning them with a bouquet of flowers.

Come Live with Me – Invitations and Betrayals

In its politics *The Jew of Malta* follows from Part Two of *Tamburlaine*, it being 'an easy transition for a playwright to pass from the feuds and treacheries of Scythians, Turks, and Christians in the Orient to those of Jews, Turks, and Christians in the Mediterranean.'[22] But *The Jew of Malta* extends and intensifies the presence of treachery and false professions. On Malta, the impulse to betray is absolutely pervasive, extending into every corner of life in this highly atomized and competitive island; virtually every conceivable relationship – political, social, familial – is fractured by lies and treachery, and at one time or another every character has reason to cry out with Barabas, 'I am betrayed' (4.3.40).

In its own way, the audience in Marlowe's theatre also suffers the experience of betrayal, for *The Jew of Malta* is full of false starts and illusory endings, of unforeseen and unforeseeable reversals, of generic paradigms invoked and exploded, of literary styles established and subverted.[23] Like the shifting winds which first place the Spanish ship at the mercy of the Turkish galleys and then suddenly reverse the relationship (2.2.10–14), the ways of the play are unpredictable and dangerous.[24] As the program note for the ground-breaking production at Reading University (1954) noted, a fundamental characteristic of the play is the 'trick played on the audience's expectations – the sudden, complete and violent reversal of a previously established mood.'[25] In *The Jew of Malta* Marlowe extends the technique he had developed in *Tamburlaine* Part Two of springing surprises on the audience, and almost half of his usages of 'sudden' and 'suddenly' occur in these two plays.[26] In spite of this common strategy, however, the two plays are strikingly different in tone and pacing. In Part Two of *Tamburlaine* the advent of the unexpected occurs infrequently and is usually an inflection of tragedy, a sudden eschatological convulsion like the mortal fits which strike down Zenocrate and Tamburlaine. But in *The Jew of Malta* the tempo of surprise is quicker and often evokes the release of sardonic laughter.

It is in variations on the invitation to 'Come live with me' that the play's political and aesthetic betrayals most clearly dovetail. A curiously persistent motif throughout Marlowe's work involves a seductive speaker's attempt to win over a listener by inviting him or her (the roles are not gender specific) to participate in a more expansive, sensuous life. In addition to providing the first line of his only lyric poem, 'The Passionate Shepherd to His Love,' the invitation to 'Come live with me and be my love' appears frequently throughout the plays, often in situations which are not explicitly amorous.[27] Indeed, Marlowe's plays can be seen as a series of extensions of this seminal lyric into dramatic form, as the poem's monological voice is translated into theatrical polyphony.[28] In none of Marlowe's plays is the transformation of the limpid pastoralism of 'The Passionate Shepherd to His Love' more striking and more ironic than in *The Jew of Malta*, where the pleasures of Cupid have been supplanted by those of cupidity. Thus, Harry Levin describes the friars' attempts to lure Barabas into their orders as a courtship which is 'the most grotesque of Marlowe's variations on the tune of "Come live with me and be my love."'[29] Indeed, the play ends with the consequences of invitations treacherously extended (Barabas' fatal banquet for the Turks) and received (Ferneze's betrayal of Bajazeth's invitation to 'live with me' [5.2.91]).

Marlowe's richest reformulation of 'come live with me' – and most blatant parody of 'The Passionate Shepherd to His Love' – is of course Ithamore's naïve attempt to seduce the predatory Bellamira:

> *Bellamira.* I have no husband, sweet, I'll marry thee.
> *Ithamore.* Content, but we will leave this paltry land,
>   And sail from hence to Greece, to lovely Greece:
>   I'll be thy Jason, thou my golden fleece;
>   Where painted carpets o'er the meads are hurled,
>   And Bacchus' vineyards overspread the world,
>   Where woods and forests go in goodly green,
>   I'll be Adonis, thou shalt be Love's Queen.
>   The meads, the orchards, and the primrose lanes,
>   Instead of sedge and reed, bear sugar-canes:
>   Thou in those groves, by Dis above,
>   Shalt live with me and be my love.   4.2.93–104

As usual in the play, the word 'Content' triggers yearning and discontent, inspiring Ithamore to disparage 'this paltry land' (cf. Barabas' 'paltry silverlings') and to invent a better one. Concurrently, his language slides into fantasy, as it begins with a single line of blank verse (earlier he had spoken homely prose) and then exfoliates into rhyming couplets which are ostentatiously poetic. His maladroit identification of himself and his beloved with figures from classical mythology points to Faustus' similarly deluded wooing of another maiden who is not what she seems, Helen of Troy. As his closing reference to 'Dis above' reveals, Ithamore ends in a state of terminal disorientation, and in this he anticipates the fate of his master.

In Ithamore's speech, as often in Marlowe, the invitation to 'come live with me' has a metadramatic dimension, as it suggests that sharing the speaker's experience involves participating willingly in a world (or work) of art. In 'The Passionate Shepherd to His Love,' for instance, the verses move from the catalogue of landscapes in stanza 1 ('valleys, groves, hills and fields, / Woods, or steepy mountain') to the longer series (stanzas 3 through 5) of gifts fashioned from natural, mainly organic materials, culminating in a 'belt of straw and ivy-buds, / With coral clasps and amber studs.' This translation of nature into artifice is apparent in the poem's two references to the shepherds, who in the second stanza 'feed their flocks' but in the sixth stanza have become performers who will 'dance and sing / For thy delight each May-morning.' Given this emphasis on art, it is no coincidence that the penultimate line of the poem contains two key terms of Renaissance literary theory. Borrowing categories from classical discussions of oratory, humanist commentators often argued that poetry has three functions: to teach (*docere*), to delight (*delictare*), and ultimately to move (*movere*).[30] Here, as throughout his writing, Marlowe shows little interest in the teaching function of literature, and so his line stresses the other two, less moral, functions: 'If these *delights* thy mind may *move* ...' By its close, the poem has become an invitation to enter a poem.

In Marlowe's plays, the invitation to 'come live with me' often occurs in an early scene or even the Prologue, thus obliquely inviting the audience to participate in the titillating world of the theatrical illusion. In the second scene of *Tamburlaine* Part One, for instance, Tamburlaine woos (in his first appearance on stage) the Arabian princess Zenocrate and then invites the Persian captain Theridamas to join up with him. In addition to convincing their on-stage hearers, these eloquent persuasions may also incline the audience to follow Tambur-laine's banner. The metadramatic function of the invitation to 'come live with me' is more obvious in the plays where it appears in the opening lines, whetting the appetites of playgoers with promises of the forbidden. In *Dido Queen of Carthage* the play's first line ('Come, gentle Ganymede, and play with me') serves as a coy invitation to both the wanton boy and the prurient audience. Similarly, in the opening lines of *Edward II*, Gaveston's prologue-like soliloquy recounts the king's graphic invitation to frolic with him, and at the same time it arouses the audience's expectation of an explicit staging of homoerotic love. In neither of these plays, however, is the invitation to the audience made good, and so the play which is promised to the spectators becomes a game played upon them.

Marlowe's most enticing and most treacherous variation on 'come live with me' is the Prologue inviting the audience into *The Jew of Malta*, and it is spoken, appropriately, by Machevil. In the late 1580s and early 1590s Elizabethans were fascinated by the insidious evil popularly associated with Machiavelli, whose writings 'often seem to have had for six-teenth-century readers the lure of a kind of forbidden knowledge, irresistible to the intellect but condemned by the moral sense.'[31] The attraction of Machiavelli must have been increased by the apparent refusal of English authorities to license the printing (in any language) of his most daring books, *The Prince* and *The Discourses*.[32] The dominant attitude was to depict Machiavellianism as a lethal Continental disease which must be kept out of the innocent, enclosed world of England at all costs. But Marlowe's Machevil disarms this view by declaring that he has been invited to 'view this land, and frolic with his friends' (4).[33] His innuendo is that Machiavelli is alive and well in England and that his true fellows are in fact present in the audience. When he declares that 'there is no sin but ignorance,' he invites the playgoers to participate with him in a worldly-wise demystification of reigning orthodoxies. *The Jew of Malta* can be seen as a kind of anti-morality play, as it gives its audience an education not in faith but in cynicism and betrayal.

The play which Machevil presents is contemptuous of gullibility and full of traps, for its audience as well as its characters. In the opening scenes this attitude is quickly conveyed by the scorn which Barabas feels (and invites the audience to share) for the credulousness of his fellow Jews. After they have expressed their fears about the arrival of the Turk-ish ships, Barabas dismisses them as merely 'silly men' who 'mistake the matter clean' (1.1.178). In the following scene, after Ferneze's extortion of Jewish wealth, Barabas has a scornful comment on his compliant co-religionists as soon as they leave stage: 'See the simplicity of these base slaves' (1.2.216). But we quickly discover that the naïve Jews are not the only people to have been taken in by Barabas, for he has deceived the audience as well. After his forceful and entirely convincing expression of outrage at having lost 'my wealth, / My ships, my store, and all that I enjoyed' (1.2.139–40), and after his fellow Jews depart, Barabas suddenly informs the playgoers that he has anticipated the seizure of his goods by hiding a massive fortune under his floor-boards. As an audience-centred interpretation of the play notes, Barabas' 'knavish confidentiality after the fact is ... a slap in the face that lumps us with the other simple "base slaves" who have underestimated him.'[34] After this initial deception, audiences will be wary of any credulous tendency to accept the events and emotions of the play at face value. In this play, to extend pity to apparent victims is to risk being made a laughing-stock. By the end of *The Jew of Malta*, the audience (like the play itself) may well have in it 'more of the serpent than the dove; that is more knave than fool' (2.3.36–7).

Even after this initial deception, an audience can scarcely avoid other traps which Marlowe sets to surprise and mock innocent moral assumptions. One of the most shocking of these moments occurs at the death of Abigail. Violating her guileless nature, Barabas deputizes her first to recover his gold by pretending to convert to Christianity and then to seduce Lodowick even though she loves his rival Mathias. She is a reluctant conspirator, and the impatient Barabas has to force this 'paltry silly girl' (2.3.286) to dissemble. Abigail is easily the kindest figure in the play and also the most sympathetic, especially after she learns (from the gleeful Ithamore) that her father has been responsible for the death of Mathias. After being poisoned by Barabas, she asks the attending friar to 'witness that I die a Christian' (3.6.41) and expires. Audiences are likely to be tricked into laughter by the very suddenness of Friar Bernardine's ruefully salacious response: 'Ay, and a virgin, too, that grieves me most.' In the 1964 Clifford Williams production, a reviewer noted that 'the audience is torn between its natural sympathy for the pathetic Abigail, and convulsions of laughter at the complete callousness of the farcical characters around her.'[35] An audience may also find itself laughing at the hapless Abigail's credulity, for only someone who is other-worldly to a fault could trust such a scurvy excuse for a friar.

Marlowe's most sustained and elaborate trick on the audience's naïveté begins with Machevil's misleading introduction of Barabas in the Prologue.[36] It would be difficult to imagine a bigger canard than Machevil's promise

> to present the tragedy of a Jew,
> Who smiles to see how full his bags are crammed,
> Which money was not got without my means.   30–2

Not only will the play prove to be a very funny 'tragedy of a Jew,' but Barabas will not turn out to be the usurer implied by the stuffed bags. Even more misleading is Machevil's request that Barabas 'not be entertained the worse / Because he favours me' (34–5). Whether one interprets 'favours' as 'resembles' or 'takes the side of,' the lines suggest a close similarity between Barabas and Machevil, and there is a good deal in the first four acts to support this connection. According to Gentillet's *Contre-Machiavel*, the true Machiavellian is avaricious, an enemy to religion and morality, concerned only with his own welfare, hypocritical in his pretence to decency, pitiless in treating his enemies, and an inveterate poisoner – all categories in which Barabas scores reasonably well. From early on, however, there are significant differences between the actions of Barabas and the conduct associated with Machiavelli. Despite Thomas Heywood's characterization of him in the play's Caroline revival as 'a sound Machevill,'[37] Barabas ultimately proves to be deeply unsound in his attempts at deviousness.

The full extent of Barabas' un-Machiavellian conduct is apparent only at the end of the play, when he naïvely trusts his life to his old enemy, the Governor Ferneze. This confidence proves to be an appalling misjudgment, especially for a person who prides himself on his politic cynicism. In addition to ignoring common sense, Barabas' faith in Ferneze violates a maxim of Machiavelli that was well known among Elizabethans: 'he is utterly undone which seeks by new good turns to root out old grudges.'[38] By the end of the play it is clear that the true Machiavel is not the flagrantly villainous Barabas but the outwardly pious Ferneze.[39] This unforeseen association of Machiavellism with Christian hypocrisy would be all the more surprising to the play's first audiences, for it appears to be unprecedented in Elizabethan literature. When Thomas Nashe in 1593 defines hypocrisy as including 'all Machiavellism, puritanism, and ... all under-hand cloaking of bad actions with commonwealth pretences,' he almost certainly has *The Jew of Malta* in mind.[40]

The Trickster Tricked

Barabas' disastrous decision to double-cross the Turks and trust Ferneze is the biggest crux in the play, and virtually every commentator has addressed it. What has not been adequately noted, however, is how much light the endings of Marlowe's other works cast on the fate of Barabas. Despite his obvious uniquenesses, Barabas is not *sui generis* among Marlovian protagonists. If we think of him in act 5 as a master game-player who is caught up in one of his own games, then his situation will be familiar. Indeed, Barabas has an interesting counterpart in what is apparently Marlowe's first protagonist, the poet-lover in *All Ovid's Elegies*. This Tantalus-like figure from Ovid, we recall, glories in his ability to play erotic games upon both his lovers and their keepers, but in the end he is betrayed and made impotent by a mistress to whom he has confided his amatory secrets. Like the poet-lover in *All Ovid's Elegies*, and all of Marlowe's dramatic protagonists who follow him, Barabas winds up internalizing his game-playing and thus playing mental tricks upon himself. As in the final scenes of his other works, in act 5 of *The Jew of Malta* Marlowe reveals a fascinated understanding of the psychology of self-delusion.

Perhaps the best way to understand Barabas' misjudgment is in terms of his fatally flawed conception of his identity. As if he has made the mistake of believing what the Prologue said about him, he comes to conceive of himself in act 5 as the essence of Machiavellism. Thus he congratulates himself on his treachery, egotism, and (a word he compulsively repeats in the final scenes) his 'policy.' But he is far from the totally disillusioned outsider whom he imagines and wishes himself to be. Despite his effusive cynicism about Malta and its professed values, Barabas is trapped inside traditional mental attitudes which he cannot alter, and indeed seems not even to be aware of. In increasingly ironic ways, the play reveals him to be truly the Jew *of* Malta. When his supposedly lifeless body is dumped outside the walls, he immediately burrows his way back into the city, which suggests that he cannot conceive of himself as the Jew *off* Malta. In this deluded belief that he is more opposed to his society than he really is, Barabas anticipates the inner contradictions of other Marlovian protagonists, especially Doctor Faustus.[41]

For the Machiavellian, the ultimate goal is to seize and maintain power, but it is precisely at the moment when he arrives at political rule that Barabas founders. He does so, quite curiously, by recurring to his earlier mind-set of being a Jewish merchant. Offering to the captured Ferneze his freedom and the destruction of the Turks, Barabas asks him three times, 'What wilt thou give me ... ?' (5.2.76,79,83). When, not surprisingly, Ferneze agrees with the very generous terms promised him, Barabas congratulates himself for having made a good deal ('And thus far roundly goes the business') and revealingly reassures himself that 'This is the life we Jews are used to lead' (5.2.115). Just before he is fatally double-crossed by Ferneze, Barabas characterizes his triumph in language which defines his new status of ruler in terms of his old profession of Jewish merchant: 'Why, is not this / A kingly kind of trade, to purchase towns / By treachery, and sell'em by deceit?' (5.5.46–8). Here Barabas comes full circle, recalling his defensive comment on his wealthy fellow Jews in the opening scene: 'I must confess we come not to be kings. / That's not our fault ... Give us a peaceful rule, make Christians kings, / That thirst so much for principality' (1.1.128,133–4). In the end, it would seem that it is Barabas' conception of his Jewishness, a conception quite different from the lurid stereotype of Jews he himself had exploited, which prevents him from becoming the Machiavel he wishes to become.[42] There is not a more subtle moment of characterization in Marlowe.

Barabas' misperception of himself and his world is manifested in his new, strangely naïve willingness to think in terms of moral emblems. Thus, exhorting himself to take advantage of his political authority, Barabas likens the ruler who does not enjoy his power to

> the ass that Aesop speaketh of,
> That labours with a load of bread and wine,
> And leaves it off to snap on thistle tops.   5.2.39–41

The picture which Barabas describes appears in emblem books (without reference to Aesop) as a symbol of the self-denying nature of covetousness. In some editions of Alciatus which Marlowe may have known, this emblem is paired with the picture of Tantalus in the underworld as another example of 'Avaritia.'[43] Like the miser and Tantalus, the ass that bears provisions but eats only thistles does not enjoy what he possesses. But Barabas' use of the emblem is richly ironic, for, while he thinks his citing of it demonstrates his shrewdness, he immediately proceeds to engage in the truly asinine act of trusting the Governor. After vowing to be 'more circumspect' than the ass, Barabas compounds his confusion by invoking another well-known image from the emblem books:

Begin betimes, Occasion's bald behind;
Slip not thine opportunity, for fear too late
Thou seek'st for much, but canst not compass it.   5.2.44–6

Once again, Barabas' counsel of prudence proves to be suicidal, as his worry about the Tantalian fate of not being able to compass his desire triggers his fall into a state of terminal frustration. For Barabas moral bromides prove to be disastrous.

It is only when, at the close of the final scene, the floor is cut away from beneath Barabas that his delusions become clear, both to him and to the audience. In this play of unexpected shifts in language, style, and genre, the audience has never enjoyed a secure and stable vantage-point from which to perceive large patterns of significance.[44] The final scene is the most sudden and violent of these disorientations. Throughout act 5 the word 'surprised' appears frequently, always carrying its military sense of 'overwhelmed by a sudden assault.' Thus Barabas informs Calymath that he knows 'a place / Where you may enter, and surprise the town' (5.1.70–1), and then he promises Ferneze to 'render you / The life of Calymath, surprise his men' (5.2.79–80). And when Ferneze proves to be the master of surprise by trapping Barabas, he does so with the connivance of the playwright, who mischievously keeps the theatre audience in the dark about the details of the counterplot against Barabas until it is sprung.[45]

The effect of this *coup de théâtre* is to suspend the audience between contrasting attitudes toward Barabas and indeed toward the entire play. From the perspective of moral literature, Barabas' sudden plunge into the cauldron which he had prepared for the Turks is fully transparent and satisfying. Even if Barabas had not earlier described it as a 'deep pit past recovery' (5.5.36), everyone in the audience would have known from woodcuts and devotional literature that the boiling cauldron was a representation of hell. Moreover, the cauldron has a particular appropriateness for Barabas, for one of Geffrey Whitney's emblems depicts a boiling, overflowing cauldron to show that 'reaching heads that think them never well / Do headlong fall,' and in many depictions of hell a boiling cauldron is identified as a punishment for avarice.[46] It is richly appropriate that Barabas be responsible for cooking his own goose, even without the biblical apophthegm 'He that diggeth a pit, shall fall

therein' (Proverbs 26:27; Psalms 7:15–16). Yet another strand of retribu-
tive logic is the resemblance of the cauldron to the pot containing the
porridge with which Barabas had poisoned the nunnery.[47] As well, the
cauldron pleasingly rounds off the play by recalling the Prologue's reference to the tyrant Phalaris, who 'bellowed in a brazen bull' (25)
because he was cooked in the roaster which, Barabas-like, he had
intended for his enemies. In this rather overdetermined image of the
cauldron, then, the play seems 'summed and satisfied': infinite justice in
a little pot.

But there is a distinct sense in which the bottom falls out of the Christian cauldron just as it does from beneath the floor, as all of this iconography is so insistent that the scene begins to look like a parody or
caricature of divine retribution.[48] Even though an audience's sudden
laughter may be primarily at the expense of Barabas, it may also stem
from the general ridiculousness of the entire scene. A woodcut of an
overflowing hell-cauldron is one thing, but Barabas splashing around in
a pot on stage is another. And certainly when the characters resume
speaking after his fall, the enclosure of Christian theology fails to contain the contents of the pot:

> *Calymath.* How now, what means this?
> *Barabas.* Help, help me, Christians, help!
> *Governor.* See, Calymath, this was devised for thee.
> *Calymath.* Treason, treason: bashaws, fly!
> *Governor.* No, Selim, do not fly;
>   See his end first, and fly then if thou canst.
> *Barabas.* O help me, Selim, help me, Christians!
>   Governor, why stand you all so pitiless?   5.5.63–70

The rapid alteration of speakers and of attitudes seems, like the changing winds in Barabas' counting-house, to fly in every direction at once.

Especially disconcerting are Barabas' urgent cries for 'Christians' to
help him, cries which address the spectators in the audience as well as
those on stage. Of course the audience has been deceived by Barabas
(and Marlowe) before, and this plea could well be another trick played
on naïve sensibilities. But if the Christian audience, like the Maltese
Christians on stage, refuses to extend pity, then complications ensue. To
see the Jew begging unyielding Christians for pity wreaks havoc with
the Elizabethan orthodoxy which says that it is precisely the ability to
feel mercy which distinguishes between Jew and Machiavel on the one

hand and true Christian on the other. Thus, in his villain's litany Barabas had urged Ithamore to 'Be moved at nothing, see thou pity none'
(2.3.173), and Gentillet's treatise charged that Machiavels watch the sufferings of their victims 'without having any commiseration or compassion upon them, no more than upon brute beasts.'[49] Suspended between
comedy and theology, between a villain pleading for mercy and a Christian denying it, an audience may not be sure how to react.

In his response to Barabas, Ferneze unintentionally undermines a conventional moral response:

> Should I in pity of thy plaints or thee,
> Accursed Barabas, base Jew, relent?
> No, thus I'll see thy treachery repaid,
> But wish thou hadst behaved thee otherwise.   5.5.71–4

This passage is particularly unpleasant in its collocation of hissing ferocity ('Accursed Barabas, base Jew') and unctuous hypocrisy ('[I] wish
thou hadst behaved thee otherwise'). In this play, and coming from this
mouth, the charge of 'treachery' can hardly fail to boomerang. Just as
earlier he had accused Barabas of covetousness while fleecing him of his
wealth, Ferneze now accuses him of treachery after having double-
crossed him. What we see simmering in the Maltese cauldron is scape-
goat.[50] If the pot stands as an image of hell, then the Governor and his
fellow Christians surrounding it are, after all, identical with the devils in
the woodcuts. And if this is justice, it is justice with a vengeance, recalling a chilling formulation at the close of Thomas Nashe's *The Unfortu-
nate Traveller*: 'The farther we wade in revenge, the nearer come we to
the throne of the almighty.'[51]

Behind the blatant Christian iconography of cauldron and hell-fire,
there is another infernal scene being shadowed, the scene of Tantalus'
punishment in the underworld. Without coming into sharp focus, a
number of Tantalian motifs are present, including a destructive banquet
(at which the Turks have been massacred). There are overtones of the
punishment of Tantalus in that of Barabas, as he too stands in water and
reaches up for relief which is not forthcoming. And when Barabas commands his tongue to 'curse thy fill, and die,' the imaging of hatred as an
insatiable appetite may be suggestive of what Sir Philip Sidney called
the 'self-devouring cruelty' of the Tantalids.[52] Most notably, the dark
humour of Barabas' being boiled in his pot catches the tone of Tantalus'
becoming the comic butt of his own game. But at the close of *The Jew of*

Malta these Tantalian motifs are finally more shadow than substance, as the contrast between this death scene and those in *Edward II* and *Doctor Faustus*, Marlowe's last two plays, reveals. In their final moments, Marlowe's English king and German necromancer will undergo torments which unmistakably call to mind the suffering of Tantalus. Not coincidentally, in these plays the audience will have a strong sense of arriving at a place where suffering continues to be ambiguous in its morality but becomes absolute in its intensity. Unlike Barabas' melodramatic and perhaps farcical last words – 'Die, life: fly, soul; tongue, curse thy fill and die!' (5.5.88) – the final utterance of both Edward and Faustus will be an unforgettable scream.

6

The Play of History and Desire: *Edward II*

In abstract, thematic terms, Marlowe's *Edward II* continues *The Jew of Malta*'s corrosive exploration of hypocrisy, as in both plays political self-interest dresses itself in the rhetoric of moral outrage. But the two plays' effects on a theatre audience prove to be as different as they can be. Through its exhilarating fantasies, caricatures of good and evil, and unforeseen plot twists, *The Jew of Malta* invites playful collusion and subversive laughter from its audience. In *Edward II*, however, the play does not entertain the audience, release its fantasy, or engage its humour. Though it begins with the promise of imaginative and sexual release, as Piers Gaveston fantasizes about the gratifications he will enjoy as the lover of the king, *Edward II* proceeds to depict a world of frustration and futility, a world in which desire is finally incarcerated. In *Edward II* this emphasis on futile hopes and unalterable constraints afflicts the playgoers as well as the dramatis personae. Especially for Elizabethans with fresh memories of *The Jew of Malta* (or, more distantly, the *Tamburlaine* plays), attending a production of *Edward II* must have felt like an unexpected and unpleasant confrontation with intransigent reality. Compared to even the least stagy moments in Marlowe's earlier plays, *Edward II* has the dry force of disenchanted documentary.[1]

The account of Edward's reign in Marlowe's principal source, Holinshed's *Chronicles of England, Scotland, and Ireland* (1587), reads like a dismal litany of judicial hangings, decapitations, and disembowellings, as by turns the king's men and the barons frustrate and execute each other. And, while Marlowe adroitly shapes and compresses Holinshed's account of episodes sprawling over Edward's twenty-year reign, he refuses to prettify the picture by discovering a high providential design in English history, as Shakespeare had recently done in *Richard III*. This is to say that Marlowe's play does not perform the idealizing and consolatory functions which for Sir Francis Bacon characterized the relationship of Poesy to History, in which 'Poesy seems to bestow upon human nature those things which history denies to it, and to satisfy the mind with the shadows of things when the substance cannot be obtained.'[2] Contrary to Bacon's formulation, Poesy in *Edward II* insists on History's denials and deprivations. The play's sombre reading of history receives visual definition through an ironic twist on the conventional triumphal procession. What we see repeatedly enacted on the stage is not the triumphal entrance of a victor but rather the humiliating exit of the subdued. On more than a dozen occasions, characters are forcibly removed from the stage and led to a destination which is either prison or, more frequently, the chopping block.[3] The element of humiliation and impotence in these scenes is increased by the fact that the people who drag the status-conscious victims from the scene are always of lower social degree, often nameless soldiers or attendants.[4] The removal to the chopping block is the march of history.

Edward II is a disconcerting work, as Clifford Leech pointed out in a landmark essay, because of the frequency with which violence is inflicted on characters who are powerless to escape or to protect themselves.[5] When the barons confront the king, one of the emblems which they display (2.2.22–8) shows a hapless flying fish pursued by predatory fish in the water and by ravenous birds in the air; in Whitney's emblem book this picture carries a painfully simple motto: 'Weakness is exposed to violence.'[6] In *Edward II* the assault on the helpless begins in the opening scene, when Gaveston and Edward lay 'violent hands' (1.1.188) on the Bishop of Coventry for having exiled Gaveston. If Edward's command is actually enacted, the king and his favourite 'Throw off his golden mitre, rend his stole / And in the channel christen him anew' (1.1.186–7). There is a chilling hint of worse to come (which Derek Jarman's film version strongly suggests is rape) when Edward awards the bishop to Gaveston as a plaything: 'I give him thee; here, use him as thou wilt' (1.1.195). As commentators have pointed out, this brief but disturbing episode has multiple correspondences with the climax of the play, the excruciatingly drawn out and unspeakably cruel murder of the king himself.[7] That which is hinted at in the humiliation of the Bishop of Coventry is fully elaborated at play's end. The feculent dungeon in which Edward is murdered, even more than the scenes of torture in Marlowe's other plays, is pervaded by images evoking the underworld.

In both his physical situation and his mental state Edward is punished in ways that call to mind the torment of Tantalus.

Marlowe's *Edward II* is remarkable not only for its violence against the vulnerable but also for the immediacy with which that violence is felt by the audience, which in its own way is equally helpless. Spectators watching *Edward II* may well sense that they have been manhandled no less than its characters. Marlowe's history play works on its audience as Bacon said that History works on the human understanding, not (like Poesy) 'accommodating the shows of things to the desires of the mind' but rather 'buckling and bowing down the mind to the nature of things.'[8] More than any of Marlowe's other works, its impact is stiflingly oppressive. Even a bowdlerized production of the play (Frank Benson's in 1905) was sufficiently disconcerting to provoke a reviewer to sniff that *Edward II* 'is not of a character calculated to raise the spirits of the playgoer.'[9] Indeed, some of the best criticism of the play has expressed a sense of personal affront. Wilbur Sanders reveals the play's power to disturb in a jeremiad branding it as an incoherent product of neurosis which expresses 'an ecstatic impulsion to "do dirt on humanity", to humiliate and grind into the dust, and then again to humiliate.'[10] Even the author of a measured defence of *Edward II* against Sanders' agitated charges of moral and artistic incoherence concedes that it is 'a grim, disquieting, even disagreeable work.'[11] One can see these outbursts of the critics, like those of Edward in prison, as frustrated responses to a world which denies hopes of meaning and fulfilment. To watch this play, or even to read it sensitively, is to be overwhelmed. Extending the game-playing techniques which he had developed in his earlier work, Marlowe repeatedly places his audience in situations which invite it to internalize the helplessness of the figures whom it sees on stage.

Helplessness and Desire

In the first scene of *Edward II*, Marlowe stages an emblematic vignette which foregrounds the motif of playing with the desires of powerless people and turning them into Tantali. After Gaveston's haughty soliloquy which opens the play, a group of 'Three Poor Men' approaches him with a plea for employment. In their desperate dependency, they reflect a contemporary Elizabethan concern with 'masterless men' (especially destitute soldiers) on the streets of London,[12] and they represent the state of abjection which awaits all the characters in the play. After first dismissing the men with contempt, Gaveston quickly changes his mind in an aside: 'But yet it is no pain to speak men fair. / I'll flatter these and make them live in hope' (1.1.41–2). And so in an act of gratuitous malice, he plays with their expectations, teasing them with the promise that 'If I speed well, I'll entertain you all' (1.1.45). As Tamburlaine and Barabas had done, Gaveston demonstrates his power to himself by tantalizing others. But, unlike these earlier figures, Gaveston has the taste of powerlessness in his mouth when the play begins. His exile from and return to England have depended on forces beyond his control, and now he places these supplicants in exactly the same position of dependence – on himself. Indeed, just before the Poor Men enter, Gaveston mocks 'the multitude' in terms that suggest how his own desires have been tantalized: '*Tanti*; I'll fawn first on the wind / That glanceth at my lips and flieth away' (1.1.22–3). In this play, fawning dependency and supercilious defiance are two sides of the same coin. (Marlowe's suggestion that the courtier is inevitably a Tantalus, always hoping and always being disappointed, is made explicit two decades later in the complaints of John Webster's melancholy Bosola.)[13] When the 'Three Poor Men' exit, they declare that 'We will wait here about the court' (1.1.48).

Gaveston's teasing of the Poor Men's hopes anticipates what is to come, for in this play history tantalizes through the ironic concatenation of events. As Eugene Waith noted, *Edward II* is a 'play of blocking – of characters crossing each other and reacting to the frustration of being crossed.'[14] Thus, to take an example from an incident already mentioned, the animus which Edward and Gaveston feel toward the Bishop of Coventry is intensified by the frustration stemming from their just-finished altercation with the nobles. The general situation is neatly summed up by one of the king's men, who coldly exults at a moment of advantage that 'These barons lay their heads on blocks together; / What they intend, the hangman frustrates clean' (3.2.90–1); 'they' refers to both the barons and their heads, which are full of intentions but severed 'clean' from the bodies necessary to realize them (Tudor hangmen performed beheadings). As is usually the case in the play, the speaker's expression of sardonic irony turns against himself, for he too will fall prey to the executioner, to be followed in due course by his master the king, by the king's assassin, and finally by Mortimer, the usurper who ordered the killing. In an icon of futility, the play closes with two theatrical props at the centre of the stage: the head of the usurper perched on the coffin which holds the corpse of the murdered king.)

In *Edward II*, characters repeatedly imagine themselves to be on the

verge of realizing their schemes and desires, only to be crushingly disappointed. This denial of self-aggrandizing expectation informs the parallel downfalls of its two most antagonistic characters, Piers Gaveston at
the middle of the play and the Mortimer Junior at its end. Both Gaveston and Mortimer exult in the unlimited power which (they think) they
have gained through their sexual alliance with the person on the throne,
Gaveston with the king and Mortimer with the queen.[15] But of course
both would-be overreachers are monstrously deluded and meet igno-
minious deaths. Gaveston's fantasies of control over the king and the
kingdom are terminated by the dry, documentary manner in which his
off-stage death is reported to the king (and to the audience):

> Warwick in ambush lay,
> And bare him to his death, and in a trench
> Strake off his head, and marched unto the camp.   3.1.118–20

The sudden violence of 'Strake off his head' (echoing how Pyrrhus
'struck off his [Priam's] hands' at Troy [*Dido* 2.1.242]) is balanced in the
second half of the line by the resumption of the world's banality: 'and
marched unto the camp.' Though Gaveston disappears, history and the
play go on.[16]
   The death of Mortimer is equally ironic. Shortly after Gaveston's murder, Mortimer proudly identifies himself as the possessor of 'virtue that
aspires to heaven' (3.2.73), but despite the Icarian pretensions he, too, is
trapped in the snare of quotidian events. In his final words, Mortimer
grandly characterizes himself as a man who has freed himself from
bondage to fortune's wheel so that he can undertake a heroic voyage
into the beyond:

> Farewell, fair queen; weep not for Mortimer,
> That scorns the world, and, as a traveller,
> Goes to discover countries yet unknown.   5.6.63–5

When it is read in context, however, this noble resolution is savagely
undercut by the command of the young King Edward, who has just
been mocked by Mortimer as a 'paltry boy': 'What! Suffer you the traitor
to delay?' (5.6.66). The effect is similar to the moment in *King Lear* when
Edmund punctures Lear's fantasy about a contemplative life in prison
with Cordelia, another futile attempt to escape from fortune, with the
blunt command 'Take them away' (5.3.19). Mortimer may *speak* as if he

is lifting sail on a voyage of discovery, but we *see* him, as we had seen Gaveston earlier, being taken on a trip to the chopping block. If Edward's earlier command to 'Bring him unto a hurdle, drag him forth' (5.6.51) is now implemented, Mortimer will be strapped flat on his back to a sled and hauled away to be hanged, drawn, and quartered.

The play's most complex web of frustration is the erotic and political entanglement of Edward, Gaveston, and Isabella. In a sombre transformation of the Ovidian pattern of flight and pursuit, the essential rhythm of frustrated desire in *Edward II* involves lovers who almost come together but are kept apart. At one time or another, each of these figures becomes a Tantalus who is momentarily ravished by the hope of possessing the loved one but is deprived of him (only men are desired in this play) by a rival's machinations. The effect of this teasing is to breed vindictiveness, as a baron implies when he says his wife will feel cheated if he does not visit her: 'We that have pretty wenches to our wives,/Sir, must not come so near and balk their lips' (2.5.100–1). Throughout the first half of the play, Isabella has the recurrent but fading hope that the husband with whom she has shared intimacies in the past will return to her. And her wishes seem to be realized when, in gratitude for her arranging Gaveston's restitution, Edward announces 'a second marriage 'twixt thyself and me' (1.4.334). But of course the return of Gaveston spells the end of her hopes. For Isabella the breaking point comes when Edward embraces Gaveston and even Gaveston's wife, but not her:

> From my embracements thus he breaks away;
> O that mine arms could close this isle about,
> That I might pull him to me where I would,
>
> ...
>
> That, when I had him, we might never part.   2.4.16–21

Frustrated by how Edward eludes her, Isabella fantasizes (Dido-like) about an embrace which will be inescapable and terminal. Like so much of the play's language, her image suggests a forceful manipulation of a subject's body (her phrase 'pull him to me' recalling Mortimer's threat against Gaveston to 'pull him from the strongest hold he hath' [1.4.289]). It is the frustration of this wilful desire which leads to Isabella's coldly calculated violence against Gaveston and then Edward himself.

Unlike Isabella's pursuit of Edward, the passion of Edward and Gaveston is largely mutual, but it too is repeatedly frustrated, as they seem to be always either greeting each other or bidding each other farewell.[17] In a pattern which foreshadows the identification of Edward with Tantalus in the final scenes, the king remains stationary while the object of his desire is constantly in motion; in a teasing oscillation, Gaveston repeatedly moves toward Edward but is withheld from him. Thus Gaveston is banished by the old king Edward before the action begins, recalled by the new king Edward in the opening scene, banished again through the coercion of the nobles (1.4), recalled through the crafty intervention of the queen, forced to flee after the king's defeat (2.4), and then pursued, captured (2.5), and killed by the barons. Like his life, Gaveston's death is characterized by expectations raised and dashed. No sooner has Gaveston been seized by the barons than hope arrives in the form of an emissary bearing the king's desire to 'see him / Before he dies' (2.5.36–7). At first Warwick refuses the king's request, thus eliciting Gaveston's sarcastic question 'Why, my lord of Warwick, / Will not these delays beget my hopes?' (2.5.44–5). But Pembroke presses the idea of taking Gaveston for a final visit to Edward, Warwick seems to relent, and Gaveston's hopes are again begotten: 'Sweet sovereign, yet I come / To see thee ere I die' (2.5.92–3). But Warwick's acquiescence proves to be a trick, and he proceeds to seize Gaveston on his way to Edward and brutally murder him.

It is fitting that, in a land where desire is so frequently teased and frustrated, the king increasingly takes on the lineaments of Tantalus. Following his permanent separation from Gaveston, Edward progressively descends into an infernal world of deprivation and degradation. Gaveston's first words to Edward declare that 'since I went from hence, no soul in hell / Hath felt more torment than poor Gaveston' (1.1.145–6), and several scenes later he responds to the news that he must be banished from Edward by wondering 'Is all my hope turned to this hell of grief?' (1.4.116). In a typical irony of the play, Gaveston's perhaps casually hyperbolic 'hell of grief' is fully and terribly realized at the end – but for Edward. In the progressive isolation which he undergoes, Edward's role and social identity are ruthlessly stripped away and, in the case of his beard, shaved away. Ironically, his unsuccessful attempt to retain his crown, which he had never taken as a serious responsibility while on the throne, marks his last struggle to remain connected to the world of the living.

The most frequently quoted lines in the play articulate Edward's sense of deprivation: 'But what are kings when regiment is gone / But perfect shadows in a sunshine day?' (5.1.26–7). Since he had been associ-

ated with the sun earlier in the play, Edward's characterization of himself as a 'perfect shadow' marks his striking progress toward non-
being.[18] In addition to suggesting his loss of authority and subsequent
loss of his role as king, 'shadow' (like the double sense of the Latin
umbra) can mean both the shade cast by an object and the shade of a person, a ghost. The word is used in this latter sense when Warwick, about
to execute Gaveston, says to him, 'Come, let thy shadow parley with
King Edward' (2.6.14). In the dungeon scenes, the clear suggestion is
that Edward himself has become a ghostly shadow of himself, a shade
in the kingdom of shades. At one point he invokes the spirits of his dead
friends in a manner which suggests that he already shares their condition: 'The Spencers' ghosts, wherever they remain, / Wish well to mine'
(5.3.44–5).

As Edward is ever more acutely deprived of the essentials of his existence, he comes to resemble Tantalus in increasingly literal terms. Not
only is Edward imprisoned in a cistern-like dungeon which is a foul,
Tartarean underworld, but in that infernal setting he assumes the posture of Tantalus. Thus, from one of his jailers we learn that he stands 'in
a vault up to the knees in water' (5.5.2). He is also like Tantalus in being
starved. In matter-of-fact language which is curiously moving (the contrast with Bajazeth's rage at his imprisonment is instructive), Edward
complains that he suffers from lack of food and water:

> Within a dungeon England's king is kept,
> Where I am starved for want of sustenance,
> My daily diet is heart-breaking sobs ...   5.3.19–21

The sheer unendingness of Edward's torment is emphasized by his
muted repetitions two scenes later:

> They give me bread and water, being a king,
> So that for want of sleep and sustenance
> My mind's distempered, and my body's numbed,
> And whether I have limbs or no I know not.   5.5.61–4

In both scenes, Edward unknowingly complains to the keepers whose
charge it is to destroy him. As we shall see, there is a disturbing parallel
between his captors' playing with him and the dramatist's teasing of his
captive audience.

Teasing and Punishing Voyeurs

As criticism is beginning to realize, *Edward II* manifests a strong interest in how theatre works, and especially in how plays manipulate audiences.[19] This metadramatic concern is announced at the beginning of the play when Gaveston relishes his plan to use theatrical shows to 'draw the pliant king which way I please' (1.1.52). The pièce de résistance of his imagined spectacles is a provocative transformation of Ovid's myth of Diana and Actaeon (*Metamorphoses* 3:138–259):

> Sometime a lovely boy in Dian's shape,
> With hair that gilds the water as it glides,
> Crownets of pearl about his naked arms,
> And in his sportful hands an olive tree
> To hide those parts which men delight to see,
> Shall bathe him in a spring; and there, hard by,
> One like Actaeon, peeping through the grove,
> Shall by the angry goddess be transformed,
> And, running in the likeness of an hart,
> By yelping hounds pulled down, and seem to die.
> Such things as these best please his majesty ...   1.1.60–70

This scenario radically revises Ovid's story, in which the 'chaste Diana' is mortified to be seen naked by a man, and her attendant maidens do 'all they could to hide both her and eke themselves from shame.'[20] In Ovid these attempts to cover the too-tall goddess are in vain, and he stresses how Diana's acute embarrassment makes her even more beautiful, 'standing naked in his sight' and blushing like a lovely sunrise. In Gaveston's version, however, the motif of voyeurism is much more explicit and titillating. The desperate attempt of Ovid's Diana to cover herself now becomes a game, and she is transformed into a teasing exhibitionist in whose 'sportful hands' the olive branch is a prop to focus attention on what is barely hidden.[21] Gaveston's version is also more disconcerting than Ovid's, since, despite the virtual strip-tease with which she entertains Actaeon, his Diana nevertheless insists on the Ovidian punishment: that he be ripped apart by his dogs for spying on her. In a motif which will be re-enacted at the end of the play, erotic enticement gives way to brutal violence.

Gaveston hopes that his little playlet will arouse the gaze of the king, and it is likely to exert some of that titillating effect upon the audience in the theatre. (Even Gaveston's syntax teases, as four lines of sensuous description follow the subject and delay the revelation of the predicate, thus arousing curiosity about what the 'lovely boy in Dian's shape' is doing with himself. There is also a calculated coyness in Gaveston's reference to 'hid[ing] those parts which men delight to see,' since it is not clear whether he refers to the female parts of Diana or the male parts of the 'lovely boy' impersonating her. Though the playlet nominally represents the story of Actaeon spying on the goddess, Gaveston clearly assumes that Edward will derive much of *his* pleasure watching the 'lovely boy' (instead of the 'boy playing lovely Diana'). In addition to raising questions about Gaveston's motives and Edward's sexual preferences, the passage invites the audience to think about what kinds of shows, what kinds of theatrical and anatomical parts, it takes most pleasure in seeing.

Though commentators have usefully related Actaeon to the fates of Edward and Gaveston, who are pursued and destroyed by enemies imaged as hunters and hounds, the larger significance of the Actaeon myth may have gone unnoticed.[22] In addition to thinking of Actaeon as a lacerated victim, it is important to remember that he is also an onlooker or audience who is caught up in the action which he observes. In the opening scene, this fate befalls Gaveston, who first chooses to 'stand aside' (1.1.72) and make caustic asides when Edward and the nobles enter the stage and quarrel. But Gaveston forfeits the privileged pleasures of detached spectatorship when he announces his presence. After Edward embraces him, Gaveston is effectively trapped within the world of political strife and well on his way to meeting the end of Actaeon. Another, more suggestive, application of the Actaeon story to spectatorship is not to onlookers within the play but rather to the audience in the theatre. Like Diana suddenly turning on the voyeuristic Actaeon, the play inflicts injuries on the audience for whom it promised to provide pleasure. At the emotional climax of the play, the degradation and murder of Edward, the allusion is most relevant to the audience: Actaeon's aroused watching of the naked goddess bathing in a spring finds a grim counterpart in the audience's pained observation of the near-naked king standing in a cesspool. Simply to watch that compelling scene is a lacerating punishment for curiosity.

Like Marlowe's earlier work, *Edward II* creates and disappoints an audience's expectations, but it does so with a wounding violence which is largely new. This process begins with an invitation to enter the play through an antechamber calculated to raise false expectations about the structure lying behind it. In Gaveston's prologue-like opening speech, the 'amorous lines' of Edward's letter provoke him to imagine the satisfaction of desires which have been frustrated by Edward's father and the clergy:

> Sweet prince, I come. These, these thy amorous lines
> Might have enforced me to have swum from France,
> And, like Leander, gasped upon the sand,
> So thou wouldst smile and take me in thy arms.
> The sight of London to my exiled eyes
> Is as Elysium to a new-come soul;
> Not that I love the city or the men,
> But that it harbours him I hold so dear –
> The king, upon whose bosom let me die.   1.1.6–14

No other Elizabethan history play begins so provocatively – a pun on orgasm marks the climax of the speech. For a contemporary audience, these lines would be especially striking because of their remarkable and perhaps unprecedented violation of the taboo on explicitly expressing homoerotic desire, sodomy being in the jurist Edward Coke's words 'that detestable abominable sin, amongst Christians not to be named.'[23]

Marlowe's principal historical source, Holinshed's *Chronicles*, repeatedly hints at a sexual relationship between Edward and Gaveston but never spells it out (e.g., 'through his [Gaveston's] company and society he [Edward] was suddenly so corrupted, that he burst out into most heinous vices').[24] Unlike his circumspectly orthodox historical sources, Marlowe foregrounds the erotic nature of Edward and Gaveston's relationship, just as he foregrounds an erotic relationship in the opening lines of *Dido Queen of Carthage* when Jupiter dandles Ganymede on his knee. In both plays, however, the sensationalist introduction is misleading, for it promises a far more explicit and more sustained treatment of homoeroticism than the play actually delivers. At the outset of *Edward II* the audience is, like Gaveston, invited to imagine a world of sexual frolic, but what the play finally arrives at is the invisible and passionless political adultery of Isabella and Mortimer. In place of the 'lovely boy' playing the part of Diana, at the end of the play we see a boy king who has learned to decapitate his enemies.

The discomfort which the audience experiences in *Edward II* cuts deeper than mere disappointment, for the play actively works to subject its spectators to the conditions affecting its characters, and especially Edward himself. Mortimer's command to his henchman suggests the play's attitude to its spectator: 'Seek all the means thou canst to make him droop' (5.2.53). To droop is to feel futility and powerlessness, to despair of the possibility of taking action. In a verbal formula which pervades the play, and which will also appear prominently in *Doctor Faustus* and *Hero and Leander*, the adverbs 'in vain' and 'vainly' negate active verbs of striving and labouring. These terms toll in a litany of hopelessness when Edward is set upon by his prison-keepers, who '*wash him with puddle water and shave his beard away*':

> *Matrevis.* Why strive you thus? Your labour is in vain.
> *Edward.* The wren may strive against the lion's strength,
>   But all in vain; so vainly do I strive
>   To seek for mercy at a tyrant's hand.   5.3.33–6

After this brief and futile struggle – the shaving of his beard suggests his emasculation as ruler and man – Edward is so exhausted and shadow-like that he, unlike Shakespeare's Richard II, is no longer capable of assertion or even verbal defiance.

The effect of Marlowe's play in the theatre is to induce in its audience a kind of muted exhaustion similar to Edward's. His growing lack of control is a mirror in which the audience can see its ongoing experience of the play reflected. Following the deceptive lyricism of Gaveston's early speeches, the action hurries forward with a compelling force which hales the audience along on the tide of events. As Robert Fricker noted in a sensitive analysis of the play's dramatic construction, 'Marlowe's grip on the attention of his audience is ... tightened by a reduction to a minimum of the elements creating relief from the forward urge of the action.'[25] The play's events occur at breakneck speed, as actions are performed almost as quickly as they are planned, often before characters or the audience are ready for them. Repeatedly, the audience is thrown off balance, as it is forced to move faster than it wishes to, and taken to places where it may prefer not to venture.

In the circumstances surrounding the death of Gaveston, there is an anticipation of the audience's helpless watching of Edward. After Pembroke withdraws to visit his wife, the keeping of Gaveston is temporarily left to one James, who appears to be a young servant of Pembroke. When Warwick and his men work their double-cross and seize Gaveston, James and his fellows attempt for a moment to protect their prisoner but quickly surrender him. James apparently heeds Warwick's warning ('strive you no longer' [2.6.7]), for after Warwick's exit (with Gaveston in chains) he says rather feebly to his companions, 'Come, fellows, it booted not for us to strive' (2.6.18). In the Royal Shakespeare Company production of 1990, the intermission came after this line, and the effect was to make 'this statement into more of a question for the spectators. Would they have tried to protect Gaveston?'[26]

The discomfort which the audience may feel in this scene is amplified by its similar but much deeper engagement with the king's brother, Edmund Earl of Kent. As many people have testified, Kent is perhaps the least unattractive figure in the play. Unlike virtually all the other characters, he is sincere when he speaks of his 'love to this our native land' (2.3.1), and though his allegiances shift, his motives do not appear to be self-aggrandizing. Indeed, his reluctant transfer of allegiance from the king to the nobles and back to the king parallels (and helps to shape) a similar trajectory in the audience's sympathies. Thus, critics have attributed to Kent the reassuring function of 'a barometer of moral feeling,' or 'a sort of weathervane whose turnings veer with the rectitude of the situation,' or 'a kind of ethical norm,' or a man whose 'sincere concern for England makes him a kind of choric character.'[27] As a reviewer has noted, this sympathetic attitude to Kent is apt to be evoked even more strongly from audiences watching a production than from readers of the play.[28]

For an audience it is distressing that, since Kent is 'the one character in the play upon whom the affections can rest,' he is also a virtual personification of futility.[29] Beginning with his failure to prevent Edward and Gaveston from humiliating the Bishop of Coventry (1.1.188–9), every word of advice which Kent utters in the play falls on deaf ears, serving merely to offend the person he addresses. When Kent's interventions take the form of action, they continue to be futile. Ironically, his only successful action is to free Mortimer from the Tower (4.1), a deed which Mortimer will later reward by putting his benefactor to death. The audience's strongest identification with Kent comes after Edward has been usurped, imprisoned, and forsaken by everyone else. But, when the audience most desires Kent's successful intervention, his attempt is most pitifully ineffective. Immediately following his futile attempt to seize the protectorship of Prince Edward from Isabella, Kent articulates in an aside his decision to 'haste to Killingworth Castle / And rescue agèd Edward from his foes' (5.2.119–20). But Kent's plan to rescue his brother will surely strike an audience as hopeless, for earlier in the same scene Mortimer had been warned by a friendly bishop that 'Edmund laid a plot, / To set his brother free' (5.2.32–3). Immediately the prudent Mortimer warns his soldiers guarding the king to take precautions to 'dash the heavy-headed Edmund's drift' (5.2.39), and thus the audience sees him taking steps to frustrate the plot *before* Kent resolves to undertake it.[30]

To no one's surprise except his own, Kent's single-handed attempt to free Edward from a band of forewarned guards fails. Indeed, the failure is coeval with the attempt, for when Kent commands Mortimer's men to 'Lay down your weapons,' they respond by manhandling him (5.3.55–7). In the following scene, the soldiers deliver Kent to Mortimer, and the young king pleads for his uncle's release, but with as little success as Kent had met in his attempt to rescue Edward. As he is being dragged away, Kent asks 'whither will you hale me?' (5.4.105), and his question is answered not by anyone on stage but by a sardonic (and almost certainly authorial) stage direction: '*They hale Edmund away, and carry him to be beheaded.*'[31] Thus, the figure who is closest to being a projection of the audience's ethical sense is subdued and unceremoniously disposed of. Kent's unsettling futility is vividly apparent if we compare him to his namesake in *King Lear*, another loyal figure who functions as a surrogate for the audience.[32] Unlike Marlowe's, Shakespeare's Kent is vigorous; though he cannot prevent Lear's tragedy, he is at least able to express feelings of anger and bereavement through which the audience can find some satisfaction.

With the elimination of Kent, the last chance for the rescue of Edward is nullified. The effect is to place the audience in an extreme version of what Marjorie Garber has characterized as the 'dichotomous position' of the audience of a Shakespearean tragedy, which is 'at once active – in emotional response, in pity and terror, in sympathy or identification – and passive – in its entrapment in seats or boxes, and its inability to intervene.'[33] In the prison scenes the audience can neither withhold its sympathy from Edward's extreme suffering nor escape from the feeling of being subjected to an entrapment similar to his.[34]

The Play in Prison

Critics in search of points of contact between Marlowe and Shakespeare have often discussed the influence of *Edward II* on *Richard II*, another play depicting the deposition of a weak English king. But, despite its many similarities to *Edward II* in image and event, *Richard II* is far less disquieting in its dramaturgy, being leisurely and ritualized where Marlowe's play is pressing and immediate.[35] The Shakespearean play on which *Edward II* made the greatest impact is not *Richard II* but the later, more imposing, *King Lear*.[36] In Shakespeare's handling of the blinding of Gloucester and Marlowe's treatment of Edward's murder, these two plays stage acts of violence which are 'obscene' in the word's etymological sense: not fit to be presented on stage. Both are also plays in which the violence inflicted by characters on each other is shared to an uncommon degree by the audience. Like *King Lear*, *Edward II* is a play which cultivates the power to hurt its audience.[37]

The most obvious source of *Edward II*'s power to disturb is its climactic scene (5.5), which 'stages the extremest imaginable physical cruelty' as the helpless Edward is brutally murdered.[38] This scene has elicited much hyperbole from critics, beginning with Charles Lamb's famous remark that it 'moves pity and terror beyond any scene, ancient or modern with which I am acquainted.' F.P. Wilson added, after quoting Lamb's statement, 'But I wonder if there is not too much horror in the terror, if the scene is not so painful that it presses upon the nerves.'[39] Similarly, Clifford Leech characterized Edward's final scenes as 'painful to read or to see or to speak of ... The Jacobean playwrights could think of strange ways of torment and murder, but they never tear at our nerves as Marlowe does in this play.'[40] As the critics' somatic metaphors indicate, the violence is directed against and felt by the audience as well as the king. *Edward II* is a play in which both a king and an audience lose the privilege of detached spectatorship.

The almost unbearable oppressiveness of Edward's prison scenes stems in part from a change in tempo. Prior to Edward's death scene, the play is distinguished by what a director characterized as its 'extraordinary speed of events, the way the play leaps from event to event – it is like hurdle jumping.'[41] But in 5.3 and 5.5 the torment and murder of Edward take place in slow motion. Here Marlowe deviates from Holinshed's account, in which the murder of Edward occurs with merciful dispatch; attempts to poison him having failed, the murderers 'came suddenly one night into the chamber where he lay in bed fast asleep' and fatally assaulted him (2:587). In Marlowe's version, however, the murder is prefaced by a sinister kind of teasing foreplay, as both Edward and the theatre audience are reduced to powerless waiting, fearful of the impending doom but uncertain when and how it will fall. The element of teasing begins in earnest with the appearance of Lightborn, who is entirely Marlowe's creation (in Holinshed Matrevis and

Gurney commit the murder). Lightborn is the last of a series of increasingly pitiless keepers (Leicester, then Berkeley, then Matrevis and Gurney) to whom Mortimer assigns the care of Edward, and there are several suggestions that he is less than human. His name, as many commentators have noted, translates 'Lucifer' into English, and earlier it belonged to a devil in the Chester cycle of Corpus Christi plays.[42] As Mortimer's sudden conjuration of him ('Lightborn, come forth') suggests, he is a *diabolus ex machina*, a figure created for the express purpose of making the gratuitously horrific possible.

What makes Lightborn a distinctly Marlovian devil is the pleasure he takes in playing cat-and-mouse games with his victim. Lightborn's predilection for teasing is already apparent when Mortimer commissions him to perform the murder. After Mortimer asks him if he has decided 'how to accomplish it,' Lightborn evasively responds 'Ay, ay, and none shall know which way he died' (5.4.23–4). More is involved in this desire for secrecy than the professional killer's desire to cover his tracks. Indeed, Lightborn seems intent on whetting Mortimer's curiosity about his mode of killing. First he lists the forms of murder which he has mastered, several of which involve invading the orifices of passive victims:

Or whilst one is asleep, to take a quill
And blow a little powder in his ears.
Or open his mouth and pour quicksilver down.   5.4.33–5

When Lightborn chillingly concludes 'But yet I have a braver way than these,' Mortimer reaches for the bait: 'What's that?' But Lightborn withholds the information: 'Nay, you shall pardon me; none shall know my tricks' (5.4.36–7). And of course this teasing of Mortimer engages the morbid curiosity of the theatre audience.

In the following scene, Lightborn's instructions to his subordinates provide appalling hints as to what the 'braver way' may be:

I know what I must do. Get you away.
Yet be not far off; I shall need your help.
See that in the next room I have a fire,
And get me a spit, and let it be red hot.   5.5.27–30

When Lightborn requests 'a table and a featherbed,' some members of Elizabethan audiences would have recalled Holinshed's account of the murder:

and with heavy featherbeds or a table (as some write) being cast upon him, they kept him down and withal put into his fundament an horn, and through the same they thrust up into his body an hot spit, or (as other have) through the pipe of a trumpet a plumber's instrument of iron made very hot, the which passing up into his entrails, and being rolled to and fro, burnt the same, but so as no appearance of any wound or hurt outwardly might be once perceived.   2:587

Even an audience which does not know Holinshed can scarcely resist imagining the worst. In the mind's eye, the glowing spit is suspended over the ensuing dialogue between Edward and Lightborn.

When he enters the dungeon for the first (and last) time, Lightborn deepens our dread and our curiosity by promising himself that 'ne'er was there any/So finely handled as this king shall be' (5.5.38–9). 'So finely handled' is a terrible echo of Gaveston's intention to 'draw the pliant king which way I please,' and many modern productions emphasize the likeness of Lightborn and Gaveston by doubling the parts and employing similarly flamboyant costuming for both.[43] The most important parallel between the characters is that Gaveston's plan at the beginning to manipulate Edward by staging 'Sweet speeches, comedies, and pleasing shows' (1.1.55) is grotesquely realized by Lightborn at the end when he creates a playlet in which he acts the part of the bosom friend and lover whom Edward so desperately needs.[44] Gaveston's theatrical fantasy involved Edward as the spectator and ultimately the victim of a play about Actaeon's spying on an almost naked boy-Diana in a fountain. In Lightborn's little play, the places are changed: the audience gazes at the nearly naked Edward in a cesspool and is punished to the (considerable) degree that its curiosity has been aroused.[45] Regardless of how it is staged, the visual power of the scene will be intense because it is the first murder in this violent play which occurs in sight of the audience.

One cannot be certain about how the murder was staged in the earliest productions. The text is vague, as there are no stage directions, and the only references to the table, featherbed, and spit are Lightborn's commands to his helpers to 'Run for the table' (5.5.109) and then to 'lay the table down, and stamp on it,/But not too hard, least that you bruise his body' (5.5.111–12). The lack of reference to fetching the heated spit need not imply that it was not used, as it is possible that dialogue or stage directions were withheld from the printed text.[46] In any event, the recent stage history of *Edward II* shows a decisive shift away from the reticence of early twentieth-century productions, of which grateful reviewers commented that the death scene was 'rightly curtailed' and 'robbed of its horrors.'[47] Since Toby Robertson's Edinburgh Festival production in 1969, directors have presented audiences with fairly explicit versions of Holinshed's account. Regardless of the exact stage business which the audience sees, it is surely misleading to say with Harry Levin that 'The horrendous details are decently obscured.'[48] The truth is closer to the opposite: in so far as the audience must strain to see what exactly is being done to Edward (the 'pliant king' is presumably lying on his stomach and facing the audience), the effect of the partial obscuring will be quite indecent, a teasing of the audience's curious gaze. Even if the murder is totally hidden by a transverse curtain, as it was in William Poel's historic Elizabethan Stage Society revival, the effect will be obscenely tantalizing.[49]

Edward's death is so distressing that, like Cordelia's in *King Lear*, it has driven commentators to invoke ideological nostrums in order to explain it away.[50] In the past these palliations were often homophobic, as they maintained or, more frequently, implied that the manner of Edward's death was invented by Marlowe as a just punishment for the sin of sodomy.[51] While some of the visual imagery of the scene does have analogues in punitive Christian iconography (e.g., medieval representations of hell in which sodomites are impaled on spits),[52] the play as a whole does not present the relationship of Edward and Gaveston as intrinsically sinful, and the extreme pleasure which Lightborn takes in murdering Edward renders the victim pitiable and the justice dubious. In the parallel case of Barabas' fall into the cauldron, Marlowe undermines a familiar emblem of justice through caricature and comic exaggeration. In *Edward II* he takes the opposite tack, emphasizing what a critic has called the troubling 'collision between iconographic tradition and tormented individual.'[53] Edward's pain will not be moralized away.

In a tradition beginning with Bertolt Brecht's extensive rewriting of *Edward II*, many commentators have maintained that, far from being a sinner, Edward is presented as a secular saint.[54] In a direct reversal of the older view, Edward's sainthood has been linked with his homosexuality, his death being said to represent a process of 'spiritual elevation by debasement' in which 'the more he is abused the more he is resolved to a type of martyrdom.'[55] Similarly, in a new historicist inflection, Edward's death is significant because it subverts the rituals of state violence and thus transforms him from a mere sensualist 'into a martyr to the moralizing of history.'[56] Like its antithesis, however, this interpretation requires evidence which the text pointedly does not supply. As he does not exhibit much understanding of his fall and scarcely acknowledges any responsibility for it, Edward does not seem a likely candidate for sainthood of any sort.[57] But perhaps a more serious objection to this sanctification of Edward is that, like the claim for his damnation, it does what the play refuses to do – draw attention away from the terrible impact of his death.

In a particularly revealing attempt to find edification in Edward's death, several commentators have found solace in the belief that he 'is not merely a victim, for his agonizing cry raises the town and helps effect the restoration of order and distribution of justice on which the play ends.'[58] But the evidence for the argument that Edward's scream helps to restore order is explicit only in Holinshed:

> His cry did move many within the castle and town of Berkeley to compassion, plainly hearing him utter a wailful noise, as the tormentors were about to murther him, so that diverse being awakened therewith (as they themselves confessed) prayed heartily to God to receive his soul, when they understood by his cry what the matter meant. 2:587

In Marlowe the cry is reduced to a shadow of the efficacy (but not the agony) which it carries in the chronicle. The play's only reference to the scream comes from one of the murderers immediately after the king's death: 'I fear me that this cry will raise the town, / And therefore let us take horse and away' (5.5.113–14). Not only is there no reference to compassion in Marlowe, but the very power of the scream to escape the dungeon and enter the world has become problematic.

What is not at question is the force with which the scream pierces the audience in the theatre, the one group of people which is sure to have heard it. Indeed one continues to hear this cry long after the play is over – and after the young Edward III has avenged his father and restored some semblance of political order. A contemporary testimony to the scream's lacerating force appears in a most unlikely context, George Peele's poem celebrating the installation (26 June 1593) of the Earl of Northumberland as a Knight of the Garter. In the course of naming the original members of the Order of the Garter, Peele mentions Sir Roger Mortimer and then pauses to distinguish him from the earlier Mortimer who had usurped Edward's throne:

> And Mortimer a gentle trusty Lord,
> More loyal than that cruel Mortimer

That plotted Edward's death at Killingworth.
Edward the second, father to this King,
Whose tragic cry even now methinks I hear,
When graceless wretches murthered him by night.[59]

Peele's vivid recollection of the cry suggests that a performance of Marlowe's play rather than a reading of Holinshed's account lies behind his words, and the hypothesis is supported by the reference to 'night' (Holinshed does not specify the time) and the tell-tale presence of the word 'tragic.' Significantly, it is earlier in this same poem that Peele characterizes the recently deceased Marlowe as 'Fit to write passions for the souls below.' The association in Peele's mind is clear, for there is scarcely a setting in all of Marlowe more hellish than the dungeon at Killingworth with its 'graceless' killers, and Edward's scream must have reminded Peele of the cries of the damned. For a witness of such cruelty, even a witness in the theatre, there can be no catharsis, no forgetting.

7

Damnation as Tantalization: *Doctor Faustus*

Though opinion remains divided whether it is Marlowe's last play, in many ways *Doctor Faustus* has the force of a summary or conclusive vision.[1] In no other work by Marlowe are the farthest reaches of desire articulated so fully and then frustrated so conclusively as in this play about a magician with delusions of omnipotence. In *Doctor Faustus* images associated with Icarus and Tantalus, Marlowe's archetypes of aspiration and frustration, occur with uncommon force and frequency. Indeed, Marlowe conceives of Faustus' career in symbolic terms as the grim transformation of a would-be Icarus into a tormented Tantalus. The association of Faustus with Icarus is immediate and unmistakable. The opening Chorus, which functions as a prologue, clearly alludes to Icarus when it describes Faustus as a man whose 'waxen wings did mount above his reach' (AB:21).[2] But, as a comparison of this line with its source in Geffrey Whitney's *Choice of Emblemes* reveals, Marlowe's Icarus already has overtones of Tantalus.[3] By the end of the play, Faustus' associations with Icarus have been superseded by a powerful stage-image depicting him as Tantalus, as the spiritually parched protagonist reaches in vain for the blood of Christ which he sees, or thinks he sees, streaming in the firmament. Ultimately, it is not the heroic Icarus but the tormented Tantalus who comes to represent the essential relationship of human beings to what the Epilogue dryly refers to as 'heavenly power.'

In addition to evoking the connected figures of Icarus and Tantalus, *Doctor Faustus* is Marlowe's fullest, most explicit treatment of many motifs of the Tantalus myth. In no other play of Marlowe's, for instance, are food and drink so much in evidence and the subject of so many games of tempting and withholding. In the play's stage-imagery, the spectacle of nourishment being withheld is the core of several scenes. Also, for the first and indeed the only time, Marlowe associates the punishment of Tantalus in Hades with a protagonist who is damned. Unlike the metaphorical hells of Barabas and Edward, the hell of Faustus is as literal as can be. Not only do we see Faustus carried off to hell at the close, but the play explicitly articulates the idea of damnation as deprivation and teasing that was hinted at in earlier plays, and especially in *Edward II*. In the world of *Doctor Faustus* religion is inseparable from tantalization. While devils are plentiful in *Doctor Faustus* and hell is everywhere, heaven is characterized as an enticing absence. Repeatedly the face of God, the blood of Christ, and the oil of grace are evoked in the presence of Faustus, only to be denied him. To be in hell is not only to be deprived of the vision of God (a conventional idea) but also to be teased by that deprivation. These numerous Tantalian motifs appear in both authoritative versions of *Doctor Faustus*, the 1604 and the 1616 texts. It is, however, in act 5 of the longer version of 1616 that the Tantalian nature of Faustus' damnation is most fully elaborated in verbal and stage imagery.

Marlowe's intense thematic focus on tantalization in *Doctor Faustus* is accompanied by a transformation of the theatre into a hellish, Tantalian environment. In the works discussed in previous chapters, Marlowe's interest in tantalization had led him toward a dramaturgy of enticement and frustration, as the plays created expectations which they did not fulfil. In *Doctor Faustus* he takes the process of teasing a step farther. Instead of simply frustrating narrative expectation, Marlowe's toying with his audience takes the more fundamentally theatrical and more disconcerting expedient of undermining the audience's confidence in the substance of what it sees on stage. No other play of Marlowe's concentrates so heavily on the problematic reality of visual spectacle and on the epistemological difficulties facing the audience. In *Doctor Faustus*, the world inside the theatre becomes a phantasmagoria; what the audience thinks is substantial often proves to be illusory, and what was not visible sometimes proves to have been present. By the end of this troubling play, the audience is likely to have come to share the desire which Faustus had expressed – and which it had doubtless dismissed – in the opening scene, the desire for some higher power to 'Resolve me of all ambiguities' (AB:1.1.82). But finally the play refuses to resolve its teasing ambiguities, and this is reflected in the fact that no other work by Marlowe has provoked so much commentary and so little consensus.[4]

Food and Games

For many commentators *Doctor Faustus* is a troubling play because of its mixture of high tragedy and low comedy, its oscillation between game-playing and damnation. Like the Elizabethan printer's omission of 'some fond and frivolous jestures' from what he termed the 'tragical discourses' of *Tamburlaine*, numerous attempts have been made to excise the comic material from *Doctor Faustus*, often by attributing it to putative collaborators or revisers. These arguments have never been convincing, however, for broad humour so pervades the play that very little besides Faustus' opening and closing soliloquies would be left if all the comedy were eliminated. Instead of lamenting the fact that *Doctor Faustus* is not a Greek tragedy, we would do better to think about the ways in which its game-playing intersects with the idea of damnation. In an influential defence of comedy in the play, Robert Ornstein argued that *Doctor Faustus* 'is not the tragical history of a glorious rebellion' that many readers wish it to be, because it is informed by 'the disenchanted vision of the aspiring mind – the knowledge that the Comic Spirit hovers over the Icarian flight of the self-announced superman.'[5] While this view is on the right track, the phrase 'Comic Spirit' obscures the fact that the humour in the play grows increasingly dark and sadistic as the plot progresses. The game-playing and pranks have less to do with an orthodox demarcation of the human and the divine than with questions of power and control. After all, the closing words of the Epilogue do not warn the audience about the moral limits of human action, nor do they smile knowingly at the inevitable failure of an Icarian flight. Rather, their tight-lipped reference to what 'heavenly power permits' suggests that what really matters to the heavens is less morality than control. In *Doctor Faustus*, as in Marlowe's earlier work, tantalization is a game which creates power through the manipulation of desire. To think of Faustus' damnation in terms of tantalization is to highlight the sadistic nature of his punishment, for the damnation scene is the nastiest and most conclusive of the play's games.

As many commentators have noted, *Doctor Faustus* is extraordinarily rich in its reference to food and drink, and this motif has been interpreted variously: in theological terms as a manifestation of Faustus' gluttonous pride, in psychological terms as a sign of his inner emptiness, in psycho-theological terms as a compensation for the substance of the Communion denied by Protestant theology.[6] Though there is something to be said for each of these interpretations, they do not pay adequate attention to the specific *uses* of food and drink within the play. Virtually every appearance of food and drink is in the context of a game, often a game which involves tempting a person with nourishment and then withholding it. The pervasive hunger and thirst of the play are presented not as a given of the human condition so much as the effect of appetites being provoked and played with. In *Doctor Faustus* the relationship of the heavens to man unnervingly recalls Tamburlaine's treatment of Bajazeth in the banquet scene.

The manipulative power of enticement is apparent early in the play in an exchange (in 1616 only) between two clownish stable-boys called Robin and Dick.[7] Robin, who has pinched one of Faustus' conjuring books, begins by stating his willingness to perform whatever Dick wishes ('Do but speak what thou'lt have me to do, and I'll do't'). But without waiting for his response, Robin proceeds to entice Dick with a catalogue of wines: 'Or if thou'lt go but to the tavern with me, I'll give thee white wine, red wine, claret wine, sack, muscadine, malmsey, and whippincrust, hold belly hold' (B:2.2.29–32). Dick's response is most revealing; although to this point he has not shown any signs of being thirsty, he now declares 'O brave! Prithee, let's to it presently, for I am as dry as a dog.' The abundance of Robin's imagined wine-list induces in Dick (in an uncanny intimation of Pavlov) a dog's thirst. Like most of the comic subplot scenes, this one nicely mirrors Faustus' situation; Robin entices Dick much as the master magicians Valdes and Cornelius have enticed Faustus with their promise of spirits who 'can dry the sea / And fetch the treasure of all foreign wrecks' (AB:1.1.146–7).

This connection between withholding food and exercising power is most striking in a prank which occurs at the centre of the play, Faustus' disruption of the 'troublesome banquet' at the papal court (3.1 in 1604, 3.2 in 1616). The trick is anticipated in the play's first reference to Faustus' visit to the Pope; in a pun appearing twice in both the 1604 and 1616 texts, we learn that Faustus will 'take some part of holy Peter's feast.'[8] Marlowe is careful to show that the manner of Faustus' taking casts the Pope in the role of Tantalus:

Pope. My lord, here is a dainty dish was sent me from the Bishop of Milan. [*He presents a dish.*]
Faustus. I thank you, sir. *Snatch it.*
Pope. How now, who's that which snatched the meat from me? Will no man look? – My lord, this dish was sent me from the Cardinal of Florence.
Faustus. [*Snatching the dish.*] You say true. I'll ha't.

Pope. What again? – My lord, I'll drink to your Grace.
Faustus. [*Snatching the cup.*] I'll pledge your Grace.   A:3.1.64–72

The corresponding scene in the English Faust Book (chapter 22) emphasizes theft rather than teasing, specifying only that on separate occasions
Faustus steals food and Mephistopheles wine from the table in front of
the Pope.[9] Marlowe, however, creates the stage-image of the Pope as
Tantalus by showing that the food and drink are 'snatched' directly
from his hands, and the comment 'I'll drink to your Grace' suggests that
the cup should be snatched away just as it comes to his lips. By adding
to his source the stealing away of a second plate of meat, Marlowe intensifies the comic repetition of the game. Like Tantalus, the Pope does not
learn. Though Faustus proceeds to box the Pope on the ear, it is his
snatching away of the food and drink which makes the greatest impression on the gluttonous papal court. When the friars curse Faustus with
bell, book, and candle, their solemn malediction begins and ends with
curses aimed at persons not mentioned in the English Faust Book: 'he
that stole away his Holiness' meat from the table' (AB:3.1.90) and 'he
that took away his Holiness' wine' (AB:3.1.98).

Faustus' tantalization of the Pope is mirrored in the immediately following scene, in which Robin and a companion steal a drinking vessel
('silver goblet' in A; 'cup' in B) from another blustering authority figure,
the Vintner. Clearly the vessel is intended to recall the snatched chalice
holding the Pope's wine in the previous scene, and perhaps the point
was emphasized in performance by the use of the same prop. The motif
of tantalization is acted out in an equally obvious fashion, for Robin and
Dick ('Rafe' in A) withhold the goblet from the Vintner in a distinctly
teasing fashion. In the 1616 text, which is the fuller account, Dick hands
the cup to Robin before he is searched, and then Robin hands it back
before his turn to be frisked. When the frustrated Vintner declares that
'sure the cup is between you two,' Robin answers 'Nay, there you lie.
'Tis beyond us both' (B:3.3.25–6), which suggests that he has set it on the
ground. The recent discussion of this stage-business with the cup as an
example of 'formulaic dramaturgy' deriving from folkloric sources has
obscured its thematic relevance to the previous scene and to the pervasive concern with tantalization in the play.[10]

As the plot progresses, it becomes increasingly apparent that Faustus stands in the same relationship to the fulfilment of his desires as
the Pope stands to his supper, or the Vintner to his cup, or Dick to his
imagined wines. Though (because?) magic promises him everything,

he is never contented with anything. Unlike the pregnant Duchess of Vanholt, who is completely satisfied by the ripe, out-of-season grapes which Faustus procures, the magician himself is always empty, and there is poignancy in his response to her thanks: 'I am glad they do content you so, madam' (A:4.2.29–31). What Faustus needs cannot be supplied by the fetchings of Mephistopheles. In Faustus, as in Tamburlaine, there is a clear connection between the games of tantalization he plays upon the appetites of others and the teased state of his own. Indeed, Faustus' snatching of the Pope's food and drink is a slapstick re-enactment of Tamburlaine's feast in the presence of the starving Bajazeth. In both cases there is an implied mirror-relationship between tantalizer and tantalized, since Tamburlaine in Part Two becomes increasingly frustrated and since Faustus will soon find himself in the Tantalian situation of the Pope as he reaches for sustenance which is withheld.[11]

In so far as we conceive of Faustus as being teased by the very nature of his insatiable and multiplying desires, he can be adequately described in the moral terms with which Renaissance humanists characterized Tantalus: a figure of self-frustrating avarice. But, as we would expect of Marlowe, this traditional moral interpretation of Tantalus is not sufficient to account for the darker connections between desire and Christianity in the play. Perhaps the dominant feature of the play's religious vision is an emphasis on absence and deprivation. In physical terms, we can see this deprivation in the contrast between the devils, who are always at hand whether Faustus wants them or not, and the paucity of benign manifestations of God in the play. This absence of positive images of religion is stressed by the demonic Christianity represented by the Pope, who is himself a proud conjurer of hocus-pocus in Latin like Faustus. God is manifested only in the form of signs which seem calculated to tease and frustrate Faustus; ironically, heavenly intervention usually serves to torment Faustus through tantalization. The play never presents the traditional vision of God as the state of felicity in which human striving is fully satisfied. What we get, instead, are expressions of deprivation.

The tantalizing promise and denial of grace are strongly apparent in the presentation of the Old Man. On the one hand, he appears to represent perhaps the strongest evidence for the active intervention of divine grace in the world; like a Christian version of Daedalus, he warns his charge about the sin of overreaching.[12] On the other hand, the vision of grace with which the Old Man supposedly reassures Faustus has a distinctly teasing element. When he sees Faustus on the verge of killing himself with Mephistopheles' dagger, the Old Man exclaims:

Ah, stay, good Faustus, stay thy desperate steps!
I see an angel hovers o'er thy head,
And with a vial full of precious grace
Offers to pour the same into thy soul.
Then call for mercy and avoid despair.   AB:5.1.53–7

While it is appropriate for the Revels editors to note the many references to vials of mercy and damnation in Revelation, it is more important to notice the connection between this vial and the drinking-vessels which have been used in previous scenes to tease the Pope and the Vintner. Moreover, the fact that the angel 'hovers' makes the vial seem just barely out of reach, and the fact that he 'offers' to pour the vial suggests (whether or not the Old Man intends the effect) a teasing enticement, a miming of an intervention which is not actualized.[13] The liquid that can save will not be poured into empty Faustus.

It is in the context of this repeated snatching-away of sustenance that we can best understand what is in many productions the most intense moment in the play. During the climactic scene of his damnation, Faustus cries out more in panic than contrition:

O, I'll leap up to my God! Who pulls me down?
See, see where Christ's blood streams in the firmament!
One drop would save my soul, half a drop. Ah, my Christ!   A:5.2.77–9

In the first line, the desperate burst of Icarian aspiration is immediately inverted by a cry of Tantalian frustration. Faustus, like Tantalus, is in a crazed state of unbearable thirst, and the liquid which he sees but cannot reach represents the possibility of life. These lines invite the actor delivering them to assume the posture of Tantalus with outstretched hand and gaping mouth. Thus, in the 1966 Oxford University Dramatic Society production, Richard Burton as Faustus was 'electric in agony as he sees Christ's blood streaming in the firmament outside the reach of his imploring hand.'[14] The stage-tableau of Faustus as Tantalus in the underworld suggests that (in Mephistopheles' words) 'where we are is hell' and that Faustus himself is already suffering the torment of damnation. In the 1616 version, this vision of the streaming blood is the climax of a series of tantalizations which are not in the 1604 text. But, before we examine that sequence, we must first see how this moment also caps a series of scenes in which the audience is teased by the spectacle which it sees on stage.

Leading the Audience's Eye

In *Doctor Faustus*, as in Marlowe's other plays, tantalization is not restricted to being a theme depicted on stage through word and visual image. It is also realized in the action of the play upon its audience. Along with *Hero and Leander*, *Doctor Faustus* is the most daring of Marlowe's works in the misdirections and confusions into which it leads its audience. What Faustus thinks he knows at the beginning of the play will later prove to be illusory, and the same is true for the audience. For both the protagonist and the people watching him, complacent certitudes about reality give way to painful disorientation. When Faustus declares 'Come, I think hell's a fable,' Mephistopheles dryly responds, 'Ay, think so still, till experience change thy mind' (AB:2.1.130–1). For the audience, no less than for Faustus, experience will prove to be disconcerting and will change minds, as callow, theoretical knowledge is superseded by an engagement with pain. There is, however, a key difference in the certainties which Faustus and the audience lose. While Faustus is disabused of his facile belief in magic, the audience may well suffer at least the momentary loss of doctrinal certainty. Even more than in the death scenes of Barabas and Edward II, the violence at the close of *Doctor Faustus* swamps with suffering the formulas of justice.

The action of the play upon its audience can best be described as inducing an insidious progress from clarity to confusion.[15] In the closing lines of the Chorus to act 1 and in Faustus' long soliloquy which immediately follows, his intellectual pretensions and spiritual failings are transparent. This is one of very few scenes about which critics largely agree, and there are many discussions of Faustus' weak logic, his cavalier rejection of traditional learning, and especially his twisting of three biblical passages into a perverse syllogism justifying his despair. Because of their knowledge of scripture, Elizabethan audiences presumably would have felt quite certain in their grasp of Faustus' errors.[16] It is important that this scene occurs in Faustus' study and against a backdrop of authoritative books, both sacred and magical. (Anyone who has seen a production in which Faustus throws the Bible to the ground knows what a *frisson* that action still conveys.) Indeed, early in the play the conflict between Christianity and magic is represented as a battle of the books, the Good Angel's first words being a command to Faustus to 'lay that damned book aside' and to 'Read, read the Scriptures' (AB:1.1.72,75). But the scriptural authority which allows an audience a secure judgment of Faustus quickly disappears, to be replaced by such problematic manifestations of divine writ as the writing on Faustus' arm. Progressively, the play's theology can be understood only in terms of highly complex issues which were themselves controversial in Elizabethan England, such as the conflict between free will and predestination, hotly debated at Cambridge during Marlowe's years.[17]

An audience's innocent, theologically secure response to the opening scene (and to scripture) is most violently bedevilled by a passage which appears only in the 1616 text. When late in the play Faustus blames Mephistopheles for having led him astray, his companion responds with a staggering declaration:

> I do confess it, Faustus, and rejoice.
> 'Twas I that, when thou wert i'the way to heaven,
> Dammed up thy passage. When thou took'st the book
> To view the Scriptures, then I turned the leaves
> And led thine eye.   B:5.2.97–101

Faustus' immediate response is to weep (for the first time in the play), and the effect on the audience may be scarcely less convulsive. Even more shocking than Mephistopheles' dropping his amicable mask is his boast of having controlled Faustus. In the opening scene, the audience had seen Faustus alone on stage, or so it thought, as he tossed his books aside and wilfully decided to espouse black magic. Of course, Elizabethans knew that devils are liars, and Mephistopheles may well not be speaking the truth.[18] But Elizabethans also knew that their senses were vulnerable to infernal tampering and that, as Stephen Gosson noted in an anti-theatrical treatise, 'the Devil stands at our elbow when we see not, speaks, when we hear him not.'[19]

The spectators' sense of the ground shifting beneath their feet is exacerbated by the fact that these lines sharply contradict what Mephistopheles himself had said earlier in response to Faustus' charge of having led him astray: "Twas thine own seeking, Faustus. Thank thy self' (B:2.3.4). The pointedness of Mephistopheles' contradiction ("Twas thine own seeking' vs. "Twas I') suggests that his reversal is not, as some commentators have argued, merely an incoherent textual revision demonstrating the inferiority of the 1616 text.[20] It is, I think, a daring reversal calculated to disorient the audience. (This effect is of course neutered if the audience, unlike Faustus, actually sees Mephistopheles turning the pages, as in Adrian Noble's 1981 production.)[21] What in the opening scenes appeared to be a wilful transgression revealing Faustus' 'self-conceit' is now characterized as an invisible form of manipulation, perhaps part of the plot by which 'heavens conspired his overthrow' (AB:Prologue, 22). As a rather dismayed commentator remarks, 'The renowned scholar thus is transformed into a puppet whose very act of reading is determined by the devil.'[22] In addition to upsetting audience expectation, the sudden suggestion that Faustus may have been a puppet from the beginning plays havoc with any attempt to understand the action in moral or religious terms other than the harshest, most unpalatable form of Calvinist predestination.

This spectacular reversal raises troubling questions about the reliability of eyesight, for if Mephistopheles was present at the beginning of the play then he was invisible to both Faustus and the audience. Ironically, he was as invisible as Faustus himself was to the Pope and friars in their banquet scene. The suggestion is that reality is not necessarily apparent to the senses, and that what is visible is not necessarily real. On a mundane level, this state of ocular uncertainty is symbolized by the eyeglasses which Faustus wears (and which the horse-courser threatens to smash).[23] More pervasively, these visual ambiguities are sustained throughout the play in a number of 'shows' in which ravishing spectacles are conjured up for the hungry eyes of characters on stage (and of course for those of the theatre audience).[24] (There is a suggestive parallel between the 'pleasing shows' in *Edward II* which Gaveston plans to stage in order to 'draw the pliant king which way I please' [1.1.53] and the dumb shows which Mephistopheles stages in order to lead Faustus' eye.) Given the play's magical conjurations of hyper-real spectacles of ambiguous substance, most notably of Helen of Troy, it is revealing that several seventeenth-century theatrical anecdotes speak of the terrifying, unscripted appearance on stage of 'the visible apparition of the Devil' or of 'one devil too many' among the actors.[25]

The problematic relationship between seeing and knowing is made explicit in the second appearance to Faustus of the Good Angel and Bad ('Evil' in 1604) Angel:

Faustus. Contrition, prayer, repentance – what of them?
Good Angel. O, they are means to bring thee unto heaven.

Bad Angel. Rather illusions, fruits of lunacy,
That makes men foolish that do trust them most.   AB:2.1.16–19

In addition to their disagreement about what is illusion and what reality, the two Angels are themselves of problematic reality. As several commentators have pointed out, they are more elusive than their allegorical counterparts in morality plays – they may be objective figures sent on a ministry by God and Lucifer, and they may equally well be expressions of Faustus' inner self.[26] Like Faustus, the audience is confronted – or should be confronted – with the problem of distinguishing between the subjective and the objective. Orson Welles' production of *Doctor Faustus* for the Federal Theatre Project exploited this problem by being 'designed and executed as a magic show' employing many *trompe l'œil* effects.[27] Some directors, however, have suffered from a misguided concern about confusing audiences and thus have been careful to resolve all of these ambiguities. Thus, in his Royal Shakespeare Company production of 1974, John Barton reduced the cast of characters to the status of mere figments of Faustus' imagination, with the two Angels becoming hand puppets manipulated by him.[28]

Even more teasing than such alluring spectacles of ambiguous substance are those which Faustus sees (or says he sees) and the audience does not. Marlowe's most sophisticated playing with illusion comes from his manipulation of Elizabethan theatrical conventions about the reality of the unseen. Of course, audiences of the time were accustomed to being asked to piece out the imperfections of the bare stage with their minds. There was also a convention of Elizabethan theatre which allowed characters to have a privileged vision enabling them to see spiritual entities not visible to other people on stage or even to the audience in the theatre.[29] Marlowe effectively plays with this convention in Faustus' conversation with the scholar in 5.2. Gesturing toward what is presumably an empty space on stage, Faustus suddenly exclaims: 'Look, comes he not? Comes he not?' (AB:5.2.4–5). A few lines later, he declares:

Ah, my God, I would weep, but the devil draws in my tears. Gush forth blood instead of tears, yea, life and soul. O, he stays my tongue! I would lift up my hands, but see, they hold them, they hold them.   AB:5.2.30–4

With their confusing shifts of pronoun, these intense lines may be as confusing for an audience as for Faustus' friends. Even in the 1616 version, in which Lucifer, Beelzebub, and Mephistopheles are on stage from the beginning of the scene, we may wonder whether Faustus' hands are being held down or not. These complications are compounded by the fact that in 1616 it is only thirty lines later that Mephistopheles speaks of having led Faustus' eye in the opening scene.

Surely the play's most unsettling treatment of an ambiguous vision occurs in Faustus' final soliloquy, when he cries out, 'See, see, where Christ's blood streams in the firmament!' (A:5.2.78). As we noted earlier, Marlowe is creating on the stage an image of Tantalus in the person of Faustus, and at the same time he is also playing a Tantalian game upon his audience, who cannot be sure whether the blood which Faustus sees (or thinks he sees) is illusion or vision, imagined or real. On the one hand, the blood could well be the divine revelation which Faustus thinks it is; the fact that the audience does not see it need not mean that it is unreal. On the other hand, the streaming blood could be illusory, since Faustus is desperate and his overwrought mind is ripe for hallucination. When Thomas Nashe discusses how melancholy 'engendreth many misshapen objects in our imaginations,' one of his examples of common delusions is seeing 'bloody streamers' in the sky.[30] Not surprisingly, given this radical ambiguity, modern commentators have reached diametrically opposed conclusions about the ontological status of the blood, some calling it 'hallucinatory'[31] and others an 'actual miracle.'[32]

This moment in Doctor Faustus echoes – with a key difference – lines in the final scene of Dido Queen of Carthage, in which the deserted and deluded queen insists that she sees Aeneas returning to her. Faustus' 'O I'll leap up to my God' is a more desperate form of Dido's resolution to 'soar unto the sun' (5.1.244). In both speeches, the failure to 'leap' or 'soar' upward is followed by a frenzied vision of what cannot be reached. Again there is a close verbal parallel, as Faustus' 'See, see where Christ's blood streams in the firmament' recalls Dido's 'See, see the billows heave him up to heaven' (5.1.252). Both Dido and Faustus visualize and reach for a fulfilment which they cannot touch. There is, however, a key difference in the scenes with regard to the audience's involvement in the protagonist's tantalization. In the lines from Dido Queen of Carthage, the audience can be sure that the speaker is deluded; not only does Aeneas fail to reappear, but also Dido's sister Anna immediately urges her to 'leave these idle fantasies' (5.1.262). In Faustus, however, there is no one but the crazed magician on stage, and thus no one either to dismiss his claim as idle fantasy or to corroborate its substance. If, as seems likely, Dido was one of Marlowe's first plays and Doctor

Faustus was one of his last, the latter play's deeper frustration of the audience is an index of Marlowe's development as playwright.

In *Doctor Faustus*, Marlowe's teasing ambiguity extends beyond the question of whether the blood is in the magician's mind or in the sky, for in neither case can we be sure of the significance of the vision/illusion. Is it a sign of Christ's love of man, emphasizing the suffering which Christ accepted in order to save mankind? If so, the implication may be that divine grace continues to be present and available, if only Faustus can open himself to it.[33] But the contrary interpretation is equally plausible: that the purpose of the blood is to tantalize Faustus with what he cannot have. Just as moments earlier the Good Angel had tortured Faustus by showing him the heavenly joys which he had lost, the streaming blood may be a calculated heavenly torment, an instance of what Melville termed 'the devilish tantalization of the gods' (*Moby Dick*, chapter 110). Marlowe has constructed the play in such a way that the interpretation of its theology rests on an image which flies beyond the audience's reach.

Terminal Tantalization: The 1616 Ending

Since material relevant to Tantalus appears in both of them, sometimes in different forms, I have been treating the 1604 version and the longer 1616 version of *Doctor Faustus* as essentially interchangeable. In so doing, I have avoided the complex, ongoing debate about which text more closely reflects Marlowe's intentions.[34] With regard to the final act of the play, however, the 1604 and 1616 versions are so different that conflating them is impossible. For the purposes of this study, which are critical rather than bibliographical, the 1616 text is greatly preferable, for its version of the second scene of act 5 is some sixty lines longer than that of 1604, and virtually all of these lines contribute to the sustained process of tantalization to which Faustus is subjected. It is the longer, 1616 text in which the connection between Tantalus and the damnation of Faustus becomes most explicit and most unsettling. The enactment of tantalization in the 1616 text is so similar to the sadistic sense of play in Marlowe's other works as to support his authorship of the scene. If these lines were not written by Marlowe, they are an inspired elaboration of a vision which is distinctly Marlovian.

Though several studies have commented on various ideas of hell in the play, the predominance of tantalization in the 1616 text's hell has not been noted.[35] This motif sets the hell of 1616 apart from that of the Eng-

lish Faust Book and indeed that of most sixteenth-century representations. Perhaps because Tantalus was so vividly associated with the
pagan underworld, Christian accounts of hell rarely included tantalization among the torments inflicted upon the damned.[36] To be sure, hunger and thirst almost invariably appeared in catalogues of hell's
torments (as in chapter 61 of the English Faust Book), but they were not
represented as being provoked by teasing or enticement. Hunger and
thirst, like the burning and freezing with which they were often paired,
were significant merely as opposite (and thus inclusive) extremes of
physical pain. Teasing rarely occurs among the punishments of Christian hell, and when it does (as in the bizarre game of snakes and ladders
which the English translator adds to the hell of the Faust Book)[37] it is not
connected with food.

The only contemporary of Marlowe who repeatedly associated the
Christian hell with the punishment of Tantalus was Marlowe's friend
Thomas Nashe. In *Pierce Penniless* (1592), a work which has interesting
connections with *Doctor Faustus*,[38] Nashe clearly has Tantalus in mind
when Pierce asks the devil whether hell 'be a place of horror, stench,
and darkness, where men see meat but can get none, or are ever thirsty
and ready to swelt for drink, yet have not the power to taste the cool
streams that run hard at their feet.'[39] Notwithstanding the conventional
idea of hell as a place where people cannot see God, the devil's response
confirms that one may easily 'discern heaven from the farthest part of
hell, and behold the melody and motions of the angels.'[40] Nashe's most
explicit and most powerful association of hell with the punishment of
Tantalus appears in *Christ's Tears over Jerusalem*, which he dates just a
few months after Marlowe's death:

it were hell and the profundity of hell to any sharp transpiercing soul that had
never so little inkling of the joys of heaven, to be separate from them; to hear and
see triumphing and melody, and, Tantalus like, not be suffered to come near
them or partake them; to think when all else were entered, he should be
excluded.[41]

It is not fortuitous that two imaginative and frustrated University Wits
like Marlowe and Nashe should, 'Tantalus like,' understand the pains of
hell in terms of pleasures which can be seen but not possessed.[42]

In act 5 of the B-text, this unconventional idea of Christian hell as a
place of tantalization assimilates to itself the play's more traditional idea
of hell as a mental state characterized by *poena damni*, the pain stemming

from the sinner's sense of spiritual loss.[43] According to a tradition stretching back to the Church Fathers, to be damned is to fall away from participation in the godhead and thus to lose sight of the face of God. The Scholastic notion of hell as a loss of the sight of God remained an article of orthodoxy even in Protestant theology. Thus Richard Sibbes, a seventeenth-century Puritan divine, declares that 'when God the fountain of all good shall hide his face altogether from the creature, that is Hell.'[44] In *Doctor Faustus* we hear this conception when the Old Man warns Faustus of what happens if 'repentance come too late': 'Then thou art banished from the sight of heaven' (B:5.1.42–3). The most eloquent statement of this view occurs early in the play, but already it is coloured by suggestions of tantalization. In response to Faustus' callow query as to why his companion is not in hell, Mephistopheles responds:

> Why, this is hell, nor am I out of it.
> Think'st thou that I, who saw the face of God
> And tasted the eternal joys of heaven,
> Am not tormented with ten thousand hells
> In being deprived of everlasting bliss?   AB:1.3.75–9[45]

What is striking are the uncommonly strong sensory terms, especially '*tasted* the eternal joys of heaven'; a torment which consists of being 'deprived' of tasting sounds suspiciously like the punishment of Tantalus. Indeed, as Emily Bartels has argued recently, Mephistopheles appears to be creating in Faustus the very deprivation which he is talking about.[46] The idea of deprivation will continue to appear throughout the play, increasingly suggesting not merely the conventional ontological state of the *privatio boni* but also a teasing withdrawal of heaven.

In the 1616 but not the 1604 text, the great tantalization scene (5.2) begins with the ascent from hell of Lucifer, Beelzebub, and Mephistopheles, and this unholy trinity remains on stage for the duration of the scene, perhaps looking down upon Faustus from the balcony and certainly remaining invisible to him. These grim figures constitute an on-stage audience which, like that of Ferneze and his cronies at the end of *The Jew of Malta*, is pitiless in the extreme. When Beelzebub wonders how Faustus will 'demean himself,' Mephistopheles responds by characterizing Faustus as a futile Icarus:

> How should he, but in desperate lunacy?
> Fond worldling, now his heart-blood dries with grief;

His conscience kills it, and his labouring brain
Begets a world of idle fantasies
To overreach the devil. But all in vain.   B:5.2.11–15

As David Bevington noted in the Introduction to the Revels edition, 'The final act in the B-text places considerable stress on vertical movement and position.'[47] Taking the observation a step farther, we can say that these lines in 1616 are animated by the tension between the Icarus which Faustus aspires to be and the Tantalus which his objective situation reveals him to be.

Faustus' climactic torture by tantalization begins with the final appearance of the Good Angel and the Bad Angel. This appearance follows immediately after Mephistopheles' boast that when Faustus was reading the Bible he led the scholar's eye, and it similarly upsets the expectations of both Faustus and the audience. In their earlier manifestations, the Good and Bad Angels had set themselves in black and white opposition to one another, each flatly contradicting the other. In 5.2, the two Angels at first seem to retain their adversarial relationship, as they enter the stage '*at several doors*' (s.d.). But as soon as they speak they are suddenly revealed to be (in William Empson's phrasing) 'so frankly in cahoots that they finish one another's sentences:'[48]

> *Good Angel.* O Faustus, if thou hadst given ear to me,
>   Innumerable joys had followed thee.
>   But thou didst love the world.
> *Bad Angel.*   Gave ear to me,
>   And now must taste hell's pains perpetually.
> *Good Angel.* O, what will all thy riches, pleasures, pomps,
>   Avail thee now?
> *Bad Angel.*   Nothing but vex thee more,
>   To want in hell, that had on earth such store.   B:5.2.104–10

It would appear that the erstwhile opposing Angels have joined together to conspire the overthrow of Faustus' mind. Implying that damnation is a foregone conclusion, the Good Angel engages in the ultimate 'I-told-you-so,' while the Bad Angel moralizes on Faustus' doom with scarcely concealed pleasure. In a sadistic turn of wit, Faustus is told that the only thing he will have 'more' of is the sharp torment which stems from being deprived of 'store.' The lesson that starvation is an apt punishment for gluttony would have been familiar to Elizabethans, for it was periodically preached from pulpits as part of the government's attempt to prevent hoarding of grain.[49] But these lines stand out in their fierce irony, with the Bad Angel's curse that Faustus will 'taste' hell's pains echoing Mephistopheles' comment that 'his store of pleasures must be sauced with pain' (B:5.2.16).

This brutal teasing of Faustus is momentarily relieved but ultimately intensified by a fine stroke of stage spectacle involving a flying throne.[50] With the Good and Bad Angels joining against him and with the trinity of senior devils watching him from above, Faustus would seem inexorably trapped. But for Faustus, and perhaps for the audience as well, there is a sudden hope of escape in the spectacle announced by the stage direction: '*Music while the throne descends.*' This throne, which is lowered by winch from the canopy or 'heavens' above the stage, represents the celestial seat awaiting the saved. Since the play has been almost totally devoid of unproblematic signs of saving grace, the allurement of this glittering throne which descends to the harmonies of ravishing music would be difficult to exaggerate. But, when the throne touches down and the music ceases, the Good Angel quickly destroys all hope: 'O, thou hast lost celestial happiness, / Pleasures unspeakable, bliss without end' (B:5.2.111–12). Following the Good Angel's scornfully perfunctory farewell to Faustus ('poor soul'), the throne ascends, perhaps – to compound the insult – with the Good Angel sitting smugly in it.[51] The flying throne is calculated to demonstrate to Faustus, as tantalizingly and painfully as possible, that he is an Icarus without wings.

In an appalling symmetry, the ascent of the elusive throne is followed by the revelation of the descent which Faustus must take. First, a stage direction indicates that '*Hell is discovered.*' Exactly what this hell revealed on stage consists of is not clear, but it is probably the 'hell-mouth' inventoried by Philip Henslowe in 1598. The verbal picture supplied by the Bad Angel evokes a 'vast perpetual torture-house' and reaches its climax in a thematically rich evocation of food and deprivation:

> These that are fed with sops of flaming fire
> Were gluttons, and loved only delicates,
> And laughed to see the poor starve at their gates.   B:5.2.128–30

Editors have not noted that these lines allude to and transform the biblical parable of Dives and Lazarus (Luke 16:19–26). The phrase 'at their gates' calls to mind that the beggar Lazarus 'was laid at his [Dives']

gate,' and the reference to the starvation of the poor derives from Lazarus' desire 'to be refreshed with the crumbs that fell from the rich man's
table.' And Marlowe's gluttons ('fed with sops of flaming fire') reflect
the fate of Dives, who, because he 'fared sumptuously every day,' is sent
to hell to be tormented in flame. There is, however, a sadistic twist in the
Bad Angel's version, a twist that emphasizes the pleasures of tantalizing
people. Unlike the scriptural account, which according to the gloss in
the Geneva Bible concerns 'those who live deliciously and neglect the
poor,' in Marlowe the gluttons take delight in actually *watching* the poor
people starve at their gates. So Marlowe assimilates Lazarus to the figure of Tantalus, and Dives to the gods who sit as an audience. As the
crime is more cruel in Marlowe, so is the punishment; whereas Dives
begs for a drop of water to cool his tongue, Marlowe's gluttons are
force-fed 'sops of flaming fire.'

In recent years it has become a fixture of Marlowe criticism to depre-
cate the 1616 form of Faustus' damnation as full of 'pious moralising,'
and as 'a text which lends itself to interpretation as a more or less orthodox morality play.'[52] As we have seen, however, the emphasis on tantalization in the 1616 damnation is scarcely typical of Christian doctrine or
of English morality plays. Moreover, I believe that it is extremely misleading to characterize this repellent material as 'pious moralising,'
since the term implies the author's approval of the message. In fact the
1616 passages are so drastically unpleasant (Empson entitles his chapter
on them 'The Sadistic Additions') that they cast the justice of Faustus'
damnation in a very cold and dubious light, perhaps even implying a
radical questioning of that justice.[53] Far from being un-Marlovian, these
lines push punishment to an excess which resembles the hideous orthodoxy in the final scenes of *Edward II* and *The Jew of Malta*. In all three
cases, there is in abstract terms an eye-for-an-eye appropriateness in the
punishments meted out, but this appropriateness is so nasty and
inflicted by such dubious moral agents (the devils, Lightborn, Ferneze)
that it begins to look like a travesty of itself.

As I noted earlier, the emphasis on tantalization in the 1616 passages
colours the nature of Faustus' final soliloquy, which immediately follows. In particular, the line 'See, see, where Christ's blood streams in the
firmament' takes on even stronger overtones of tantalization in the context of these other teasing passages. (This crucial line appears only in
1604; presumably it was deleted from 1616 in response to a parliamen-
tary act of 1606 forbidding blasphemy in the theatre.)[54] With Faustus'
insistence that 'one drop' of this streaming blood would save him, there

is a further connection between the soliloquy and the 1616 passage alluding to Dives and Lazarus. Just as Dives, with the tables turned, cries out for Lazarus to 'dip the tip of his finger in water, and wet my tongue,' so Faustus in his agony calls out for 'one drop' of Christ's saving blood.[55] And perhaps the parallel can be extended, for the biblical 'great gulf [which is] fixed' (Luke 16:26) between Dives in hell and Lazarus in Abraham's bosom has its counterpart in the gap between Faustus' outstretched hand and the streaming blood in the firmament. In keeping with the spirit of the Chorus' statement in the Prologue that 'melting heavens conspired his overthrow' (AB:22), Christ's blood may be teasingly proffered to Faustus only to be withheld, like Tantalus' fruit and water. Such a torture turns the saving gift of grace into a mocking torment.

Throughout the body of this final soliloquy, we see Faustus in the extremities of terror and desire as he feverishly attempts to find the words which will save him. Some of the most celebrated words of the speech are the Latin words of Ovid which Faustus speaks as if they were a magical conjuration: 'O lente, lente currite noctis equi' (AB:5.2.74). But words of course fail, and the speech becomes a series of verbal notations of physical actions. As a theatre critic noted of Paul Daneman's effective delivery of the lines, Faustus is reduced to being 'convulsed and clawing at salvation.'[56] If this unedifying punishment of Faustus is indeed Christian, in contemporary terms it can only be likened to a perverse Christian snuff movie in which the infinitely vulnerable and terrified victim is ravaged by God's merciless instruments. Or, in slightly less contemporary terms, Faustus' death can be characterized as a scene in which 'Marlowe offers us the Theatre of the Absurd or the Theatre of Cruelty, as if to voyeurs under constraint.'[57] This deeply repellent ending turns the conclusion of *The Jew of Malta* inside out. Whereas the gloriously unrepentant Barabas resists Ferneze's triumphal gloating, the hapless Faustus attempts to repent but is subjected to remorseless punishment. In this scene, the psychology of the torturer is no different from that in Marlowe's earlier plays, and thus God as well as Lucifer must be placed in the sadistic company of Tamburlaine, Ferneze, and Lightborn.

In the strangely ambivalent homily of its Epilogue, *Doctor Faustus* refuses the final clarity that Elizabethans weaned on morality plays might have expected (and that the English Faust Book duly delivered).[58] After three lines of classicizing lament for Faustus, the tone abruptly shifts to ham-fisted alliteration and cautionary threat:

Faustus is gone. Regard his hellish fall,
Whose fiendful fortune may exhort the wise
Only to wonder at unlawful things,
Whose deepness doth entice such forward wits
To practise more than heavenly power permits.

These lines place the 'forward wits' of the audience in precisely the situation of Faustus, which is to say that of Tantalus. We are left with a vision of enticement and punishment, perhaps enticement as punishment. Since what is unlawful is compellingly attractive, one can only hope to wonder at it rather than reach for it. Having persistently played with the fascination of inderdicted issues ('unlawful things'), *Doctor Faustus* itself quite blatantly contradicts the advice that it now proffers.[59] Like much else in the play, the Epilogue suggests that tantalization is at the centre of Marlowe's bitter understanding of being a Christian and damned.

8

Frustrating the Story of Desire: *Hero and Leander*

Quite apart from the possibility that it may be Marlowe's last, *Hero and Leander* is the appropriate work with which to end this study, for it provides especially striking evidence of his proclivity to equate desire with tantalization. Unfortunately, *Hero and Leander* has rarely been read in the context of Marlowe's oeuvre, and thus its centrality has not been appreciated. Being Marlowe's only narrative poem, *Hero and Leander* has suffered from the simple fact that it is not a play, and a consequence of its generic uniqueness has been the common strategy of situating it in a non-Marlovian context: the group of Elizabethan verse narratives, most of them modelled on Marlowe's poem, which retell erotic mythological narratives in an Ovidian manner.[1] These studies often describe *Hero and Leander* as if Marlowe's imagination had gone on holiday, and thus in an influential book Douglas Bush declared that 'the poem in its total effect is an almost unclouded celebration of youthful passion and fullness of physical life.'[2] If, however, we see its relation to the tragedies, we will be alerted to the poem's deep disenchantment. By the time *Hero and Leander* reaches its problematic ending, it has transformed an archetypal story of youthful romantic love into a tale of teasing and frustration which ends in hell.

It seems likely that *Hero and Leander*, like Shakespeare's *Venus and Adonis*, was written during the period when the plague closed London's theatres (1592–3). In some obvious ways Marlowe's departure from the theatre in *Hero and Leander* involves a return to his largest body of non-dramatic writing, his translation of Ovid's *Amores* (*All Ovid's Elegies*). Like many of Ovid's lyrics, *Hero and Leander* tells a story of seduction and erotic sport, and indeed there are numerous verbal resemblances between Marlowe's translations and his narrative.[3] But *Hero and Leander* returns to

Ovid and erotic poetry with a difference. Though its subject matter and diction glance backwards to the early verse, its method derives from and extends the mode of teasing which Marlowe developed in the mature plays. Though the plague may have closed it to Marlowe, he carried with him what he had learned from the theatre, most notably an imperious facility for teasing and frustrating his audience's expectations.

Marlowe's most illuminating anticipation of *Hero and Leander* appears in a play which he had probably only recently written. In the opening scene of *Edward II*, Piers Gaveston ponders means of pleasuring, and thus maintaining his hold on, his lover the king; he plans to stage 'Italian masques by night, / Sweet speeches, comedies, and pleasing shows' in order to 'draw the pliant king which way I please' (1.1.52–5). *Hero and Leander* is the realization in narrative terms of one of Gaveston's glittering theatrical seductions. In this story of erotic discovery, as in Gaveston's voyeuristic enactment of the Diana and Actaeon story, classical myth is re-presented with a sexual interest calculated to engage and provoke its audience.[4] To enter this 'amorous poem' (as the entry in the Stationers' Register describes it) is to become a pliant reader, drawn any which way the narrator pleases. Given the narrator's pronounced homoerotic interest in Leander, whose body he describes with far more attention than Hero's, it should not be surprising that he (again like Gaveston) tells a story in which heterosexual love is by turns foolish and violent, but never mutual and never fulfilling.

Young Love and Artful Teasing

In one regard *Hero and Leander* casts more light on the working of Marlowe's imagination than do any of his other works, for it contains his most decisive and revealing transformation of his source material. It is not an exaggeration to say that he turns the traditional story of Hero and Leander inside out, as in his mischievous hands what had been a tale of heroic Icarian daring becomes one of ironic Tantalian frustration. In the best-known versions of the story available to Marlowe, the verse narrative by the Alexandrian poet Musaeus and Ovid's treatment in *Heroides* *18* and *19*, the late-classical myth of Hero and Leander stresses the overreaching desires and mortal limits of youthful love.[5] Separated from Hero by parental decree, Leander regularly swims to her across the Hellespont at night, guided through the waves by the blazing torch which she holds high in her tower. But Hero's torch finally burns out, and the disoriented Leander drowns in raging winter seas – not far from where Icarus had met the same fate.[6] Ovid's Leander makes the parallel between himself and Icarus explicit when he desperately yearns for wings:

Now would that Daedalus could give me his daring wings – though the Icarian strand is not far hence! Whatever might be I would endure, so I could only raise into air the body that oft has hung upon the dubious wave.   49–52[7]

As many commentators have observed, Marlowe echoes this passage when his Leander cries out, 'O that these tardy arms of mine were wings' (689).[8]

What commentators have not observed, however, is that Marlowe's handling of the story as a whole undercuts this Icarian association, for in every possible way he denies the heroism of Leander's undertaking. Though Leander does swim the Hellespont, it is by day rather than night, and thus Hero's torch, the symbol most frequently mentioned in allusions to the story, becomes superfluous and disappears. Moreover, Leander's swimming is impeded not by a winter storm but by the unwanted solicitude of Neptune, who is greatly attracted (only in Marlowe) to naked boys. Like Neptune, the narrator of Marlowe's poem reveals himself to be very aware of Leander's effeminate beauty, and, as we will see, his sexual preference for Leander complicates what was in Marlowe's sources a tale of (heterosexual) love in which gender divisions are as distinct and separate as Sestos and Abydos.

The obverse of Marlowe's undercutting of the story's traditional Icarian motifs is his unprecedented emphasis on sexual tantalization. To be sure, there is likely to be some form of teasing in any telling of the Hero and Leander story, given the geographical proximity-yet-separation of the lovers. Thus, before he takes his fatal plunge, Ovid's Leander likens himself to Tantalus: 'I can almost touch her with my hand, so near is she I love ... What else than this was the catching at elusive fruits, and pursuing with the lips the hope of a retreating stream?' (*Heroides* 18:179–82). In Marlowe's poem, however, Tantalian frustration is not merely a function of geography but part of the essential psychology of sexuality. When Marlowe's Leander is likened to Tantalus (559–60), he is standing not on the far shore of the Bosporus but rather in the bedchamber of the elusive Hero. By contrast, the Heroes of Ovid and Musaeus are anything but coy. The former begins her letter to Leander by declaring 'delay but a little longer, and I shall die!' (19:8), and the latter, upon Leander's arrival at her tower, invites him to 'Come, lay all thy labors / On my all-thankful bosom' (384–5).[9] In Musaeus Leander's response is equally unequivocal: 'He straight ungirdled her; and both parts paid / To Venus, what her gentle statute bound' (386–7). Marlowe's Hero, however, is deeply divided; as 'Venus' nun,' she attempts to devote her chastity to the goddess of love, and it is not until well into Leander's second visit to the tower and after much vacillation and teasing that their desires are – momentarily – consummated.

While this interest in tantalization is deeply rooted in Marlowe's previous work, it is relevant to point out that in the literature of the 1580s and 1590s the figure of Tantalus is associated by many writers with the frustrations of (male) desire. The word 'tantalize' first appears in English in an Elizabethan love sonnet published in 1597, and in his discussion of the Tantalus myth Sir Walter Raleigh's initial observation is that 'some poets have applied [it] to the passion of love.'[10] This is not to imply, of course, that erotic game-playing and sexual frustration were invented by late Elizabethan writers. After all, the denial of consummation had been the rule in Renaissance love poetry since Petrarch.[11] But usually this erotic frustration was treated with a degree of decorous abstraction which made references to Tantalus and his punishment inappropriate. With the shift toward deplatonizing love, however, the frustrated physical appetite of Tantalus begins to take on a new relevance to the poet/lover. An early indication of this change occurs in John Lyly's *Euphues and His England* (1580), in which Philautus mocks his friend Euphues' traditional praise of disembodied love and emphasizes the importance of physical satisfaction. To relate to women only through conversation, Philautus dryly complains, 'worketh as much delight in the mind of a lover as the apples that hang at Tantalus' nose or the river that runneth close by his chin.'[12] More sensuous is Michael Drayton's lyric 'To His Coy Love,' where the poet feasts his eyes on the 'snowy breasts' which he cannot touch and then declares 'O Tantalus, thy pains ne'r tell, / By me thou art prevented; / 'Tis nothing to be plagu'd in Hell, / But thus in Heaven tormented.'[13]

In the course of *Hero and Leander* the tenor of erotic tantalization grows steadily darker, just as it grows darker as it moves through Marlowe's oeuvre. At the outset of the poem, Marlowe depicts the lovers' game-playing in terms of a motif which he had found in Ovid's *Amores* and elaborated in *Dido Queen of Carthage*: the idea of a flight which entices pursuit, and a pursuit which stimulates flight.[14] This game of fleeing and following is broadly comic in tone, as is apparent in the passage following Hero's sudden faint and even more sudden recovery and escape. First, an amusingly compressed couplet gives us Hero's flight as a coy response to Leander's kiss: 'He kiss'd her, and breath'd life into her lips,/Wherewith, as one displeas'd, away she trips' (487–8). The phrase 'as one displeased' implies that Hero is playing a role, and the suggestion is confirmed by her attempt to entice Leander to follow her: 'Yet as she went full often look'd behind,/And many poor excuses did she find/To linger by the way' (489–91). To ensure that in her 'idle flight' from him she will be followed, Hero archly drops her fan. Unfortunately, he 'being a novice, knew not what she meant,/But stay'd, and after her a letter sent' (497–8). The comedy is reminiscent of some of the exchanges between Marlowe's Dido and Aeneas, where the African queen's quite blatant enticements are lost on the hopelessly naïve Trojan warrior. Like Aeneas, Leander does not know the name of the game which he is supposed to be playing.

As the poem unfolds, the roles of the lovers crisscross (as they do in *Dido*), with Hero lapsing into passivity and confusion, while Leander becomes more active and single-minded. Gone is the opening situation in which she controlled the erotic play: 'Thereat she smil'd, and did deny him so,/As put thereby, yet might he hope for mo' (311–12). Increasingly Hero loses her self-possession, and her language moves from artful denials to slips of the tongue. By the same token, Leander becomes less gullible and more frustrated, eager to impose himself on Hero. In the course of the narrative there is a growing emphasis on physical contact, as the amorous strife of tantalization is first played out through the lovers' words and later through their bodies.[15] This tendency reaches its troubling climax when Hero's movement in the act of love-making is likened to the frantic fluttering of a bird 'which in our hands we wring' (773). But there is a hint of these sadomasochistic elements as early in the poem as Leander's first sighting of Hero. When he sees her and falls to his knees in adoration, she 'blush'd as one asham'd/Wherewith Leander much more was inflam'd' (181–2). Here the rhyming of antithetical words nicely suggests how his desire is aroused by the spectacle of her discomposure. The ending of the poem, when Leander possessively leers at Hero's naked humiliation, is already in sight.

In the second half of the poem, the situation of Leander more and more resembles that of Tantalus, and his frustrated desire for Hero is increasingly associated with the sordid crime and punishment of Tantalus. At first this association is merely implied in Marlowe's descriptive terms, as in 'With that Leander stoop'd, to have embrac'd her,/But from his spreading arms away she cast her' (341–2). But the central allusion connecting Leander to Tantalus is explicit and unmistakable. Near the end of his first visit to Hero's tower, Leander begins to 'scorch and glow':

> She, with a kind of granting, put him by it,
> And ever as he thought himself most nigh it,
> Like to the tree of Tantalus she fled,
> And, seeming lavish, sav'd her maidenhead.   557–60

Since 'ever as' means 'as often as' (*OED* I.3.c), we are to imagine an intensifying of frustration, which is created (like that of Tantalus) through sheer frequency of repetition. Hero entices and escapes from Leander not just once but many times. The changing nature of their interaction is reflected in the fact that Hero's fleeing from Leander is less a premeditated ploy than an act of desperation, an attempt to keep her body intact. The fully explicit allusion to the punishment of Tantalus introduces a darker sense of deprivation and frustration than in the earlier, relatively innocent games of arousal by denial.

As its action unfolds, *Hero and Leander* increasingly stresses the violence which is born of frustration, much as *Edward II* and *Doctor Faustus* do. Given the logic of the poem, Leander's return home without having enjoyed Hero suggests that his fire will burn still more intensely. If the keynote of Leander's first visit to Hero was his willingness to be tantalized, that of his second is his aggressiveness, his willingness to be violent. This second visit plays variations on the maxim that 'love resisted once, grows passionate' (623). In its context, this line characterizes Leander's response to his father's chastisement, but it serves equally to foreshadow the tenor of Leander's ensuing lovemaking. Precisely because he has been repeatedly frustrated on his first visit, Leander now responds with force from the outset. This violence asserts itself with surprising quickness. Leander arrives at the tower in poor shape, suffering from 'numbing cold, all feeble, faint and wan' (730), but without warning he suddenly thaws: 'His hands he cast upon her like a snare' (743). This time, for Hero there will be no escaping.

The darkening tenor of tantalization during Leander's second visit is apparent in Marlowe's allusion to the Harpies, a myth (like that of Tantalus) involving a grotesque banquet in which food is snatched away from the hungry:

And now she lets him whisper in her ear,
Flatter, entreat, promise, protest and swear,
Yet ever as he greedily assay'd
To touch those dainties, she the Harpy play'd,
And every limb did as a soldier stout
Defend the fort, and keep the foeman out.   751–6

The lines 'ever as he greedily assay'd / To touch those dainties, she the Harpy play'd' clearly echo the phrasing of the earlier description of Leander as Tantalus ('And ever as he thought himself ...'). More is involved than mere repetition, however, for 'greedily assay'd' suggests greater exigency of desire, and the Harpy allusion indicates sharper conflict between the lovers. In the earlier Tantalus allusion, Hero was imaged as the disappearing food; now she is both the toothsome 'dainties' and the loathsome Harpies who snatch it away and befoul it.[16] Behind the military simile which Marlowe develops is the recollection that Aeneas and his men engaged in fierce combat with the Harpies before driving them off (*Aeneid* 3:210–43). This association of tantalization with violent physical action immediately continues in the lines (to be discussed in detail later) which link Leander with Sisyphus, who 'toil'd in vain' (761) by repeatedly shouldering a boulder up a hill.

The well-established rhythm in which frustration leads to violence is apparent at the sexual climax of the poem, which describes Leander's conquest of Hero in terms which recall and transform his association with Tantalus:

Leander now, like Theban Hercules
Enter'd the orchard of th'Hesperides,
Whose fruit none rightly can describe but he
That pulls or shakes it from the golden tree.   781–4

Earlier Hero was likened to the elusive fruit on the 'tree of Tantalus'; now the comparison is with the apples hanging from the 'golden tree' in the Garden of the Hesperides.[17] Like the apples which tease Tantalus in hell, the golden apples of the Hesperides were forbidden and unattainable, guarded by a dragon. In one of his final labours, however, Hercules slew the dragon and seized the forbidden fruit. Marlowe's phrase 'pulls or shakes it' graphically suggests the violence with which Leander handles his previously elusive love-object, as if her maidenhead is a fruit to be ripped off the bough. The impotent frustration of Tantalus has given way to the triumphant forcefulness of Hercules, a forcefulness which cannot be distinguished from rape.

It is these motifs of teasing, frustration, and violence that link the elaborately digressive tale about Mercury and the country maid (386–482) to the rest of the poem. The nominal function of this 'shaggy god story'[18] is etiological, an explanation of why the Destinies are unalterably opposed to Cupid and love. But the story about Mercury's wooing of the maid also mirrors and generalizes many of the impulses in the interplay between Hero and Leander. In the course of being wooed by the god, the innocent girl suddenly makes the same realization that Hero had earlier; she realizes that she has the power – in a key Marlovian phrase – to 'provoke his liking' (423). Hero-like, she adopts an ambivalent, evasive stance toward her wooer, as she 'yet was mute, / And neither would deny, nor grant his suit' (423–4). Her Tantalian strategy is to 'feed him with delays,' thereby exacerbating his hunger. Finally, conceiving an ambition consonant with her power over him, she

> Impos'd upon her lover such a task
> As he ought not perform, nor yet she ask.
> A draught of flowing nectar she requested,
> Wherewith the king of gods and men is feasted.   429–32

Suddenly this shy country lass has become a Tamburlaine or Faustus, hungering for what is most forbidden and indeed 'thirsting after immortality' (427). When Mercury complies with her wish, he re-enacts one of the crimes for which Tantalus suffered the punishment of tantalization: sharing the divine secrets of nectar and ambrosia with mortals.[19]

The punishment as well as the crime of Tantalus hangs over this story of Mercury and the maid, for virtually all of the figures remain frustrated at the end. As for the maid, there is no reference to her enjoying the immortality which she presumably received from the stolen nectar. Though Mercury does appear to have received the sexual reward which he pursued, his success is mentioned only obliquely in a dependent clause ('As soon as he his wishéd purpose got' [460]). The narrative's emphasis falls not on Mercury's success but rather on his jilting of the Destinies and its far-reaching consequences, including the release of Jove from Stygian captivity and the denial of fulfilment to all human love. The widening ring of frustration even extends to scholars and poets, the followers of Mercury. The revenge of the Destinies entails that 'fruitful wits that in aspiring[20] are / Shall discontent run into regions far'

(477–8), a fate that comments on the wayward digression in which it appears and on the manic energies and recurrent frustrations inform-ing/deforming the poem as a whole.)

Narration as Tantalization

Marlowe's strategy of creating and then disappointing expectation begins in the poem's opening lines, which clearly indicate, even adver-tise, their indebtedness to Musaeus:

> On Hellespont, guilty of true love's blood,
> In view and opposite two cities stood,
> Sea-borderers, disjoin'd by Neptune's might:
> The one Abydos, the other Sestos hight.   1–4

These lines are so closely modelled on a passage in 'divine Musaeus' (52) that a scholar has used them to draw inferences about which Latin translation of the Greek text Marlowe used.[21] Like the prologues to the plays, however, this opening allusion serves to misdirect the reader, for the poem moves steadily away from the ambit of Musaeus.[22] Indeed, these lines heavily foreshadow a tragic ending which never happens. Marlowe's *Hero and Leander* ends not with the death of the lovers but with the consummation of their drawn-out love-making.

One can argue, of course, that it is improper to speak of an *ending* to Marlowe's *Hero and Leander*. Until fairly recently, most commentators (including the Revels editor) have assumed that Marlowe left the poem unfinished, and in this they follow the lead of the poem's first publisher. In the earliest extant text of the poem, the (posthumous) printed version of 1598, Marlowe's last line is followed by the comment 'Desunt non-nulla' (meaning 'something is missing'). As Roma Gill noted in her recent edition, this statement 'is probably the conclusion of the pub-lisher, trying to explain the absence of the expected ending of the story.'[23] It would appear that the publisher Edward Blount thought that Marlowe intended to write the entire story of Hero and Leander. Hence Blount's dedicatory epistle describes the poem as 'this unfinished trag-edy' and refers to 'the effecting of his [Marlowe's] determinations pre-vented by the stroke of death.' The 'Desunt nonnulla' statement provided an invitation for the poetaster Henry Petowe, who wrote a sequel finishing the story and thus erasing the abrupt Marlovian end-ing, which he said was 'contrary to all men's expectations.'[24] In the same year a much more accomplished poet, George Chapman, divided Marlowe's lines into two 'Sestiads' and wrote four more of his own, thus creating a composite *Hero and Leander* which (as its title-page claimed) 'finished' what Marlowe had 'begun.' Whether or not Marlowe intended to tell all of the traditional story, there is abundant reason to detach his lines from Chapman's moralizing appropriation of them, to say nothing of Petowe's feeble continuation.[25]

Though one cannot be certain about Marlowe's intention, there is considerable internal evidence to suggest that, instead of being an unintended fragment, *Hero and Leander* may be complete as it stands. Many sensitive readers of the poem have been troubled by Blount's view of it as 'unfinished tragedy,' since (with the exception of the starched ominousness of its opening lines) Marlowe's touch is so light. Thus, Brian Morris observed that *Hero and Leander* is informed by a 'comic method' which works through 'the frustration of normal expectations' and that 'Marlowe's bias is increasingly towards the full burlesque, and away from the impending tragic end of the story.'[26] What expectation of the poem would be more predictable, especially given its Musaean opening lines, than that it would tell the whole sad story of the lovers? Just as he has omitted any reference to the most important symbol of the traditional story – the lantern in Hero's tower – so Marlowe perhaps deliberately withholds the deaths which elevate the story to the status of myth.

The absence of the traditional ending is only the most striking of the narrative's many strategic dislocations of form. Instead of attributing the poem's oddities of design to Marlowe's supposedly artless Elizabethan vigour and 'formless unrestraint,'[27] we need to think of their highly disingenuous, manipulative effects on the reader. While it may be true that the course of true love never did run smooth, Marlowe's story of Hero and Leander hardly runs at all. The narrative has so many retarding devices (set speeches, detailed descriptions, digressive episodes) that it often seems to be stalled, leading a commentator to declare that 'the mode of the poem is not narrative at all.'[28] It would be better, however, to describe the poem's mode as a kind of *narratus interruptus*, always promising but deferring the pleasure of fulfilment. As Gordon Braden noted, 'to Mousaios's story Marlowe adds three unconsummated sexual encounters – Mercury and the country maid, Neptune and Leander, and Hero and Leander in their first night at the tower.'[29] What he did not note, however, is the skill with which Marlowe provokes the reader's participation in these ultimately frustrating scenes.

Like the other Ovidian mythological poems of Elizabethan England,

Hero and Leander appears to have been written for an audience of male readers.[30] There is some biographical support for this inference, in that the posthumous first edition (1598) was dedicated by the publisher to Marlowe's patron, Thomas Walsingham, whom the poet may have intended as its recipient. But the most compelling evidence for an intended male readership is to be found within the poem, and especially in the way that the narrative looks at desire (Neptune's desire for Leander as well as that of males for females) from a distinctly masculine point of view. In a perceptive analysis of gender and desire in the poem, David Lee Miller has spoken of its 'circuit of masculine desire' in which various male figures 'assume the position of desiring subject' and into which the narrative invites the (presumably male) reader.[31] As we will see, the poem turns on repeated scenes in which a man casts a possessive gaze on a woman.

Early in the poem a slyly self-referential passage sets forth the power of art to attract and misdirect desire. The tantalizing effect on bees of Hero's flowery veil and honey-sweet breath serves as a model for the poem's manipulation of its readers:

> Her veil was artificial flowers and leaves,
> Whose workmanship both man and beast deceives.
> Many would praise the sweet smell as she pass'd,
> When 'twas the odour which her breath forth cast;
> And there for honey bees have sought in vain,
> And beat from thence, have lighted there again.   19–24

These lines play an erotic variation on Pliny's popular anecdote about Zeuxis' painting of grapes which is so compellingly illusory that birds peck at it.[32] (In Shakespeare's *Venus and Adonis*, which is virtually a companion poem to *Hero and Leander*, the Zeuxis anecdote is explicitly linked to Tantalus and erotic frustration.)[33] The pervasive dynamic of denial creating desire is present in the suggestion that it is the vigorous beating away of the bees which provokes them to land in the same place again. Also, the bees' futile attempts to extract honey from artificial flowers is clearly relevant to the reader's attempt to derive sexual pleasure from reading a cleverly manipulative poem. In this context, the repeated sounds ('beast,' 'bees,' 'beat') suggest the exigencies of compulsive, frustrated desire.

Again and again, Marlowe uses his provocative 'workmanship' to create in the reader a desire for forbidden honey which is never satisfied⸢Take, for instance, his handling of the love-making of Mercury and the maid. There is every reason to think that Mercury's seduction will be successful, as he begins with sweet music, then locks her in his arms, and finally

> As shepherds do, her on the ground he laid,
> And tumbling in the grass, he often stray'd
> Beyond the bounds of shame, in being bold
> To eye those parts which no eye should behold.   405–8

Here the narrator invites the reader to participate vicariously – and voyeuristically – in Mercury's transgression of 'the bounds of shame.' But, just as the god is ready to 'discover / The way to new Elysium,' the maid suddenly jumps up and runs away. Before she allows more eyeing of her secret parts, she will demand immortality for the privilege.⸥A similarly unconsummated sexual encounter between a god and a mortal occurs when Neptune attempts to waylay Leander on his swim to Hero. With coy evasiveness, the narrator describes how Neptune would 'dive into the water, and there pry / Upon his breast, his thighs, and every limb' (672–3). The progression from 'breast' to 'thighs' to '*every* limb' is suggestive. But, once again, nothing comes of it; like the country maid, Leander suddenly decamps, leaving Neptune and the reader in the lurch.

It is, however, during the protracted account of Hero and Leander's wooing that Marlowe's readers are apt to do their most frustrated buzzing. Initially, Marlowe seems to promise what Musaeus had delivered, a quick consummation upon Leander's first visit to the tower. Awaiting Leander's arrival with impatience, Hero has suggestively 'spread the board' (another connection of sex with food) and 'with roses strew'd the room' (505). The following lines seem to present the act of love which we, scarcely less than the lovers, have awaited:

> At last he came; O who can tell the greeting
> These greedy lovers had at their first meeting?
> He ask'd, she gave, and nothing was denied;
> Both to each other quickly were affied.   507–10

The exclamation 'O who can tell the greeting' invites the imaginative participation of the reader, and the progression from 'greedy lovers' to 'nothing was denied' and then to 'quickly were affied [affianced]' seems to constitute a euphemistic description of sexual congress. Indeed, when one of Marlowe's inattentive imitators wrote an erotic narrative based on the poem, he used the derivative line 'He gives, she takes, and nothing is denied' to indicate the actual moment of sexual consummation.[34] But in *Hero and Leander* something *is* denied, both to the novice lovers and to the reader. After six more lines which misleadingly stress the mutuality of their love, the narrator suddenly reveals that he has made the reader's 'anticipations rocket ahead of the innocent lovers' performance.'[35] What the reader cannot help but interpret as endgame proves to have been only foreplay.

Appropriately, the teasing of both Leander and the reader is most intense in the passage which names Tantalus. The striving of Hero, we hear, generates 'a gentle pleasing heat' in Leander,

> Which taught him all that elder lovers know.
> And now the same 'gan so to scorch and glow,
> As in plain terms (yet cunningly) he crav'd it;
> Love always makes those eloquent that have it.
> She, with a kind of granting, put him by it,
> And ever as he thought himself most nigh it,
> Like to the tree of Tantalus she fled,
> And, seeming lavish, sav'd her maidenhead.   553–60

Several details recall the passage late in the *Elegies* (3.6.46–52) in which the impotent lover likens himself to Tantalus, but here the rhetoric of teasing is far more clever. The reference to being 'taught all that elder lovers know' teasingly licenses the reader to conjure up images of sexual fulfilment – images which the remainder of the passage will finally deny. The phrase which the narrator applies to Leander's sophistry – 'in plain terms (yet cunningly)' – nicely characterizes his own teasing language, in which the terms are never as plain as they first appear. It is unclear, for instance, exactly what 'the same' is which begins to scorch and glow. All of Leander or a particular organ? Particularly brilliant is the extended play on the plain but cunning word with which four consecutive lines end: 'it.' As often happens in Marlowe, the most suggestive pronouns have the most unclear antecedents, and the anatomical possibilities of 'it' shift with every inflection. We would do well not to laugh at Leander because – *de te fabula* – the passage says as much about our reading of the elusive poem as it does about Leander's reading of the coy Hero.

In *Hero and Leander* Marlowe demonstrates to his reader, as he had to his spectator in *Edward II* and *Doctor Faustus*, that he or she is not in control of the process of interpretation, and is in fact dependent on the author's whim for crucial information which can easily be withheld. Consider the important question in *Hero and Leander* of how efficacious linguistic persuasion is for successful wooing. Early in the poem, Leander delivers to Hero what must be the longest, most bravura seduction speech in all of English literature (199–294, 315–28). But this elaborate argumentation is really beside the point, as the narrator indicates immediately after Leander's conclusion: 'These arguments he us'd, and many more, / Wherewith she yielded, that was won before' (329–30). After all this verbiage which accomplishes so little, the reader may be surprised later to learn that, at a crucial moment of intimacy during Leander's second visit, he wins over Hero by saying 'something' to her. But, after having recorded in great detail Leander's inefficacious arguments, Marlowe teases the reader by refusing to specify what the lover's winning words were: 'Wherein Leander on her quivering breast, / Breathless spoke something, and sigh'd out the rest; / Which so prevail'd ...' (763–5). In *Edward II* there is a close parallel to this teasing of the eavesdropping reader when Isabella draws Mortimer aside and whispers to him presumably seductive words which neither the characters on stage nor the audience in the theatre can hear (1.4.228–37).

As *Hero and Leander* moves toward its climax, Marlowe's teasing increasingly takes the form of the narrator's voice conspicuously interposing itself between the reader and the story. A passage which ends with Sisyphus, who like Tantalus is endlessly doomed to futile labour in hell, highlights the jarring presence of the narrator:

> For though the rising ivory mount he scal'd,
> Which is with azure circling lines empal'd,
> Much like a globe (a globe may I term this,
> By which love sails to regions full of bliss),
> Yet there with Sisyphus he toil'd in vain,
> Till gentle parley did the truce obtain.　　　　　757–62

In these lines the reader is distanced from the intimate sexual contact of the lovers by the narrator's cool detachment and obtrusive figurative language. Though commentators are divided about the precise anatomical reference of the line, the notion of *scaling* Hero's 'rising ivory mount' is comically incongruous, a misplaced Icarian ascent. In the following lines, the simile of the mapmaker's globe suggests that the mount being scaled is one of Hero's breasts, but the complication added by the narrator's intrusive parenthesis renders the globe idea silly. Then, in a transitionless colliding of opposed tones, the parenthetical reference to love's voyage 'to regions full of bliss' is immediately followed by the allusion to how Sisyphus 'toil'd in vain.' Moreover, the allusion to Sisyphus contains a final fillip of incongruity, since the image of the sweaty sinner rolling his boulder up the hill cannot help but recall both Leander's scaling of 'the rising ivory mount' and his vigorous handling of the 'globe' of Hero's breast. Thus, the narrator's direct address and recherché imagery have the effect of forestalling the reader's emotional participation and instead encouraging a number of comically un-erotic visualizations. Like Sisyphus, then, the reader finds himself labouring in vain.

Even after Hero's tantalization of Leander ceases, Marlowe's toying with the reader continues, extending into the lines which mark the belated sexual union of the lovers. Ironically, after so many teasingly presented false climaxes, the real climax of their love-making is presented so elliptically that first-time readers invariably pass over it without realizing its significance. Only after we have read on do we realize that the reference to fruit which 'none rightly can describe but he / That pulls or shakes it from the golden tree' was the narrator's elusive way of saying that Leander's pleasure in intercourse cannot be communicated. After so much teasing of the reader into imagining events which turn out not to be forthcoming, these lines pass over the central erotic moment before we know it is there. Perhaps like Leander himself, the reader is rushed past the climax, unable to savour its sweetness. What the closing lines rush into is not the satisfaction of either lover but the shame of Hero at her loss.

Lovers and Readers in Hell

It might seem plausible to think that, since the prolonged play of sexual frustration in the narrative finally does reach a climax, *Hero and Leander* can be said to transcend Tantalus. Indeed, several of the critics who have been alert to the theme of teasing in the poem have argued that at the close Marlowe takes his two lovers (and, by implication, his readers) from frustration to fulfilment. Thus, after noting that Marlowe's Hero is often coy and a tease, Roma Gill quickly declares that following her union with Leander 'The poem ends in glorious and harmonious fulfillment – the apotheosis of comedy.'[36] Similarly, Gordon Braden concludes his treatment of sexual frustration in the poem with the sanguine remark that 'the various hindrances to consummation are merely means to an end.'[37] By dint of carefully selective quotation, one can find some textual evidence for such sunny views. Thus, one can cite the striking lines in which we learn that while Hero

> trembling strove; this strife of hers (like that
> Which made the world) another world begat
> Of unknown joy.   775–7

What is not clear from the quotation, however, is that the sentence beginning mid-line after 'unknown joy' starts with the phrase 'Treason was in her thought' (777). Only a period and a small blank space separate 'joy' from the 'treason' which immediately ensues. Similarly, every potentially climactic moment is quickly undone.

On close inspection, the argument that *Hero and Leander* concludes on a note of fulfilment collapses. As we have seen, the very passage that marks the sexual union of the lovers is more an ellipsis than an apotheosis, and it is difficult to see how Marlowe's hurrying the reader past this climax is compatible with a celebration of fulfilment. More tellingly, the argument for consummation can be maintained only by the desperate expedient of ignoring the poem's last thirty lines, in which there is scarcely anything glorious or harmonious. Instead of resolving the tensions of the poem on the note of satisfaction that readers might well expect, the closing lines re-enact, for a final time, the Tantalian rhythm which previously has frustrated every promised fulfilment of sexual or interpretive desire. This is to say that the sexual climax is followed by a climactic frustration.

The most pointed of all the poem's ironic anticlimaxes occurs within a few lines of its close. In a sequence which re-enacts her earlier attempts to elude Leander and his response of violent seizure, Hero attempts to sneak from bed and hide 'in some corner,' but Leander suddenly grasps her and gazes at her nakedness:

> Thus near the bed she blushing stood upright,
> And from her countenance behold ye might
> A kind of twilight break, which through the hair,
> As from an orient cloud, glims here and there.
> And round about the chamber this false morn
> Brought forth the day before the day was born.

So Hero's ruddy cheek Hero betray'd,
And her all naked to his sight display'd.
Whence his admiring eyes more pleasure took
Than Dis, on heaps of gold fixing his look.   801–10

The image of Hero's blush becoming a 'kind of twilight' has a delicate beauty, especially in the detail that the cloud-like effect is created by the diffusion of light through her hair. But these lines have an ominous subtext, since they are closely based on Ovid's description (*Metamorphoses* 3:183–5) of the naked, humiliated Diana just before she destroys the voyeur Actaeon.[38] The passage appears to be on the verge of a climactic hyperbole with the phrase 'Whence his admiring eyes more pleasure took / Than ...' But the upward sweep suddenly collapses, and the ironic final line descends to Dis and his underworld kingdom. When Braden says of this passage that Hero 'draws herself up to the full dignity of her erotic presence' (150), he prudently refrains from quoting the lines likening her to 'heaps of gold.' Erich Segal's succinct formulation is preferable: 'At what should be a celestial moment, Marlowe makes a hell of heaven.'[39]

It would be hard to exaggerate the ironic, Marlovian ('My daughter! My ducats!') force of the simile likening Leander's gaze at Hero to Dis' looking on his money-bags. Even without the reference to Dis, there is a note of futile anticlimax in ending on a gaze, since the poem has begun with great emphasis on gazing and then moved toward progressively more intimate touching. Now the poem returns to its beginning, but with a crucial difference, for earlier Hero had gained amorous power through the gaze of men.[40] Now the gaze of Leander exacerbates the shame which Hero already feels, and it confirms her newly devalued status as an object possessed by him. The simile may also suggest that Hero is a captive of Leander, as the only woman with whom Dis is associated is Proserpina, whom he seized from the world of the living. And of course the likening of a woman's attractiveness to that of gold is calculated to make a reader think twice; in Renaissance treatises on love, a frequent topic of debate was 'Whether it is possible for a miser to love.'[41] The image of Leander's miser-like enjoyment of Hero becomes even more unpleasant when we recall his earlier attack on virginity as a kind of self-hoarding. After warning her that 'treasure is abus'd, / When misers keep it' (234–5), he applied to her the traditional image of the miser as a Tantalus who denies himself: 'Less sins the poor rich man that starves himself / In heaping up a mess of drossy pelf / Than such as you ...'

The entire passage is doubly disconcerting because, in addition to its ironic treatment of Leander's possessive gaze, it implicates the voyeuristic (male) reader in that gaze, presenting him with an unpleasant image of himself in the act of watching. The line 'her all naked to his sight display'd' – with its countermetrical emphasis on 'all' and the assonance of 'naked' and 'display'd' – promises a climactic revelation of a body which always has been at least partly veiled from the sight of Leander and the reader. Like Mercury in pursuit of the country maid (and Edward in Gaveston's playlet), the reader is enticed to become 'bold / To eye those parts which no eye should behold' (407–8). What follows, however, is not a picture of the beautiful Hero but instead a depiction of Leander gazing at her. The reader is invited to peep through the keyhole, but what he sees is a reflection of himself.

This scene reveals its full force only if it is read in the context of Marlowe's plays as well as that of his Ovidian poetry. Though commentators have noted resemblances to Marlowe's translation of the love-elegy in which Corinna visits Ovid's chamber in a thin gown (*Elegies* 1.5), this passage has a deeper similarity to a situation which recurs near the end of many of the plays: the theatre audience watching a scene in which a victorious character observes with pleasure the helpless suffering of his victim. More specifically, the scene may conjure up images of Tamburlaine watching Bajazeth in his cage, or Ferneze watching Barabas in his cauldron, or Lightborn eyeing Edward in the dungeon, or Mephistopheles enjoying Faustus' panic. In *Hero and Leander*, no less than in the plays, one effect of the final scene is to discomfit the audience, inducing self-consciousness about the gaze with which it watches, and perhaps enjoys, the abasement of the victim. In the plays, it is important to note, the primal scene of gazing at torture always contains imagery of hell (hell is where we watch criminals suffer), and in the poem this association with the underworld occurs quite unmistakably with the appearance of Dis.

If we look back over the poem, we can see that Dis does not exactly come from nowhere. In *Hero and Leander*, as in Marlowe's plays, attempts to separate the heaven of consummated desire from the hell of frustrated desire are futile. (In *The Jew of Malta* Ithamore speaks for all of Marlowe's lovers when he concludes his invitation to love by invoking 'Dis above' [4.2.103]). At the centre of the tale of Mercury and the country maid is a futile attempt to compartmentalize heaven and hell. Exulting in his (very temporary) power, Mercury decides that Jove should be 'banish'd into hell,' and accordingly for a while 'Murder, rape, war, lust and treachery / Were with Jove clos'd in Stygian empery' (453, 457–8). As Clifford Leech astutely noted, 'The implication is evident that with his [Jove's] restoration we are living once more in a Stygian darkness.'[42] And Mercury himself engages in amorous 'treachery' by being untrue to the Destinies, who in turn free Jove, and the brutalities associated with him, from the underworld. So, although lovers in the first rush of excitement may hope, like Mercury, to 'discover / The way to new Elysium' (410–11), eventually they find themselves in hell. Throughout *Hero and Leander* desire cannot be isolated from crime and punishment, and we recall that it was a stereotypically innocent country maid who commissioned Mercury to re-enact the crime of Tantalus.

The complex in which erotic desire is associated with crime and punishment, and in particular the crime and punishment of Tantalus, is presented richly in the initial description of Leander:

> His body was as straight as Circe's wand,
> Jove might have sipp'd out nectar from his hand.
> Even as delicious meat is to the taste,
> So was his neck in touching, and surpass'd
> The white of Pelops' shoulder ...   61–5

In a sly metamorphosis, the allusion to Ganymede, the boy who served nectar to the gods, quickly becomes an allusion to Pelops, the boy who was himself served to the gods. Pelops was the son of Tantalus, who cut him up and fed him to the gods, presumably in a blasphemously prideful test of their omniscience. His shoulder is white because it contains a prosthesis of ivory which was used to substitute for the one irreplaceable mouthful of his flesh eaten by Ceres (*Metamorphoses* 6:404–11). Read in the light of the Pelops/Tantalus story, the lovely synaesthesia of 'Even as delicious meat is to the taste, / So was his neck in touching' points directly to the crime of cannibalism and colours the poem's many subsequent associations of desirable bodies with food.[43] Moreover, the reference to the 'nectar' of Jove may call to mind the alternative food-crime of Tantalus, his violation of the taboo against sharing the gods' nectar and ambrosia with other mortals.

The appearance of Dis at the close of the poem strongly chimes with this pervasive association of erotic desire with crime and punishment. It is not fortuitous that *Hero and Leander* contains important allusions to three of the exemplary criminals who are punished in the realm of Dis: Tantalus, Sisyphus, and Ixion.[44] Just as it had alluded to Tantalus and

Sisyphus in passages which we have discussed, the poem refers to Ixion and his offspring the centaurs in the context of powerful but frustrated sexual desire: 'Wretched Ixion's shaggy-footed race, / Incens'd with savage heat' (114–15). Moreover, Marlowe mentions as a parallel to Mercury's theft of nectar (437–8) another notable punishment (sometimes located in hell by mythographers), the punishment of Prometheus for stealing fire from the gods.[45] This density of allusion to infernal punishment is increased by a reference to one of the punishing instruments; Renaissance mythography associated the Harpies with the Furies and described them as 'employed by the gods in punishing the sin of mortal men ... in the infernal kingdom.'[46]

The ending of *Hero and Leander* resonates with and gives new imaginative life to a commonplace of Elizabethan poetry in which 'The lover declareth his pains to exceed far the pains of hell.'[47] The usual strategy is for the poet to compare his frustration to the punishments of one, and sometimes all, of the famous sinners in the underworld. For instance, Marlowe's friend Thomas Watson begins a lyric by declaring, 'In that I thirst for such a Goddess' grace / As wants remorse, like Tantalus I die.'[48] Then, after likening himself to all the other exemplary sufferers (Ixion, Tityus, Sisyphus, and even the female Belides), Watson concludes with a summary statement: 'A wondrous thing, that Love should make the wound, / Wherein a second Hell may thus be found.' In Elizabethan lyrics, this notion of love as a 'second Hell' almost always carries a whiff of pedantic posturing, for a true kinship of suffering would disable the learned eloquence with which the poets make the claim. Marlowe's more sophisticated treatment makes the point without explicitly declaring that, as an imitator of *Hero and Leander* put it, 'who ever the like tried, / Knows 'tis a hell to love, and be denied.'[49] And Marlowe makes the point with a twist, for in his poem the hell of love persists beyond sexual denial and the woman suffers it as much as the man does.

The subdued but pervasive emphasis which *Hero and Leander* gives to punishment in hell provides a good reason for thinking that the poem's final lines are an appropriate ending rather than an arbitrary breaking-off point. The closing passage records a final descent to the underworld and a final reversal of image and expectation:

By this Apollo's golden harp began
To sound forth music to the Ocean,
Which watchful Hesperus no sooner heard,

But he the day's bright-bearing car prepar'd,
And ran before, as harbinger of light,
And with his flaring beams mock'd ugly Night,
Till she, o'ercome with anguish, shame, and rage,
Dang'd down to hell her loathsome carriage.   811–18

The first four lines presage the musical coming forth of dawn, an appropriate ending for the romantic story which has been repeatedly promised to the reader. The phrase 'harbinger of light,' however, leads to a
description not of the expected sunrise but of the conquest over Night
with which the poem ends.

The triad of 'anguish, shame, and rage' has a climactic force because it
emphasizes how *Hero and Leander* has depicted the frustration rather
than the fulfilment of love. 'Anguish, shame, and rage' have an obvious
relevance to the spurned and vengeful Destinies in the Mercury digression, and the emotions are equally applicable to Neptune's state of mind
after his failure to win Leander's love.[50] But the most powerful association is with Hero, who has just been humiliated by Leander, much as
(female) Night has been mocked by (male) Hesperus. In both cases, it is
the gaze (or 'beams') of masculine assessment which humiliates; though
Leander takes pleasure in Hero's beauty and Hesperus mocks Night's
ugliness, the effect on the objectified female is markedly similar.[51] The
correspondence between Hero and Night is so strong that on a first
reading of the poem students often assume that the final lines describe
the death of Hero (and indeed the passage may gesture toward the traditional ending of the story in which Hero throws herself from her
tower). It is appropriate that, in this poem where every outgoing
impulse is ultimately frustrated, the last lines suggest suicide. In the
context of the traditional Hero and Leander story, this image of a precip-
itous, self-destructive descent into hell could scarcely be more surprising or more inappropriate. In the context of Marlowe's whole corpus,
however, it feels eerily familiar.

Afterword

In one of his Oxford Lectures, Seamus Heaney praises Marlowe for 'extending the alphabet' of expression in English verse, and especially for being 'boldly liberating' in his treatment of language and desire.[1] The invigorations which Heaney finds in Marlowe are important and not to be dismissed, but they are also – as I hope to have shown – part of a larger, finally ironic rhythm. To illustrate Marlowe's work with passages of lyric brio, as Heaney does, is to create an attractive but misleading picture, for these local exhilarations inevitably terminate in frustrated desire. What seductive lyricism places on offer, reductive plot finally withholds. And when Marlowe's writing is viewed as a whole, this note of diminishment and repetition resonates with considerable power. Though his plays and poems are full of brilliant images, exotic settings, and colourfully varied protagonists, this rich inventiveness is always dogged by signs of obsessive recurrence. In each of his works, Marlowe creates a freshly imagined world, but invariably he proceeds to reduce this world to a stage on which to tell, yet again, his Tantalian tale.

In place of the customary and usually invidious (to Marlowe) comparison with Shakespeare, I want to end with a link to a writer far removed in place and time but, like Marlowe, deeply interested in the tantalizing nature of life: Ralph Waldo Emerson. In an eloquent essay titled 'Tantalus,' Emerson feelingly explores the intimation that both nature and culture promise mankind a fulfilment which cannot be grasped:

There is in woods and waters a certain enticement and flattery, together with a failure to yield a present satisfaction. This disappointment is felt in every landscape ... It is the same among the men and women, as among the silent trees; always a referred existence, an absence, never a presence and satisfaction.[2]

Though Tantalus is never mentioned in the body of the essay, his image hovers over Emerson's language and is evoked with increasing clarity as the essay unfolds. In his last paragraph, Emerson finally acknowledges the troubling thought that man may indeed be the plaything of a superior, teasing power:

What shall we say of ... this flattery and baulking of so many good well-meaning creatures? Must we not suppose somewhere in the universe a slight treachery, a slight derision? Are we not engaged to a serious resentment of this use that is made of us? Are we tickled trout, and fools of nature?   121–2

Emerson, however, raises this troubling spectre of Tantalian punishment only to exorcise it.[3] In language that protests too much, he immediately declares that 'there is not the smallest prospect of advantage from such considerations,' adding that 'One look at the face of heaven and earth puts all petulance at rest, and soothes us to wiser convictions.'

When Christopher Marlowe's protagonists look at the face of heaven, what they see is not consoling – they see images of punishment and deprivation. And the derisive cruelty of their common fate realizes Emerson's worst suspicions about humankind as a toy of higher powers. Splendidly and frighteningly free of the transcendentalist's 'wiser convictions,' Marlowe never acquiesces to the belief that a benign purpose lies behind the arousals and frustrations of human desire.

Notes

Introduction

1 Leech, *Christopher Marlowe*. While Leech does not discuss 'The Passionate Shepherd to His Love,' I do not discuss Marlowe's fine but Tantalus-free translation of book 1 of Lucan's *Pharsalia*. Cheney's comprehensive study of Marlowe's 'career idea' arrived too recently for me to assimilate its findings.

2 Though it was probably written before the *Tamburlaine* plays, 'The Passionate Shepherd to His Love' is discussed in the chapter on *The Jew of Malta*, which contains a parody of it. *The Massacre at Paris*, almost certainly one of the latest plays, is discussed in chapter 1.

3 See, for instance, Boas, and Ribner, in Marlowe, *The Complete Plays of Christopher Marlowe*, xx–xxiv. Ribner, however, does not mention *Hero and Leander*.

4 For 'the centrality of ambiguity in Marlowe's plays,' see Duane, 51–67.

5 For discussion of this general phenomenon, see Seán Burke.

6 Orgel, 'What Is a Text,' 86. Cf. the assertion in the editors' Introduction that 'In the English Renaissance theatre, the text is structured by the multiple and complex collaborations that the theatre demanded between patrons and players, playwrights and printers, playhouses and playgoers' (2).

7 For politics, see Shepherd; imperialism, Bartels; sodomy, Bredbeck; espionage, Sales; militarism, Shepard; treason, Karen Cunningham; heresy trials, Maus, 72–103; courtly surveillance, John Michael Allen, 67–94. Many of these topics are visited in *Christopher Marlowe and English Renaissance Culture*, ed. Grantley and Roberts, a collection which 'conveys the impression that Marlowe is little more than a convenient peg on which to hang details of Elizabethan England' (Bugliani-Knox).

8 For the crucial hermeneutical importance of authorial intention, see Harris, 90–106. Patterson concludes a searching discussion of 'Historical Criticism and the Claims of Humanism' by emphasizing intention as an interpretive

category (73–4). For a devastating demonstration of how the denial of authorial intention has licensed ideologically strait-jacketed interpretations of
Shakespeare, see Richard Levin, 'The Poetics and Politics of Bardicide.'

9 Skura, 175. In addition to Skura's article, Parker and Zitner's volume contains informative pieces by Richard Dutton, Barbara A. Mowat, and Alexander Leggatt on authorship and Elizabethan drama. For a variant more
friendly to Foucauldian theory, see Montrose's call for 'giving greater historical and cultural specificity and variability both to the notion of Author and
to the possible functions it may serve' (92).

10 See, for instance, Jonathan Goldberg's remark that 'The historicity of the text
means that there is no text itself; it means that a text cannot be fixed in terms
of original or final intentions' (214).

11 Foakes comments that 'for all the emphasis now on the plays as ephemeral
productions collaboratively staged, hardly any traces remain of performance
for most of the plays, except in occasional notation of actors' names, or in
some kinds of stage direction, or in small textual interventions ... that may
derive from the playhouse' (115).

12 The most elaborate attempt to remove Marlowe from both *Doctor Faustus*
texts is that of Marcus.

13 Marcus, 13. Marcus' coinage of the term 'Marlowe effect' (referring to putative
attempts of hypothetical revisers to make their work seem Marlovian and
therefore commercially successful) has recently been applied to all of Marlowe's writing by Healy, 21–30. Skura uses a recurrent pattern linking the
theatre and the hunt to construct the authorship of Shakespeare (176).

14 The best discussion of shared authorship is still that of Bentley, 197–234,
though it should be supplemented with Masten's recent survey.

15 Orgel, 'What Is a Text,' 87

16 Bristol, 18

17 Gill, in Marlowe, *The Complete Works of Christopher Marlowe*, 1:121

18 Recently Rasmussen has reviewed the arguments for various collaborators,
decided that 'there is very little real evidence of Nashe's authorship of the
prose scenes in Faustus [sic],' and guardedly advanced a new candidate,
Henry Porter (62–75).

19 Wraight's *Christopher Marlowe and Edward Alleyn* contains only a brief and
extremely hypothetical discussion of the two men's relations.

20 For documentation of Marlowe's propensity to violence, see Proser, *The Gift
of Fire*, esp. 14–20; for a vivid evocation of the climate of duplicity in which
Marlowe may have worked as a spy, see Nicholl, *The Reckoning*. Empson was
mindful of these concerns when he declared with reference to *Doctor Faustus*
that Marlowe 'would be an impossible man to collaborate with' (193).

21 For the story, see Wernham.
22 For these games, see Gomme, 41–2, 208.

1: Marlowe and the Torment of Tantalus

1 Chapman, *Hero and Leander*, sestiad III, 189–91, in Marlowe, *The Poems*, ed. Maclure, 52–3. 'Subject' probably carries its obsolete philosophical meaning: 'The substance of which a thing consists' (*OED* 2:5).
2 C.F. Tucker Brooke, 358
3 For the relationship of Chapman's *Hero and Leander* to Marlowe's, see my discussion in chapter 8.
4 'The Honour of the Garter,' in Peele, *The Life and Minor Works of George Peele*, 246. For evidence that Peele had a performance of Marlowe's *Edward II* in mind when he was writing his poem, see below, page 132.
5 C.F. Tucker Brooke, 358. Peele's words were echoed (and crudely moralized) in *The Second Part of the Return from Parnassus* (1606): 'Marlowe was happy in his buskind muse, / Alas unhappy in his life and end. / Pity it is that wit so ill should dwell, / Wit lent from heaven, but vices sent from hell.' See *The Three Parnassus Plays*, 242–3.
6 Icarus, another important mythological figure in Marlowe, is also named only once, his presence also being evoked through verbal imagery.
7 The history of Tantalus in the Renaissance remains to be written. Though the emphasis is primarily on cataloguing ancient allusions, there is some citation of humanist references in Hylén's *De Tantalo*, an 1896 dissertation in Latin. Prescott compresses a good deal of information in her entry on 'Tantalus' in *The Spenser Encyclopedia*, 676–7, as does Steadman in his article. For references to Tantalus in Spanish literature of the Golden Age, see Gomez, 11.
8 Two of the fullest Renaissance accounts of Tantalus are Natalis Comes, *Mythologiae* (Venice, 1567), VI.xviii and the commentary by Claude Mignaut in many sixteenth-century editions of Andreas Alciatus, *Emblemata cum Commentariis* (Padua, 1621), 370–3. The reference to 'plures Tantali' is from Comes, 190 verso. The best account of the earliest narrative sources of the myth is Ganz, 531–6.
9 For lists of Renaissance depictions of Tantalus, see Pigler, 2:238, and Reid, 1013. A rare depiction showing Tantalus in the upperworld is an engraving in which he tumbles through the air after having been hurled from Mount Sipylus. See Strauss, ed., *Hendrik Goltzius: The Complete Engravings and Woodcuts*, 2:444–5.
10 For these Homeric punishments, see Sourvinou-Inwood. For a Freudian

interpretation (in which the punishment figures the infant's insatiable desire for the breast), see Bunker.

11 Camus, *The Myth of Sisyphus*, 90. For a contrast between 'Sisyphian and Tantalian Personality Types,' see the Introduction to Shoham. For an outline of the book, which is in Hebrew, I am indebted to my colleague Zailig Pollock.

12 Among Lucian's many references to Tantalus, the one in 'Charon' is especially suggestive (229). For Goya's Tantalus, see *Capriccio* no. 9 in *The Complete Etchings of Goya*, 18. Daumier's powerful engraving of Tantalus with glazed eyes and straining tendons is illustrated in Turner, 204. That Franz von Suppé could name a comic operetta *Tantalusqualen* ('The Torments of Tantalus') suggests that in the mid-nineteenth century the myth was losing its nasty edge.

13 Marlowe quotes in Latin from *Thyestes* in *Edward II* (4.7.53–4), and in the final two acts of *Tamburlaine* Part One many motifs derive from Seneca's play.

14 The quotation is from Seneca's *Thyestes*, ed. Tarrant, 112.

15 Seneca, *Thyestes*, in *Four Tragedies and 'Octavia,'* trans. Watling, 51

16 Tarrant notes that Seneca's 'repeated emphasis on parts of his [Tantalus'] body ... make[s] him appear less than fully human, nearly equating him with the physical instruments of his appetites' (Seneca, *Thyestes*, 112).

17 When, for instance, Jewish and early Christian apocalypses included a Tantalus figure in hell, they attributed to him new food crimes, ranging from premature breaking of fasts to the bizarre category of 'wicked poor men who in life struggled to find enough to eat while their wives robbed them.' See Himmelfarb, 92.

18 In the dumb show preceding act 4 of the Tudor tragedy *Gorboduc*, Tantalus leads a procession of kings and queens who 'unnaturally had slain their own children.'

19 The motive of testing the gods' omniscience runs from Fulgentius (*Fulgentius the Mythographer*, 80) to Comes (189 verso) and Alciatus/Mignaut (370). A sign of the trivialization of the myth in the Middle Ages is the banal motive that he killed his son because the gods were coming for supper and his larder was bare. For this and other amusing medieval accretions, see Fox's note in Henryson, 419–20.

20 One of the earliest formulations of this alternate myth is in Pindar's *Olympian 1*. For the relationship of Pindar's treatment to the probably older, cannibalistic version, see Sourvinou-Inwood, 44–5, and Nagy, 128–35.

21 Sidney, 110

22 For the proverb 'Tantali talenta' ('The Talents of Tantalus'), see Erasmus, *Adages* I vi 22, in vol. 32 of *The Collected Works of Erasmus*, 17–18.

23 For the identification of Tantalus with avarice, see Hylén (110–11) and Bald-win, *On the Literary Genetics of Shakespere's Poems and Sonnets*, 133–6. Baldwin cites examples from Spenser, Sidney, and Shakespeare.

24 Erasmus, *On Copy of Words and Ideas*, 70. See also the comment in his *Enchiridion*: 'Tantalus, tormented by thirst, teaches us that it is a great curse to gaze with open mouth at heaped up fortunes without venturing to make use of them' (*Spiritualia*, 68).

25 Similarly, the depiction of Tantalus in Bartholomy Aneau's *Picta Poesis* (1552) is labelled 'Avarus Inops' (108).

26 Greenblatt, *Renaissance Self-Fashioning*, 218

27 Donne, *The Sermons of John Donne*, 8:75 (modernized)

28 Heywood, 61. Ultimately this view is rebutted by the Thomistic exposition of desire expressed by the character More, which Deakins usefully analyses (xv–xxxvii).

29 Ficino, *The Letters of Marsilio Ficino*, 2:79. Greene relates this passage to the motif of thirst in Rabelais (88). Cf. Erasmus' comment (citing Gregory Nazianzen) that the punishment of Tantalus applies to 'the delights of this world, which never satisfy the mind' (*Adages II i 1 to II vi 100*, 298).

30 There is no study of Marlowe's mythology comparable in scope or sensitivity to Bate's *Shakespeare and Ovid*. The Marlovian mythological figures most commented on are a related pair, Phaeton (see Bate, 38–46) and Icarus (see below).

31 I know of only two groupings of images which include both Icarus and Tantalus. One is a late series of drawings for medallions by Hans Holbein the Younger, including Tantalus (uncommonly young and idealized), Icarus, and Hagar and Ishmael in the wilderness. For illustrations and rather cryptic commentary, see Stein, 326–31. The other grouping is Hendrik Goltzius' set of four engravings (1588) depicting the Disgracers (Tantalus, Icarus, Sisyphus, and Phaeton), each of whom is falling through the sky. See Strauss, ed., 2:444–51. Goltzius' set is a variation on the more usual quartet of the damned consisting of Tityus, Tantalus, Sisyphus, and Ixion (deriving from Ovid's *Metamorphoses* 4:457–61). Titian, Ribera, and others executed series of paintings based on this latter grouping.

32 Ellis-Fermor, 84

33 Harry Levin, 23, 159, 161. For an example of Levin's influence, see Hussey's comment that 'For many readers what keeps Marlowe alive and exciting today is to be found in his dramatic projection of the Icarian motif in a series of compelling contexts' (77).

34 That Icarus survives his fall and lives a life of self-loathing impotence is the central conceit of Edward Field's poem 'Icarus' in *Stand Up, Friend, with Me*, 20.

35 Esler, 165–243
36 See Curtis' discussion of the frustrations of 'The Alienated Intellectuals of
    Early Stuart England,' esp. 313–14.
37 Watt, 37
38 G.K. Hunter, *John Lyly*, 34. Hunter's characterization of Lyly, another skilled
    and ambitious writer from Canterbury, is suggestive: 'At the end of his life
    he found that he had wasted his time (he had no post) and the beauty of his
    literary productions (and even their fame) was no consolation to him' (33–4).
39 'Frolic courage' is from Arthur Golding's Elizabethan translation of Ovid's
    story of Icarus, in *Shakespeare's Ovid*, 165 (8:299).
40 For the scant goods inventoried in John Marlowe's will, see Urry, 40. F.P.
    Wilson suggests that Marlowe may have been reminded of himself when he
    read in an account of the historical Tamburlaine that 'notwithstanding the
    poverty of his parents, even from his infancy he had a reaching & an imagi-
    native mind' (23).
41 Anxiety about patronage pervades *Edward II* especially, with the Poor Men's
    approach to Gaveston in the opening scene and the ongoing machinations of
    Gaveston and, later, of Spencer Junior and Baldock. Marlowe's outbursts
    against undiscriminating patrons in *Hero and Leander* are also revealing, as is
    the fact that Doctor Faustus' dreams of conquest give way to servile commit-
    ments of his services.
42 See 116.
43 Harry Levin, 159. Irony and frustration in Marlowe were given a new
    emphasis by Cole. For the recognition of Marlowe's comic, if darkly comic,
    manner, Leech's essays were crucial. See his 'Marlowe's Humor,' 167–78,
    and the posthumous gathering of his essays, *Christopher Marlowe: Poet for the
    Stage*.
44 The key formulation of this view of desire was Stephen Greenblatt's chapter
    on Marlowe in *Renaissance Self-Fashioning* (193–221). Related points were
    made by Snow, and by Lindley.
45 For a brief linking of Tantalus and Lacan, see Belsey, 'Love as Trompe-l'oeil,'
    257–8. For Lacan and the theorizing of desire, see Belsey, *Desire*, 42–71.
46 See, for instance, Rudd, 'Daedalus and Icarus (ii),' 44, and Giamatti, 535.
47 Symonds cited the lines as his first example of Marlowe's 'lust of the impos-
    sible' (489–90); Harry Levin quoted them because they represent 'Marlovian
    tragedy in stark outline' (24); and for Steane they 'state the credo of the aspir-
    ing mind as well as any in Marlowe' (239).
48 For poetic glorifications of Icarus, see Cassirer, 69–70; Rudd, 'Daedalus and
    Icarus (ii),' 37–42; Gatti, 81–9; and Ginzburg. In *The Heroic Frenzies* Giordano
    Bruno quotes Tansillo's sonnet on Icarus immediately after making a decla-

ration which resembles some of the Guise's heroically frenzied rhetoric: 'A heroic mind will prefer falling or missing the mark nobly in a lofty enterprise, whereby he manifests the dignity of his mind, to obtaining perfection in things less noble, if not base' (Bruno, 117).

49 *The Lamentable Tragedy of Locrine*, 92 (3.3.41)

50 Oliver, in Marlowe, *'Dido Queen of Carthage' and 'The Massacre at Paris,'* 100.

51 Marlowe's phrase translates Ovid's 'poma fugacia captat Tantalus.' Like Ovid's, most descriptions of Tantalus in Latin use some form of *fugere* to characterize the evasive movement of the fruit and water. In English translations the usual equivalents are to 'fly' or (less frequently) to 'flee.'

52 Tantalus' relevance to this phrase is briefly noted by Cutts, 173.

53 Hattaway cites this 'haunting' line as evidence for the Marlovian protagonists' 'wish to supplement their being: it should be complete, but the fact of desire demonstrates its incompleteness' ('Christopher Marlowe,' 212).

54 Unfortunately, the prop of 'Tantalus' tree' cannot be connected with a specific play. See Chambers, 2:168.

55 In Abraham Bloemaert's interesting drawing of Tantalus, Zeus watches his victim, and, since the back of the god's head is very close to the picture plane, the illusion is created of seeing Tantalus through his tormentor's eyes. Bloemaert's drawing (in the Courtauld Institute) is illustrated in de Bosque, 262.

56 The best example occurs in the 1616 text of *Doctor Faustus*, where the devils ascend to a vantage-point (the balcony?) from which 'To mark him how he doth demean himself' (5.2.10) in his final agony. But Lightborn gazing at the imprisoned Edward and Tamburlaine at the caged Bajazeth also come to mind.

57 See Rhodes' similar comment on the twofold effect of Marlowe's language, which works 'both to excite the appetite and then to impose boundaries upon it' (117).

58 Leggatt, 'The Critical Fortunes of Christopher Marlowe,' 93

59 Wager, *'The Longer Thou Livest' and 'Enough Is as Good as a Feast,'* Prologue, 31, 34–6. The allusion (not noted by the editor) is to Ovid, *Metamorphoses* 10:40–4.

60 See, for instance, Kelsall, 67; Birringer, 236; and Greenblatt, *Renaissance Self-Fashioning*, 202.

61 Weil, 1, 2

62 Duncan, 108–15

63 Among interesting studies of Elizabethan audience response are Berry, Jones, Cartelli, *Marlowe, Shakespeare, and the Economy of Theatrical Experience*, Cartwright, and *English Renaissance Drama and Audience Response*.

64 Gurr, 'The General and the Caviar,' 8. Gurr has collected the meagre evidence about audiences in *Playgoing in Shakespeare's London*, 50–118, and esp. appendix 2 ('References to Playgoing'), which quotes snippets from 210 contemporary works.
65 The best brief discussion of the evidence (and lack of evidence) is Astington, 'The London Stage in the 1580s,' 1–18.
66 Kenneth Burke, 'Psychology and Form' in his *Counter-Statement*, 31. For a discussion of various expectations an audience may have even before a performance begins (e.g., generic expectations), see Carlson, 82–98.
67 The translation is from Raleigh's interesting discussion of Tantalus in *The History of the World* (II.xiii.3), in *The Works of Sir Walter Raleigh*, 3:392.

2: Translation Template: *All Ovid's Elegies*

1 The most balanced account of Marlowe as a translator (which of course includes howlers) is Gill, 'Snakes Leape by Verse.'
2 Ellis-Fermor, 14
3 Knoll, 28. Significantly, these 'glimpses of things to come' invariably concentrate on the Icarian and the sublime, such as instances in which 'a sonorous word gives a rhythmical effect that presages "the mighty line"' (Boas, 39–40).
4 Steane, 299
5 Nashe quotes more frequently from the *Amores* (twenty-seven times) than from any other work by Ovid, who was his favourite classical author. See Nashe, 5:133. For the quotation from Lyly, see *Euphues and His England*, 143.
6 Jacobsen, 154. Particularly useful for its account of medieval attitudes to the *Amores* is Stapleton, though his treatment of Marlowe's translation is surprisingly sketchy.
7 Moss, 3
8 From a table in Bolgar, 530–3
9 As many commentators have noted, Marlowe's translation of Ovid's poem about the high calling of poetry (1.15) is very powerful.
10 There are at least two dozen appearances of these terms in contexts where the idea of play is not explicit in Ovid. For the equivalents for Latin terms in Elizabethan English, I have consulted the most popular Latin-to-English dictionary of Marlowe's day, Thomas Cooper's *Thesaurus Linguae Romanae et Britannicae* (1565).
11 Green, in Ovid, *The Erotic Poems*, 309
12 Du Quesnay, 10–11. For a diffuse reading of the *Metamorphoses* along similar lines ('engaging the reader in what is going on in the poem and at the same time frustrating him'), see Glenn, viii.

13 In his translation of the *Amores* in *Ovid: The Love Poems*, A.D. Melville pays homage to Marlowe's translations of 1.5, 3.6, and 3.13 by including them in lieu of versions of his own. Another indication of the excellence of these translations is that they were included in the well-chosen selection of ten which appeared in the octavo entitled *Certaine of Ovids Elegies*, which is the earliest printed collection of the *Elegies*.

14 For the influence of Ovid's poem and Marlowe's translation of it in the Renaissance, see von Koppenfels, esp. 129–30.

15 Marlowe's 'To leave the rest' translates Ovid's more subtle 'singula quid referam,' or 'why describe each feature?'

16 Du Quesnay, 10. For the opposite view, see Easthope, 52.

17 Barsby, in Ovid, *Amores, Book I*, 69

18 In several other passages as well, Marlowe imports into Ovid a pairing of the 'sweet' and the 'stol'n.' Cf. 'We scorn things lawful, stol'n sweets we affect' (2.19.3) and 'stol'n pleasure is sweet play' (3.4.31). In his 'Elegy 12' (47–8), John Donne appears to have recalled Marlowe's coupling of these terms.

19 Green, in Ovid, *The Erotic Poems*, 397

20 Ovid, *The Erotic Poems*, trans. Green, 232

21 For the convention of the shut-out lover in Ovid, see Copley, 125–40 and esp. 82–90.

22 Montaigne, 2:15

23 'An obstacle is required in order to heighten libido; and where natural resistances to satisfaction have not been sufficient men have at all times erected conventional ones so as to be able to enjoy love' (Freud, 256–7).

24 In her recent edition of the Second Book of the *Amores*, Booth makes a similar distinction between two 'epigrammatic *leitmotive*' in the poem, but she does not give enough emphasis to the element of masochism in the second. See Ovid, *Amores II*, 91–2.

25 Green, in Ovid, *The Erotic Poems*, 309

26 Ovid's line is 'quod licet, ingratum est; quod non licet acrius urit,' which Booth closely translates as 'What is allowed is unattractive; what is not allowed burns more fiercely.'

27 Marlowe's 'Nothing I love that at all times avails me' translates Ovid's 'nil ego quod nullo tempore laedat,' which Booth (89) renders as 'I love nothing that never gives pain.'

28 That the waters are 'stol'n' is Marlowe's confusing addition to Ovid. For the proverb 'You seek water in the sea' (meaning 'You look in the very place where there is nothing else to be seen'), see Erasmus' *Adages* (I ix 75), 221.

29 Throughout his love poetry, Ovid always identifies the crime of Tantalus as garrulity. See *Ars Amatoria* 2.602–7 and *Amores* 2.2.43–4; 3.11.30.

30 Howell, 75
31 Cf. 'I loathe, yet after that I loathe I run, / O how the burden irks, that we should shun' (2.4.5–6) and 'I fly her lust, but follow beauty's creature: / I loathe her manners, love her body's feature' (3.10.37–8)
32 Kenney, Introduction to Ovid, *The Love Poems*, trans. Melville, xvii
33 Davis, 44
34 Marlowe, *Doctor Faustus*, ed. Bevington and Rasmussen, 195. It is noteworthy that none of the many critical discussions of the inefficacy of language in Marlowe's plays makes reference to the centrality of the motif in the *Elegies*.
35 Booth, in Ovid, *Amores II*, 57
36 For an appreciative comment on how Marlowe 'accepts the situation and imagines himself in it,' see Gill, 'Snakes Leape by Verse,' 149.
37 In a panel discussion, Debora Shuger mentioned the 'pornography of male impotence' in the Renaissance (without referring to this poem) as a topic that requires further study (276).
38 The emendation of 'thirsts' is preferable to the apparently meaningless 'thrives' of the early quartos, which is presumably a compositor's error. See Pearcy, 435–6.
39 Compare, for instance, Faustus' attempt to deny the reality of hell and Tamburlaine's refusal to admit that Zenocrate is dead.
40 In place of the 'two-leav'd book,' Ovid abstractly speaks of being forced to see her 'probra,' meaning 'disgrace' or 'unchastity.' For a riddle from 1610 about using 'a pen with a hole in the top, To write between [a] two-leaved book,' see Gordon Williams, cited in *TLS* (21 April 1995), 6.
41 Barsby, in Ovid, *Amores, Book I*, 63

3: Playing with the Powerless: *Dido Queen of Carthage*

1 See, for instance, Cole's pithy comment that 'though the matter is Virgilian, the spirit is Ovid's' (85). For Ovidian elements in the play, see Proser, '*Dido Queene of Carthage* and the Evolution of Marlowe's Dramatic Style,' 84–5; Mary E. Smith, 103; Martin, 56–61.
2 Barsby, in Ovid, *Amores, Book I*, 17
3 Steane applies the phrase 'humour of discomfiture' to Tamburlaine's treatment of his captives (107).
4 Harry Levin notes the centrality of 'ticing' in the play but does not comment on the linked action of escaping (16).
5 In addition to its prominence in the *Elegies*, the motif of fleeing and following pervades the *Metamorphoses*, beginning with Apollo's pursuit of Daphne (1.452–552).

6 Virgil mentions Iarbas only twice, once in passing (4.36) and later (4.198–218) in more detail as Iarbas bitterly complains to Jupiter that his many sacrifices have been in vain, since he has lost Dido to Aeneas.

7 From *Amores* 2:19, Iarbas echoes a line ('hoc iuvat, haec animi sunt alimenta mei') in which the poet pleads with his mistress to say no to him, for 'This is joy, this is food to my passion' (Loeb translation).

8 Ficino, 'Marsilio Ficino's Commentary on Plato's *Symposium*,' 199

9 In *Antony and Cleopatra* Shakespeare makes what he borrows from Marlowe less ironic; Antony's 'I come, my queen' (4.14.50) and Cleopatra's 'Husband, I come' (5.2.287) are directed to each other. And the fact that Cleopatra echoes Antony's words without having heard them suggests a spiritual dimension conspicuously absent from Marlowe.

10 Gibbons, 44

11 The phrase is from Nashe, 2:153.

12 For a concise account of the love-hunt from classical literature to the Renaissance, see Don Cameron Allen, 'On *Venus and Adonis*,' 102–5.

13 *Ars Amatoria* 1.45, trans. Green, in Ovid, *The Erotic Poems*, 167. For another reference to erotic nets and snaring women in toils, see 1.264–71.

14 In a formulation often quoted in the Renaissance, Ovid begins *Amores* 1.9 by declaring 'Militat omnis amans, et habet sua castra Cupido' (translated by Marlowe as 'All lovers war, and Cupid hath his tent'). For commentary, see Thomas, and Murgatroyd.

15 Marlowe creates a pun on 'arms' in his translation of *Amores* 2.18, in which the speaker says that he wants to be writing heroic verse about 'new-sworn soldiers' maiden arms' ('prima arma'), but he is prevented by his 'wench,' who 'wreathes about my neck her winding arms ['lacertos'], / And thousand kisses gives, that work my harms' (9–10). For the pun in *Dido*, see Cupid's comment that 'I shall one day be a man / And better able unto other arms' (3.3.35–6).

16 For a discussion of the conflict between love and war in the play, as well as useful comments on the threat which Dido poses to Aeneas' identity, see Kuriyama, 53–76.

17 The most thorough study of boy acting risks few judgments about tone in its treatment of *Dido* as a 'pathetic heroine play.' See Michael Shapiro, 166–71.

18 Don Cameron Allen, 'Marlowe's *Dido* and the Tradition,' 65

19 Cope suggestively explores the self-reflexive dimensions of the play.

20 Boas, 65

21 See, for instance, Rose's comment that 'in their attempt to represent the Dido legend as tragic, Marlowe and Nashe succeed only in rendering it degrading and ridiculous' (111).

22 For the gods' abuse of power, see Summers, *Christopher Marlowe and the Politics of Power*, 20–40.

23 Steane (40) evokes the terror of the scene, and Mary E. Smith (94–100) places the murder of Priam in the context of the Marlovian contempt for weak kings.

24 Critical discussions of the links between *Dido* and *Hamlet* have not noted that this remark about 'malicious sport' and 'mincing limbs' closely describes Priam's death in Marlowe but has nothing to do with the account which the First Player has just given (2.2.468–92).

25 Spenser, 'An Hymne in Honour of Love,' lines 134–5, in *The Yale Edition of the Shorter Poems of Edmund Spenser*, 697

26 This is still another paraphrase of Ovid's 'quod fugit, ipse sequor.'

27 The bracketed stage directions are my addition.

28 See especially the references to 'Virgins half-dead dragg'd by their golden hair' (195), to 'Cassandra sprawling in the streets, / Whom Ajax ravish'd in Diana's fane' (274–5), and to Polyxena 'by the cruel Myrmidons surpris'd / And after by that Pyrrhus sacrific'd' (287–8).

29 The first configuration of the lovers in the *Dream* is close to that of *Dido*. Just as Anna pursues Iarbas, who spurns her and pursues the evasive Dido (who loves another), so Helena pursues Demetrius, who spurns her and pursues the evasive Hermia (who loves another). In Marlowe the pattern is destructive because it does not change, while Shakespeare opens the pattern to transformation and to the resolution of marriage.

30 For this parallel, see Cope, 319.

31 For a sensitive discussion of Virgil's sympathy for Dido, see Rudd, 145–66.

32 In Elegy 12 ('His Parting from Her'), John Donne uses the same rhythms and rhyme words in an explicitly Tantalian image: 'And therefore now, sooner than I can say, / I saw the golden fruit, 'tis rapt away' (*The Poems of John Donne*, 1:101).

33 For Dido's wooing of Aeneas as an attempt to 'authorize her power,' see Bartels, 45–52. For a fine discussion that links Dido's passionate lyricism to her limited power, see Henderson, 120–66.

34 See, for instance, Oliver's note in the Revels edition, 83.

35 There are some close verbal echoes in the two scenes, especially in the rhetoric of delusion. Compare 'Achates, see, King Priam wags his hand' (2.1.29) to 'And see, the sailors take him by the hand' (5.1.189).

36 Mary E. Smith notes the different responses of Virgil's and Marlowe's Aeneas but does not discuss delusion in the play (10).

37 Mulryne and Fender begin their paper with a brief discussion of this passage.

38 The fullest discussion of these three figures unfortunately does not do justice to Marlowe's artistry. See Bono, *passim*.

39 For other notable 'leaps' in *Dido*, see Hecuba leaping on the face of Pyrrhus (2.1.244), Aeneas' heart leaping out to give life to the statue of Priam (2.1.27), and, most important, Dido's invitation to Aeneas to 'leap in mine arms' (5.1.180). And compare Faustus' desire to 'leap up to my god.'

40 Leech, *Christopher Marlowe*, 40

41 Martin, 63

4: The Conqueror's and the Playwright's Games: *Tamburlaine the Great*

1 Greenblatt's placing of Tamburlaine's restlessness in the context of 'the acquisitive energies of English merchants, entrepreneurs, and adventurers' (*Renaissance Self-Fashioning*, 194) has been elaborated by Bartels, 53–81, related to the fortunes of the Muscovy Company by Richard Wilson, and linked to Spanish conquests in the Americas by Cartelli ('Marlowe and the New World').

2 Richard Levin concludes his survey of Elizabethan references to Marlowe's Tamburlaine by observing that 'the overwhelming impression created by all these allusions is that Tamburlaine was perceived as a triumphant figure who possessed and wielded tremendous power' ('The Contemporary Perception of Marlowe's Tamburlaine,' 56).

3 Heaney, 29

4 Leech, *Christopher Marlowe*, 60; Kuriyama, 1–52

5 For example, in the Introduction to his edition Bullen declared that Marlowe 'could not don alternately the buskin and the sock' and that 'Marlowe never attempted to write a comic scene' (1:xxvii–xxix).

6 The phrase is from Cunningham's Introduction to his Revels edition, 28. For the 'pervasive humour' of Peter Hall's 1976 production at the National Theatre, see Cunningham and Warren, 158.

7 Leggatt, 'Tamburlaine's Sufferings,' 29

8 Alciatus, *Andreas Alciatus, The English Emblems*, vol. 2, emblem 85

9 La Primaudaye, 446. In *Macbeth* the Porter's lament (2.3.32–3) about the effect of drink on lechery ('it sets him on, and it takes him off; it persuades him, and disheartens him') catches the same rhythm of hope and frustration.

10 Leech, *Christopher Marlowe*, 52

11 Fieler, 39

12 Tamburlaine's reproof and Theridamas' retreat are noted by Nicholas Brooke, 'Marlowe the Dramatist,' 89.

13 Cunningham and Warren, 159

14 The recent World's Classics edition assumes that these African crowns are a 'second course' to distinguish them from the Asian crowns which Tamburlaine had earlier promised (*Doctor Faustus and Other Plays*, ed. Bevington and Rasmussen, 414). More probably, the crowns are a 'second course' because the first course was 'the banquet' on the table mentioned in the stage direction at the head of the scene.

15 Waith misses the game when he reads the scene as a manifestation of Tamburlaine's heroic liberality (*Ideas of Greatness*, 54). So does Leech, from another angle, when he says that Tamburlaine 'distributes crowns carelessly among his followers' (*Christopher Marlowe*, 51).

16 Cunningham and Warren, 159

17 Bartels notes that this crowning of the jail-keeper Almeda 'replays Tamburlaine's crowning of Zenocrate' at the end of Part One (76–7).

18 See Stroup's comment that the coronation 'effects the proper reconciliation [of Tamburlaine and Zenocrate] and the play achieves an Aristotelian conclusion' (340).

19 In Peter Hall's 1976 production, a misguided realism diminished the sense of violated ceremony, as the Scythian lords sat on pillows on the ground with only small bowls of food in front of them. See the third plate in Geckle.

20 Birringer discusses the genre-mixing intensity of the banquet scene (222–34).

21 Cunningham and Warren, 160

22 Richard Levin, 'Contemporary Perception of Marlowe's Tamburlaine,' 58–9

23 Similarly, Burnett observes that 'Tamburlaine only ever metaphorically eats and drinks; before the caged Bajazeth he keeps himself at a distance from the food and resists enjoying the dainties his followers so voraciously consume' ('*Tamburlaine* and the Body,' 35). But Burnett's assertion that 'Bajazeth (at sword's point) is forced to eat' ignores the stage direction immediately after Tamburlaine's command to 'take it [food] from my sword's point': '*he [Bajazeth] takes it and stamps upon it.*'

24 In Seneca's *Thyestes*, Tantalus refers to his prison-cell ('carcer') (line 70). When John Hoskyns was imprisoned in the Tower, he wrote a poem likening his situation to that of Tantalus (Whitlock, 483).

25 Cunningham edition (322). Marlowe's other main source, Perondinus' biography, also makes no mention of tantalization: 'Indeed, so that he might be more of an object of ridicule and contempt to Tamburlaine while he was eating his meals and carousing, Bajazeth was made to eat crumbs and crusts under the table like a dog, tied to a stool' (Cunningham edition, 325). The account in Fortescue's *The Forest* is similar (printed as an appendix in Ellis-Fermor's edition of *Tamburlaine the Great*). So is that in John Foxe, for which see Brown, 38–48.

26 Thurn's discussion of Tamburlaine's visual presentation does not refer to the banquet scene.

27 Kirschbaum, in Marlowe, *The Plays of Christopher Marlowe*, 50

28 Conrad, 133

29 Earlier Tamburlaine's scarlet costume has been associated with thirst and blood; the change from white to red is explained as a shift from satiety to thirst, white signifying 'the mildness of his mind / That satiate with spoil, refuseth blood,' while red means 'Then must his kindled wrath be quenched with blood' (4.1.52–6). For classical charges that Scythians practiced cannibalism and drank their enemies' blood, see Carolyn Williams.

30 For a list of Thyestean banquets in English plays, see Hattaway, *Elizabethan Popular Theatre*, 206–7.

31 In Terry Hands' Swan Theatre production, the scene becomes a cannibal feast. See Barton.

32 G.K. Hunter, *Dramatic Identities and Cultural Tradition*, 208

33 Braden's lengthy discussion of Senecanism and *Tamburlaine* does not refer to either the banquet scene or to Bajazeth (*Renaissance Tragedy and the Senecan Tradition*, 182–97). Battenhouse, however, does note some suggestive parallels between Tamburlaine and Atreus (*Marlowe's 'Tamburlaine,'* 203).

34 For this motif in Seneca, see *Thyestes*, ed. Tarrant, 47–8.

35 For Atreus' insatiable lust for revenge, see Boyle, 210–11, and Motto and Clark, 137–41.

36 In Part Two, Calyphas' rejection of his father's appetites ('I take no pleasure to be murderous, / Nor care for blood when wine will quench my thirst' [4.1.27–30]) is echoed by a Turkish general's characterization of Tamburlaine as 'The monster that hath drunk a sea of blood / And yet gapes still for more to quench his thirst' (5.2.13–14). Thus, Tamburlaine is identified with the monstrous fish of Lake Asphaltis: 'fishes fed by human carcasses, / Amazed, swim up and down upon the waves / As when they swallow asafoetida, / Which makes them fleet aloft and gasp for air' (5.1.202–8). The last line's suggestion of a bloated Icarianism is an incisive comment on Tamburlaine.

37 Gardner, 'The Second Part of *Tamburlaine the Great.*'

38 Pavel, 60

39 For an explication of the physician's technical terms, see Parr.

40 *Tamburlaine the Great*, ed. Cunningham, 249. For a third interpretation, see the gloss in Wolff's edition of *Tamburlaine*: 'Zenocrate's light-giving powers rivalled those of the sun.'

41 The practice of conflating the plays was established by the first major revival, the Tyrone Guthrie / Donald Wolfit production at the Old Vic in 1951. The text of the acting version indicates that the Prologue to Part Two was dropped, thus obscuring the fact that the scenes from Part Two belonged to a

separate work. See Marlowe, *'Tamburlaine the Great': An Acting Version by Tyrone Guthrie and Donald Wolfit,* 48–9.

42 Kelsall, 129. Kelsall earlier notes that 'Marlowe arouses expectations which the text does not bring into any meaningful order' (115) but does not consider the possibility of his arousing expectations in order to frustrate them.

43 Hall, 256

44 Hall, 257. In addition to beginning the play with act 1, scene 3, Hall's production 'conflated IV i and IV iii and had IV ii (the death of Olympia) follow IV iii' (Geckle, 69). For rearrangements of scenes in other productions of *Tamburlaine,* see Leslie, 105–20.

45 For a detailed discussion of Marlowe's toying with *de casibus* expectations, see Summers, *Christopher Marlowe and the Politics of Power,* 55–63.

46 Greenblatt, *Renaissance Self-Fashioning,* 202

47 For the theme of 'expectation mocked' in *2 Henry IV,* see Holland's Introduction to the Signet edition. The second parts of *Tamburlaine* and *Henry IV* contain other parallels, such as a strong emphasis on disease (including the only urinanalyses in Marlowe and Shakespeare).

48 Henslowe, 26–33.

49 In a perceptive discussion of the Prologue's awkwardness, Leech (*Christopher Marlowe,* 66) wonders 'why should we have this pedestrian verse before Part II when Marlowe had given us his most challenging manner of utterance before Part I' and then answers himself by questioning Marlowe's authorship of the lines.

50 Brinker notes that the reference to 'murd'rous Fates' is 'deliberately misleading' without commenting on how comprehensive the strategy of misdirection is in the play (5).

51 Cassirer, 42–3. For the unfolding of concepts in Renaissance art and literature, see Wind.

52 For misleading promises to 'unfold' an issue, see *Hamlet* 1.5.15 (the Ghost addresses Hamlet) and *Measure for Measure* 1.1.3 (the Duke addresses Escalus).

53 Geckle, 69

54 Battenhouse's discussion of this conflict in exclusively theological terms is severely undercut by his failure to address the ironies of theatrical presentation ('Protestant Apologetics and the Subplot of *2 Tamburlaine,*' 30–43).

55 In 'Tamburlaine's Sufferings,' Leggatt incisively discusses 'the disparity between his imaginative image of Zenocrate and his understanding of the woman herself' (30).

56 In one of the few studies to take the plot of Part Two seriously, Leech

argued that its loose ends constitute a 'deliberately casual structure' which mirrors Tamburlaine's lack of command over events (*Christopher Marlowe*, 81–2).

57 Altman, 345. Altman notes the intellectual qualification created by Orcanes' remark but does not, I think, place enough stress on its unsettling effect in the theatre.

58 Kuriyama, 49

59 Leggatt, 'Tamburlaine's Sufferings,' 32. Some reviewers of Hall's production sensed that the audience was left thinking '*Maybe* Mahomet could hear, maybe not ...' (Cunningham and Warren, 158), and others felt that 'no particular connection was meant to be drawn' between the sickness and the challenge (Geckle, 71).

60 With respect to the burning of the Koran, Greenblatt notes that 'The one action which Elizabethan churchmen themselves might have applauded seems to bring down divine vengeance' (*Renaissance Self-Fashioning*, 202).

61 By contrast, in the morality-tragedy *Cambyses*, the death of the tyrant Cambyses (who has accidentally impaled himself while mounting his horse) is conclusively revealed to be an act of divine vengeance, as it is: (a) prophesied by a third party immediately before it happens; (b) expounded by Cambyses as he lies dying; (c) formulated chorically by the lords who discover his body and repeat his dying words. Bevington's attempt to find ambiguity in Cambyses' death (and thus similarities between Preston's crude play and Marlowe's) is strained (214).

62 Bevington notes that the physiological explanation of the sickness 'implicitly repudiates the moral implication of the sequence that had led to this moment of death,' attributing the resulting ambiguity to historical tensions ('the transitional use of moral structure in a secular context') rather than to Marlowe's artistry (216–17).

63 For instance, after conceding that the fever is 'a physiological phenomenon which can be explained by psychological causes,' Battenhouse cautions 'But that does not mean God has not had a hand in it' (*Marlowe's 'Tamburlaine*,' 174).

5: Playing with Avarice: *The Jew of Malta*

1 Goldman makes excellent comments on the protagonists' oscillations between rapture and disillusion.

2 See chapter 1, page 14.

3 Humfrey Gifford, *A Posie of Gilloflowers* (1580), 71. Echoing Erasmus on the

uses of mythology, Thomas Wilson makes the same point about Tantalus in his *Art of Rhetoric* (1560), 220.

4 Brecht, *Brecht on Theatre*, 11

5 Manley, 91–3 (esp. Bernard Gilpin's remark that 'now-a-days, the little thieves are hanged that steal of necessity, but the great Barabbases have free liberty to rob and spoil without all measure in the midst of the city ... Covetousness is the root of all' [92])

6 Agrippa, 249

7 For the text of the libel, which led to Thomas Kyd's arrest and a warrant for Marlowe's, see Freeman. For the Elizabethan animosity to 'stranger' residents, see Pettegree, 278–96.

8 The best evidence of the play's power to provoke dangerous emotions is its profitable revival during the sordid trial and execution of Roderigo Lopez, the Jewish physician of Queen Elizabeth. Hotine documents the revival and speculates that it 'could have been used to help create anti-Semitic prejudice' in London.

9 For economic motives in the play, see Greenblatt, 'Marlowe, Marx, and Anti-Semitism,' in *Learning to Curse*, 40–58, and Jardine.

10 Greenblatt, 'Marlowe, Marx, and Anti-Semitism,' in *Learning to Curse*, 44. Even Greenblatt's later, italicized qualification that 'wealth is gradually replaced as the *exclusive* object of his concern' still exaggerates the point (52).

11 A rare exception is Segal, who quotes the next lines and observes that 'Barabas will always be moving – and shifting with the wind' ('Marlowe's *Schadenfreude*,' 83).

12 For the presence of Jews in Elizabethan England, see James Shapiro, *Shakespeare and the Jews*, 62–76. Sanders points out that for Thomas Rogers, the Elizabethan translator of a treatise on usury, 'The identification of Jews and Usury is so complete ... that he refers to the expulsion of the Jews in the reign of Edward I, as the banishment of the *Usurers*' (384).

13 In 1579 Stephen Gosson praised a play called *The Jew* (not extant) for 'representing the greediness of worldly choosers, and bloody minds of usurers' (Chambers, 4:204). In Robert Wilson's *Three Ladies of London* (1584), the Jewish Gerontus is a usurer (though a very benign one), and in Wilson's companion play *Three Lords and Ladies of London* (1590) the figure Usury is reminded by another character that 'thy parents were both Jews, though thou wert born in London' (Robert Wilson, 86). With respect to profession, Shakespeare's Shylock is much closer to type than Marlowe's Barabas.

14 The phrase is from Zucker (87), who does not note that the 'emblematic simplicity' is deceptively simple.

15 Bartels notes that 'Barabas's career is ... shaped by a series of performances in

which he plays the Jew' (106). The reference to 'bad coin' is from Sanders, 42. Marlowe also stands the stereotype of the duplicitous Turk on its turban. See Freer, 144.

16 G.K. Hunter quotes an letter from Peter the Venerable to Louis VII urging the confiscation of Jewish property to fund the Second Crusade (*Dramatic Identities and Cultural Tradition*, 94–5). Pettegree notes that 'In 1586 Walsingham looked to the foreign churches for a substantial loan to finance the raising of new troops for the Low Countries, and when in the following year the government was attempting to raise a force of 10,000 men to defend the country in the Armada campaign the churches were again expected to contribute generously' (294).

17 Chaucer, Pardoner's Prologue, in *The Works of Geoffrey Chaucer*, 149

18 Bawcutt, in Marlowe, *The Jew of Malta*, 32

19 Marlowe's play can be seen as a violently sardonic version of George Herbert's 'Self-Condemnation': 'Thou who condemnest Jewish hate, / For choosing Barabbas a murderer / Before the Lord of Glory; / Look back upon thine own estate' (*The English Poems of George Herbert*, 176).

20 In a discussion of women as commodities in the play, Hodge points out that it is Lodowick who initiates the diamond metaphor in this scene (19).

21 After having stripped him of all his wealth, Ferneze declares: 'Content thee, Barabas, thou hast nought but right' (1.2.152). Similarly, at the close of the play he counsels his betrayed Turkish prisoner to 'content thee, Calymath, here thou must stay' (5.5.118).

22 Boas, 132

23 Shepherd is rare among critics in connecting the betrayals inside the play with those inside the theatre (174–7).

24 Similarly, Cartelli remarks that 'In order to meet *The Jew* on its own terms, we must ride the play as we ride an unfamiliar rapids, adjusting our position to fit the contours of its protean shape and texture' (*Marlowe, Shakespeare, and the Economy of Theatrical Experience*, 164).

25 Quoted in James L. Smith, 13

26 See Fehrenbach, 1140, 1188.

27 In a not very thorough or imaginative study, Forsythe noted fourteen passages in Marlowe's plays which echo his lyric (697–701).

28 For a Bakhtinian discussion of this process, see Bruster.

29 Harry Levin, 74

30 For this tripartite division, see Shepherd's note in his edition of Sidney's *An Apology for Poetry*, 181.

31 Bawcutt, 36

32 Raab, 52

33 I reinsert the quarto's comma after 'land' (which Bawcutt removed), as it suggests an ominous pause before Machevil's invitation to frolic.

34 Jones, 74

35 James L. Smith, 18

36 Though Brinker notes that 'the prologue almost totally neglects to give concrete information about the protagonist, his history, or his fate,' he does not comment on its deceptiveness (10).

37 Thomas Heywood, 'The Prologue spoken at court,' in Bawcutt, 192

38 Nashe, 2:180. Citing this 'unrefutable principle' of 'Machiavel,' Nashe is translating the penultimate sentence of chapter 7 of *The Prince*, which attributes the downfall of Cesare Borgia to his naïve trust in Pope Julius II, an erstwhile enemy. This same axiom is cited as a 'settled rule of Machiavel' in *Leicester's Commonwealth* (1584), quoted in Meyer, 29.

39 For the identification of Ferneze with true Machiavellism (and of Barabas with Gentillet's polemical distortion of Machiavelli), see Minshull.

40 Nashe, 1:220. On the same page, Nashe seems to be thinking of *The Jew of Malta* when he notes how the Machiavel will 'seek his destruction that knows my secrets; and such as I have employed in any murder or stratagem, to set them privily together ... to stab each other mutually, for fear of bewraying me.'

41 In his New Mermaid edition of *The Jew of Malta*, Siemon notes that Barabas and Faustus cannot 'escape values assumed by the social order they reject' (xxxvii).

42 Using the Marxist idea of 'false consciousness,' Hodge makes a similar point (9–10).

43 Without discussing its significance, Rusche notes that the emblem appears in Whitney (261). For the pairing of the ass and Tantalus, see Alciatus, *Emblemata cum Commentariis*, in which the emblem of Tantalus (no. 85) is labelled 'Avaritia,' and the ass (no. 86) is labelled 'In Avaros' ('On Misers'). La Primaudaye may have had Alciatus' pairing in mind when he compared the covetous man to Tantalus in hell and went on to speak of 'Mules that carry great burdens of gold and silver on their backs, and yet eat but hay' (446).

44 For a good discussion of how the play's 'complex mélange of styles' prevents the audience from 'getting a set,' see Kelsall, 132–6. For disorienting shifts in language, also see Nicholas Brooke, 'Marlowe the Dramatist,' 91–8, and Freer, 152–8.

45 Though his account of the plot is flawed by factual errors, Pavel rightly stresses the audience's surprise when Barabas falls (68).

46 See Whitney, 216, and G.K. Hunter, *Dramatic Identities and Cultural Tradition*, 93–4.

47 Garber, '"Infinite Riches in a Little Room,"' 10
48 For a lively argument that 'it would be preposterous to play the cauldron scene as anything but farce (savage if one will),' see Kelsall, 153–4. Certainly the historical Machiavelli – who recently has been characterized as 'the most original easer of hell since Origen' – would have seen the cauldron as grotesquely humorous. See de Grazia, 318.
49 Gentillet, *A Discourse ... Against Nicholas Machiavell*, trans. Simon Patericke (London, 1602), 93. Minshull (49) quotes Gentillet's passage but does not relate it to the refusal of the Christians to aid Barabas.
50 For the politics of sacrifice in the play, see Dena Goldberg.
51 Nashe, 2:326
52 Sidney, 108

6: The Play of History and Desire: *Edward II*

1 In his chapter title, Hattaway characterizes *Edward II* as a 'dramatic documentary' (*Elizabethan Popular Theatre*, 141–59). In his Revels edition, Forker notes that in Holinshed Gaveston's death is a formal execution (226).
2 *De dignitate et augmentis scientiarum*, 13, in Bacon, 407
3 The removal of characters under guard occurs in the following scenes: 1.1.199 (Bishop of Coventry); 1.4.34 (Gaveston and Kent); 2.5.108 (Gaveston); 2.6.17 (Gaveston); 3.2.65 (Warwick and Lancaster); 3.2.75 (Mortimer); 4.6.73 (Spencer Senior); 4.7.119 (Spencer Junior and Baldock); 5.3.62 (Edward); 5.3.67 (Kent); 5.4.105 (Kent); 5.6.66 (Mortimer); 5.6.91 (Isabella). In a grim variation on the motif, Matrevis and Gurney drag the corpses of Edward and Lightborn off stage at the end of 5.5.
4 These forced exits are not mentioned in the essay on stage emblems of disorder by Bevington and Shapiro.
5 Leech, 'Marlowe's *Edward II*,' revised in Leech's *Christopher Marlowe*, 121–45
6 'Weakness is subject to violence' is the translation of Whitney's 'Iniuriis infirmitas subiecta' in Manning's edition of *A Choice of Emblemes*, 52.
7 For the similarities in staging between the two scenes, see Dessen, 124–5.
8 Bacon, 408. With emphases different from mine, Haber suggests that 'The play as a whole ... records a submission to history – to history as "the dominant ideology," and (what is the same thing) to history as "the literal truth"' (179).
9 Quoted in Geckle, 79. For the 'sanitized' nature of this production, see Forker's edition of *Edward the Second*, 101.
10 Sanders, 140. Cf. Steane's remark that the play's 'dominant spirit is one of

belittlement, where dignity is undermined, nobility turned to pettiness, and man made abject, thwarted and humiliated' (228).

11 McElroy, 207

12 For the Privy Council's concern with demobbed soldiers in the early 1590s, see Peele, *The Dramatic Works of George Peele*, 5.

13 In the opening scene of *The Duchess of Malfi*, Bosola complains, 'Who would rely upon these miserable dependences, in expectation to be advanced tomorrow? what creature ever fed worse than hoping Tantalus?' Of course a dependent at court did not have to be a 'poor man' to feel tantalized. Duke Frederick of Württemberg's futile attempts to secure the Order of the Garter (promised him by Elizabeth) were so teasingly protracted that a modern commentator dubbed him 'Duke Tantalus.' See von Klarwill, 347–423.

14 Waith, '*Edward II*,' 63

15 For the parallels between the sexual politics of Gaveston and Mortimer, see Tyler.

16 McCloskey notes that the three characters (Edward, Isabella, Mortimer) who think that their fates depend on Gaveston's 'learn immediately after his death how greatly they were mistaken' (43–4).

17 Belsey notes the centrality of absence to the Edward/Gaveston relationship in 'Desire's Excess and the English Renaissance Theatre,' 84–8.

18 For a discussion of light and dark imagery in the play, see Steane, 208–9.

19 Belt examines the 'struggle for rhetorical control' within the play but says little about the theatre audience.

20 Ovid, *Shakespeare's Ovid*, 67

21 Gaveston's Diana is kin to the two 'wanton Maidens' in Spenser's Bower of Bliss, who also disport themselves in a fountain and entice Guyon by displaying only part of themselves above the water: 'The rest hid underneath, him more desirous made' (*The Faerie Queene* 2.12.66). The *locus classicus* of the idea is in Ovid's account of Apollo's pursuit of Daphne (*Metamorphoses* 1:502): 'And sure he thought such other parts as garments then did hide, / Excelled greatly all the rest the which he had espied' (*Shakespeare's Ovid*, 32–3).

22 For Gaveston's speech as an emblematic dumb show prefiguring the death of Edward, see Sunesen, esp. 246–7; for more recent commentary on the relevance of the Actaeon myth, see Deats, 310–11, and Kelsall, 48–9.

23 Quoted in Bray, *Homosexuality in Renaissance England*, 61. The explicitness of Gaveston's opening speech does not support Bray's more recent argument that Marlowe represents the Edward/Gaveston relationship with deliberate ambiguity so as to call Elizabethan constructions of friendship and sodomy

into question ('Homosexuality and the Signs of Male Friendship in Elizabethan England,' 48–9).

24 Holinshed, 2:547. For a discussion contrasting Holinshed's occlusion of
homosexuality to the play's more revealing treatment, see Bartels, 143–72.
Curiously, Bredbeck's discussion of the treatment of homoeroticism in
Renaissance accounts of Edward's reign makes no reference to Holinshed
(48–77).

25 Fricker, 216. For a similar comment see Clemen: 'The rapid sequence of
entrances and exits, the brevity of most of the scenes, the quick exchange of
dialogue, the restless movement on stage which characterizes most scenes –
all this marks the play with a distinctive, rapid, turbulent rhythm' (126).

26 Sales, 119

27 Respectively: Forker, in Marlowe, Edward the Second, 74; Harry Levin, 98;
Kocher, Christopher Marlowe, 205; Sasaki, 35–6.

28 In an interview with Toby Robertson, John Russell Brown remarked that
'Kent, who seems to be a vacillator on the page, in your production became a
most useful representative for common affection and feeling: a very important standard' (Robertson, 177).

29 The quotation is from F.P. Wilson, 94. McElroy briefly notes 'the formidable
ineffectuality that dogs his [Kent's] every move,' but does not consider the
audience's deep need for him to be effectual (213).

30 As Briggs pointed out in his edition of the play, Marlowe has conflated two
different attempts of Kent to rescue Edward (198–9). In 1327, after learning of
a plot by Kent and associates, Mortimer 'thought good to take away from
them the occasion of accomplishing their purpose' (Holinshed, 2:586) by
moving Edward from prison to prison. Two years later, after Edward had in
fact been dead for two years, the absurdly misinformed Kent attempted to
free him and was put to death.

31 Forker includes this in a catalogue of stage directions from Edward II which
exhibit characteristics 'usually taken as hallmarks of authorial copy' (Marlowe, Edward the Second, 11).

32 See Egan.

33 Garber, '"Vassal Actors,"' 72

34 Cartelli's argument that 'Marlowe encourages his audience to will Edward's
murder' (as an act of demystification of sovereignty) does not take into
account the teasing dramaturgy which I analyse in the following section
(Marlowe, Shakespeare, and the Economy of Theatrical Experience, 135).

35 For a thoughtful contrast of the dramatic rhythms of the two plays, see
Clemen.

36 Kelsall makes several brief but stimulating references to King Lear in his dis-

cussion of *Edward II* (47–69). In a long section entitled 'The Play and Its Shakespearean Relatives,' Forker notes many connections between *Edward II* and Shakespeare's history plays but makes no mention of *King Lear* (Marlowe, *Edward the Second*, 17–41).

37 For some suggestive comments on how *King Lear* afflicts its audience, see Pechter.

38 Leech, *Christopher Marlowe*, 142

39 Lamb, *Specimens of English Dramatic Poets*, London, 1808, quoted by F.P. Wilson, 101–2

40 Leech, *Christopher Marlowe*, 140

41 Robertson, 174

42 First noted by Briggs in his edition of Marlowe, *Edward II*, 193

43 For instances of this doubling, see Geckle, 100. Forker (Marlowe, *Edward the Second*, 111) notes a 1984 production which extends the doubling by having the same actor play Spencer Junior as well as Gaveston and Lightborn – all of whom are characterized as Edward's 'fatal lovers.'

44 In some productions Lightborn acts as if he is Edward's lover. In the 1990 RSC production at the Swan Theatre, Edward is 'anticipating a final moment of sexual pleasure [when] he greets as a lover Lightborn' (Burnett).

45 For the Augustinian tradition relating curiosity and the gaze, see Schwartz, 48–63.

46 In a useful comment on the staging of the scene, Craik notes the 'remote possibility' that original dialogue about the spit was omitted (84). Recently Orgel has criticized (on ethical and textual grounds) the nearly unanimous modern assumption that the spit was used in Elizabethan performances (*Impersonations*, 47–8).

47 The comments are from reviews of William Poel's revival of 1903 and Frank Benson's Stratford production two years later (quoted in Geckle, 79–80).

48 Harry Levin, 101. In their edition, Charlton and Waller comment that, although Lightborn appears to be preparing to use the spit, 'Naturally Marlowe proceeds no farther with it' (200).

49 The review is quoted in Geckle, 79. For details of Poel's handling of the murder scene, see Speaight, 179–80. In his New Mermaid edition Merchant also suggests that the murder occurs 'behind the arras of a stage pavilion or "inner stage"' (104).

50 Nicholas Brooke sensitively discusses the palliative effect of responses to Cordelia's death in 'The Ending of *King Lear*.'

51 For an acerbic critique of this approach to Edward's death, see Guy-Bray.

52 See, for instance, Taddeo di Bartolo's fresco of Hell at San Gimignano, illustrated in Hughes, 213.

53 Diehl, 'The Iconography of Violence in English Renaissance Tragedy,' 42–3
54 In his Introduction to his translation of Brecht's *Edward II: A Chronicle Play*, Eric Bentley says of Edward that 'At the end he is almost a saint' (xxv). Brecht's Edward is strengthened by his torment, and he is murdered by being choked rather than impaled.
55 Boyette, 47
56 Karen Cunningham, 218–19
57 By contrast, the conscience-stricken Edward of Michael Drayton's *Mortimeriados* has a 'vision of his bloody reign,' which includes the lords he killed as well as the 'rueful mangled host' whom he had incompetently led against the Scots (Drayton, 1:363).
58 Summers, 'Sex, Politics, and Self-Realization in *Edward II*,' 236. Cf. Boyette's remark that 'Edward's anal "crucifixion" issues not only in a cry that will raise the town but in a restorative justice for the commonweal as well' (47).
59 Peele, 'The Honour of the Honourable Order of the Garter,' in *The Life and Minor Works of George Peele*, 253

7: Damnation as Tantalization: *Doctor Faustus*

1 Though they are fairly evenly divided between an 'early date' (1589) and a 'late date' (1592) for *Doctor Faustus*, most commentators agree that the evidence is extremely slippery. For a balanced assessment leaning toward the early date, see *Doctor Faustus: A- and B-texts (1604, 1616)*, ed. Bevington and Rasmussen (Revels Plays), 1–3. For a tilt in the other direction, see *'Doctor Faustus': A 1604–Version Edition*, ed. Keefer, lv–lvi. There is a need for a thorough review of arguments and evidence.
2 Textual citations of *Doctor Faustus* are preceded by an 'A' or 'B' to indicate whether they are from the 1604 or 1616 quarto, respectively. The prefix 'AB' indicates that the quotation appears in both versions, with the act, scene, and line cited from 1604.
3 Marlowe's 'His waxen wings did mount above his reach' echoes Whitney's 'Let such beware which past their reach do mount,' but with a difference. While Whitney's phrasing is straightforward, Marlowe's blurs the issue of responsibility. As Kuriyama notes of Marlowe's line, 'it is not Icarus but his "waxen wings," not of his own but of his father's making, that do the mounting, as of their own volition' (98). We may even visualize an Icarus trying in vain to reach his wings, and Marlowe's next line suddenly – like Icarus in the woodcut – somersaults: 'And melting heavens conspired his overthrow.' Now Faustus seems less an immoral agent than the subject of a sportive conspiracy, the gift of mounting wings perhaps being part of a plot to destroy

him. The following lines are dominated by imagery which is central to Tantalus and irrelevant to Icarus: food and the underworld.

4 For a review of *Faustus* criticism stressing how 'interpretation tends toward antithesis and dispute,' see Bluestone.

5 Ornstein, 172

6 For the theological argument, see Stock. For the psychological argument, see Snow. For the psycho-theological argument, see Barber, 87–130.

7 In the 1604 text, the equivalent dialogue is between Robin and Rafe, with Robin promising him that 'I can make thee drunk with hippocras at any tavern in Europe for nothing' (2.2.24–6). Rafe does not respond with an expression of thirst, but he does become enthusiastic about Robin's subsequent offer of Nan Spit the kitchen-maid.

8 Following W.W. Greg, the Revels editors obscure the pun in 'take part of' by noting that in Marlowe's time the meaning could be 'take part in.' They do not mention that the first meaning which would come into a modern reader's mind ('take away part of') is equally relevant.

9 See *The English Faust Book*, 131–2. All subsequent references will be cited by chapter in the text.

10 Pettitt, 176–7

11 Without developing it, Alexander makes the suggestive point that 'while Faustus may play the harpy on this occasion his own desires are likely to remain for ever tantalizingly beyond his reach' (343).

12 Sheppeard, 'Icarus and the Old Man.'

13 The Old Man's teasing vial of grace follows lines of his which promise and immediately defer salvation: 'Ah, Doctor Faustus, that I might prevail / To guide thy steps unto the way of life, / By which sweet path thou mayst attain the goal / That shall conduct thee to celestial rest!' (A:5.1.36–9). Snow cites the unexpected enjambment of the third line into the fourth to illustrate the phenomenon of 'perpetual deferral, of the tendency of goals to become redundant means to further goals' (110). There may be an ironic parallel between the vial of grace and the dagger which Mephistopheles has handed Faustus just three lines earlier. Ricks shrewdly notes that, since Faustus cannot die, the dagger 'is cruelly – tantalizingly – absurd' (10).

14 From Harold Hobson's review (*Sunday Times*, 20 February 1966) of the OUDS production, reprinted in Jump, ed., 223

15 Honigmann has useful comments on what he styles the play's 'technique of uncertainty,' but he does not note the progressive deepening of confusion (175–8).

16 Ingram argues that Marlowe refers to well-known biblical passages so that

even a 'largely unintellectual audience' would 'recognize both the vastness and the perversity of his [Faustus'] intellect' (13).

17 For the relevance of Cambridge theological controversies to the play, see Sanders, 243–52, and Eriksen, 26–58. These studies are antithetical, with Sanders arguing for Marlowe's confusion about theology and Eriksen arguing for his lucid exploration of its contradictions. In a recent study, Kaufman concludes that '*Faustus* kennels packs of problems for theological interpretation' (82).

18 Eriksen's assumption (57 n96) that an Elizabethan audience would have been certain that Mephistopheles was lying does not take sufficient account of the theatrical power of the reversal.

19 *The Schoole of Abuse* (1579) in Kinney, 94. For the relevance of contemporary anti-theatrical polemics to the spectacles of *Faustus*, see Diehl, 'Dazzling Theatre.'

20 For the argument that the contradiction reflects the incompetent work of a reviser, see Daalder, 99 – a reference I owe to my colleague Michael Treadwell. In her recent edition of the play, Gill makes a similar argument (xxiv).

21 In this production, Mephistopheles also turns the pages of Robin's conjuring book later (Bevington and Rasmussen, Revels Plays edition, 60).

22 Rozett, 238. Rozett is inclined to think that the speech 'may not have been part of Marlowe's original design.' The Romantic desire to erase Faustus' passivity can be seen in Byron's *Manfred*, where his dying hero dismisses a fiend with the vaunt that '*Thou* didst not tempt, and thou couldst not tempt me; / I have not been thy dupe' (3.4.137–8).

23 The duped horse-courser exclaims of Faustus that 'I'll speak with him now, or I'll break his glass windows about his ears' (A:4.1.163–4).

24 Bluestone's fine treatment of how 'spectacle sustains ambiguity' in the play does not discuss the possible delusions of Faustus and the audience. Similarly, Hattaway characterizes the play as a 'great phantasmagoria of scenic properties' but has little to say about delusion (*Elizabethan Popular Theatre*, 160–85).

25 Hattaway, *Elizabethan Popular Theatre*, 166–7

26 The best critical discussion is in Sanders, 217. For the theological context, see Brennan.

27 Houseman, 198

28 According to Tydeman, Barton conceived of Faustus 'as a closet fantasist, an interpretation supported by the fact that none of the magical phenomena was presented as substantial, taking the form of dummies, puppets, masked creations, and dolls' (62). See also Bevington and Rasmussen, Revels Plays edition, 58–9.

29 For the convention of privileged vision, see Dessen, 59–60, 146–9.

30 Nashe, 1:354. In the 1616 text, the possibility of hallucination is increased by Mephistopheles' remark that Faustus' 'labouring brain / Begets a world of idle fantasies / To overreach the devil' (B:5.2.13–15).

31 Snow, 87

32 Weil, 77

33 Thus Bevington and Rasmussen (Revels Plays edition, 20) link the streaming blood with the Old Man's vial of grace as evidence of God's mercy.

34 Generally speaking, from the 1950s to the 1970s the critical pendulum swung in favour of the 1616 text as being closer to what Marlowe wrote, and in the last two decades it has swung back to the 1604 version. Most commentators now believe that the more than six hundred lines which are unique to 1616 include the 'additions to *Doctor Faustus*' for which Philip Henslowe paid two playwrights in 1602. It has not been proven, however, that these lines could not have been written by Marlowe, and they contain numerous echoes of unquestioned lines by Marlowe elsewhere in the play. The statement in the recent World's Classics edition is suitably cautious: 'The B-text seemingly incorporates the additions of 1602' (ed. Bevington and Rasmussen, xvi). The fullest arguments for 1616 are Greg's introductory matter to his parallel text edition, '*Doctor Faustus*' *1604–1616*, and Eriksen, 192–226. For the superiority of 1604 see, inter alia, Rasmussen, *A Textual Companion to 'Doctor Faustus'*. In the light of Rasmussen's assertion that 'Scholars who are chiefly interested in Christopher Marlowe will have to concentrate exclusively on the A-text,' it is prudent to recall Honigmann's recent observation that 'Neither of the two texts transmits the original complete play; both texts may well transmit, in debased form, material that had a place in the lost original' (183).

35 In 'The Two Hells of Doctor Faustus: A Polytheatrical Vision,' Kott argues that the play has two conceptions of hell, one tragic and modern, the other medieval and carnivalesque (Kott, 1–27). Ricks notes the play's many suggestive equivalences of hell and the plague.

36 Though various forms of tantalization appear in early Jewish and Christian apocalyptic literature (Himmelfarb, 92–3), they largely disappear from accounts of hell in the Middle Ages.

37 The Faust Book translator says that reaching from hell to close to heaven is a ladder which the damned ascend to reach God, but 'when they are at the very highest degree, they fall down again into their former miseries' (110).

38 For some of the connections between *Doctor Faustus* and *Pierce Penniless*, see Nicholl, *A Cup of News*, 94–8.

39 Nashe, 1:218

40 Nashe, 1:219. The devil refuses to resolve the contradiction, saying 'it is not for me to intimate, because it is prejudicial to our monarchy,' which recalls Mephistopheles' comment that he is bound to tell Faustus only what 'is not against our kingdom' (AB:2.3.71).

41 Nashe, 3:170

42 For the frustrated ambitions of Marlowe and other University Wits, see Watt, 37.

43 For the history of construing hell as a state of spiritual deprivation, see Patrides, 182–99, and Creasy.

44 Richard Sibbes (1639), quoted in Patrides, 194

45 Creasy calls the idea of *poena damni* in these lines 'the primary hell of *Doctor Faustus*' (52). See also Cole, 192–3, 204–7, and Briggs.

46 Bartels, 130–2

47 Bevington and Rasmussen, eds., Revels Plays edition, 45

48 Empson, 172

49 The mandated 'Homily against Gluttony and Drunkenness' (1563) cautions that 'if we in eating and drinking exceed, when God of his large liberality sendeth plenty, he will soon change plenty into scarceness' (*Certaine Sermons or Homilies*, 96). Cited in Walter and Wrightson, 29.

50 For a thorough discussion of flying thrones in public playhouses, see Astington, 'Descent Machinery in the Playhouse.' Astington refutes Glynne Wickham's argument (often brought to bear against Marlowe's authorship of this scene) that descent machinery was not available in public playhouses during Marlowe's lifetime.

51 In the 1616 quarto there is no stage direction marking the ascent of the throne; the stage direction after the Good Angel's final words reads simply '*Exit*.' For a possible exit via an ascending throne, see the stage direction in Greene's *Alphonsus* (c.1587): '*Exit, Venus. Or, if you can conveniently, let a chair come down from the top of the stage, and draw her up*' (quoted in Astington, 'Descent Machinery in the Playhouse').

52 See the editions of the play by Bevington and Rasmussen, (Revel Plays), 48; and by Keefer, xv

53 A notable exception to the view that the 1616 damnation embodies an orthodox critique of Faustus is Sinfield's argument that it dramatizes problematic aspects of Calvinist theology (234–7).

54 Bevington and Rasmussen, Revels Plays edition, 76

55 Turner connects Faustus' drop of blood with Dives without mentioning Marlowe's use of the story in the preceding lines in 1616 (168).

56 Tydeman, 60

57 Morgan, 28

58 Leech gives a perceptive account of the 'strange things' in the Epilogue (*Poet for the Stage*, 102–3).

59 Cf. 'It is quite like Marlowe to devise his tragedy out of the terrors inspired by the controversial certainties and final mysteries of Christian theology and then to turn around and exhort his audience not to think about what he has forced them to think about' (Robert G. Hunter, 66).

8: Frustrating the Story of Desire: *Hero and Leander*

1 See Bush, *Mythology and the Renaissance Tradition in English Poetry*, 121–36; Hallett Smith, 64–130; Keach; Hulse, 93–124. For sceptical comment on this approach and useful (but brief) comments on the context provided by Marlowe's work, see Adamson.

2 Bush, *Mythology and the Renaissance Tradition in English Poetry*, 122

3 For echoes of *All Ovid's Elegies* in *Hero and Leander*, see Bush, 'Notes on Marlowe's *Hero and Leander*.' To his list one can add the revealing echo of 'Then though death rakes my bones in funeral fire / I'll live, and as he pulls me down mount higher' (*Elegies* 1.15.41–2) in *Hero and Leander*: 'For hitherto he did but fan the fire, / And kept it down that it might mount the higher' (525–6).

4 In a pioneering application of reader response criticism to the poem, Sheidley noted that 'Marlowe assaults the reader, titillating and arousing his senses through artful description, suggestion, and delay' (53). He also observed that 'the punishment of Tantalus ... forms one model for the poem's rhetorical technique.' There are useful comments on the teasing of the reader's 'aural curiosity' in Royston.

5 The fullest study in English of Musaeus' poem and its Renaissance offshoots is Braden, *The Classics and English Renaissance Poetry*, 55–153. Braden does not, however, note the parallels with the Icarus story.

6 In 'Hero and Leander: Góngora and Marlowe,' 338–9, Segal notes parallels between Icarus and Leander, adding that Francisco de Quevedo links the two figures in a sonnet. Though Segal argues that Marlowe (like Góngora) burlesques the Hero and Leander story, he does not comment on Marlowe's pointedly un-Icarian treatment of Leander.

7 Ovid, *Heroides 18* (49–52) from the Loeb edition, trans. Showerman, 247

8 In quoting *Hero and Leander* from Maclure's Revels edition of *The Poems*, I have numbered the lines continuously rather than observing with him the post-Marlovian division into a first and second 'Sestiad.'

9 George Chapman's vigorous translation of Musaeus, first published in 1619, is reprinted in Donno.

10 'Ah, do not still my soul thus tantalise,' in Robert Tofte, *Laura* xii (1597), in Lee, ed., 2:408. Other sonnets in which the lover likens himself to Tantalus are Richard Lynche's *Diella* xxv (1596) and William Smith's *Chloris* iii (1596), both in Lee (2:3l4, 326). Raleigh's comment on Tantalus is from *The History of the World* (book 2, chapter 13).

11 See Kerrigan and Braden.

12 Lyly, 380

13 Drayton, 2:372

14 Ovid and *Hero and Leander* meet in Robert Burton's account of 'provocations to lust' in *The Anatomy of Melancholy* (part 3 sec.2 mem.2 subs.4), where a discussion of fleeing and following contains two quotations from Marlowe's poem (489–90, 779–80).

15 Without reference to tantalization, this general movement from seeing and talking to touching and doing has been noted by Morris, 119, and by Godshalk, 298–300.

16 Abraham Fraunce says of the Harpies that 'Virgil describeth them 3. aeneid. as the most detestable monsters that ever issued out of the Stygian lake' (28 verso).

17 In Guyon's descent to the underworld in book 2 of the *Faerie Queene*, Spenser connects the two myths, introducing Tantalus soon after mentioning the Hesperidean apples which 'Hercules with conquest bold / Got from great Atlas daughters' (2.7.54).

18 Hulse, 31

19 Harry Levin notes the parallel between Mercury's theft and Tantalus' crime (142) without pursuing the idea of tantalization in the poem.

20 The Revels edition's emendation of 'in aspiring' to 'inaspiring' makes nonsense of the passage, as Bowers notes (*Christopher Marlowe: The Complete Works*, 2:502).

21 Baldwin, 'Marlowe's Musaeus'

22 Braden (*The Classics and English Renaissance Poetry*, 135) notes that 'Marlowe's principal use of Mousaios as a direct tool of composition' concludes with Hero's invitation to Leander to visit her tower (357–9).

23 Gill, in Marlowe, *The Complete Works of Christopher Marlowe*, 1:185

24 Petowe's 'Second Part' of *Hero and Leander* is printed in Orgel's edition of Marlowe, *The Complete Poems and Translations*, 93–110. Petowe's comment that *Hero and Leander* was 'penned by that admired poet Marlowe, but not finished (being prevented by sudden death)' appears to derive from Blount's dedicatory epistle and thus to have no authority.

25 For Chapman's appropriation and containment of Marlowe for his own, very different ends, see Campbell, and James Shapiro, *Rival Playwrights*, 22–5.

26 Morris, 115, 131
27 Bush, *Mythology and the Renaissance Tradition in English Poetry*, 127
28 Campbell, 263
29 Braden, *The Classics and English Renaissance Poetry*, 141
30 Royston, 31–2
31 Miller, 781
32 For the Elizabethan interest in lifelike artifice, see Gent, 54–9.
33 When Adonis falls on his back and Venus lands on top of him, the narrator remarks that 'worse than Tantalus' is her annoy, / To clip Elysium and to lack her joy' (599–600). The next stanza begins: 'Even so poor birds, deceiv'd with painted grapes, / Do surfeit by the eye and pine the maw ...'
34 Weever, 'Faunus and Melliflora' (1600), 278
35 Sheidley, 53
36 Gill, in Marlowe, *The Complete Works*, 1:185. In an earlier version of this essay, Gill followed the statement about 'glorious and harmonious fulfillment' with the still more dubious comment that the poem leaves the lovers 'on the floor of Hero's bedroom in a triumphant, happy, consummated tangle' ('Marlowe and the Art of Translation,' 340).
37 Braden, *The Classics and English Renaissance Poetry*, 152
38 Fifty lines earlier, Marlowe had made the association of the shamed Hero with Diana explicit: 'She, overcome with shame and sallow fear, / Like chaste Diana when Actaeon spied her ...' (744–5).
39 Segal, 'Hero and Leander,' 356
40 Miller notes that 'if Hero at first seems empowered by her status as universal cynosure, this impression is soon overtaken by a predatory delight in her humiliation' (764).
41 See Nelson, 74, and Heywood, 40.
42 Leech, *Christopher Marlowe*, 181
43 When, for instance, Leander is described as having 'A brow for love to banquet royally' (86), the brow can be either the table for the banquet or (like Pelops' shoulder) the banquet itself.
44 In an unpublished essay, my former student Christopher Jackson emphasized the allusions to Tantalus, Sisyphus, and Ixion and suggestively remarked that 'In a sense, the entire poem takes place in hell.' He also characterized the poem as 'Outside, a Hallmark card; inside, verses by de Sade.'
45 An anonymous sonnet in *Tottel's Miscellany* titled 'Hell tormenteth not the damned ghosts so sore as unkindness the lover' groups 'guileful Promethus' [*sic*] with Tantalus and Sisyphus (Rollins, ed., 1:131). Geffrey Whitney's *A Choice of Emblemes* (1586) places woodcuts of Tantalus and Prometheus on facing leaves (74–5).

46 Richard Lynche, *The Fountaine of Ancient Fiction* (1599), sig. Piii. Cf. Spenser's reference to 'The hellish Harpies' (*Faerie Queene*, 2.12.36).
47 This is the title of an anonymous poem which appears in the second and subsequent editions of *Tottel's Miscellany* (Rollins, ed., 1:217–18). Also see George Turberville's long lyric 'Of the torments of Hell and the pains of Love,' in his *Epitaphes, Epigrams, Songs and Sonets* (1567), 298–302.
48 Thomas Watson, *The Hekatompathia, or Passionate Centurie of Love* (1582), 76. Watson prefaces his poem with a prose note for the 'vulgar sort' describing the punishments of the poem's mythological figures.
49 Thomas Edwards, *Cephalus and Procris* (1595) in Donno, ed., 172 (the lines occur in a passage full of Marlovian echoes)
50 For a discussion of 'anguish, shame, and rage' as 'terms [which] tie up a great many strands in the poem,' see Steane, 333. Collins notes that these terms characterize all the poem's climactic moments of frustration.
51 I owe this observation to my colleague Elizabeth Popham.

Afterword

1 Heaney, 17–37
2 Emerson, *Uncollected Writings*, 120–1. For references to Tantalus in Emerson's *Journals*, see 5:96–7, 11:146, and 12:47.
3 For a New England view which does entertain the thought of tantalization as divine cruelty, see Emily Dickinson's '"Heaven" – is what I cannot reach!' (109).

Works Cited

Adamson, Jane. 'Marlowe, *Hero and Leander*, and the Art of Leaping in Poetry.' *Critical Review* 17 (1974), 59–81.

Agrippa, Henry Cornelius. *Of the Vanitie and Vncertaintie of Artes and Sciences.* Ed. Catherine M. Dunn. Northridge: California State University, 1974.

Alciatus, Andreas. *Andreas Alciatus.* Index Emblematicus. Ed. Peter M. Daly. 2 vols. Toronto: University of Toronto Press, 1985.

– *Emblemata cum Commentariis.* Commentary by Claude Mignaut. Padua, 1621; rpt. in *The Renaissance and the Gods* 25. New York: Garland, 1976.

Alexander, Nigel. 'The Performance of Christopher Marlowe's *Dr. Faustus.*' *Proceedings of the British Academy* 57 (1971), 331–49.

Allen, Don Cameron. 'Marlowe's *Dido* and the Tradition.' In *Essays on Shakespeare and Elizabethan Drama in Honor of Hardin Craig.* Ed. Richard Hosley. Columbia: University of Missouri Press, 1962, 55–68.

– 'On *Venus and Adonis.*' In *Elizabethan and Jacobean Studies Presented to F.P. Wilson.* Ed. Herbert Davis. Oxford: Clarendon, 1959, 100–11.

Allen, John Michael. *Sovereignty and Intelligence: Spying and Court Culture in the English Renaissance.* Palo Alto: Stanford University Press, 1993.

Altman, Joel B. *The Tudor Play of Mind.* Berkeley: University of California Press, 1978.

Aneau, Bartholomy. *Picta Poesis.* Lyon: Bonhomme, 1552.

Astington, John H. 'Descent Machinery in the Playhouse.' *Medieval and Renaissance Drama in England* 2 (1985), 119–33.

– 'The London Stage in the 1580s.' In *The Elizabethan Theatre XI.* Ed. A.L. Magnusson and C.E. McGee. Port Credit, Ont.: P.D. Meany, 1990, 1–18.

Bacon, Francis. *Francis Bacon: A Selection of His Works.* Ed. Sidney Warhaft. Toronto: Macmillan of Canada, 1965.

Baldwin, T.W. 'Marlowe's Musaeus.' *Journal of English and German Philology* 54 (1955), 478–85.
– *On the Literary Genetics of Shakespere's Poems and Sonnets.* Urbana: University of Illinois Press, 1950.
Barber, C.L. *Creating Elizabethan Tragedy: The Theatre of Marlowe and Kyd.* Ed. Richard P. Wheeler. Chicago: University of Chicago Press, 1988.
Bartels, Emily C. *Spectacles of Strangeness: Imperialism, Alienation, and Marlowe.* Philadelphia: University of Pennsylvania Press, 1993.
Barton, Anne. 'Eloquent Carnage.' *Times Literary Supplement.* 11 Sept. 1992, 19.
Bate, Jonathan. *Shakespeare and Ovid.* Oxford: Clarendon, 1993.
Battenhouse, Roy W. *Marlowe's 'Tamburlaine': A Study in Renaissance Moral Philosophy.* Nashville: Vanderbilt University Press, 1941.
– 'Protestant Apologetics and the Subplot of 2 *Tamburlaine.' English Literary Renaissance* 3 (1973), 30–43.
Bawcutt, N.W. 'Machiavelli and Marlowe's *The Jew of Malta.' Renaissance Drama* 3 (1970), 3–49.
Belsey, Catherine. 'Desire's Excess and the English Renaissance Theatre: *Edward II, Troilus and Cressida, Othello.'* In *Erotic Politics: Desire on the Renaissance Stage.* Ed. Susan Zimmerman. New York: Routledge, 1992, 84–99.
– *Desire: Love Stories in Western Culture.* Oxford: Blackwell, 1994.
– 'Love as Trompe-l'oeil: Taxonomies of Desire in *Venus and Adonis.' Shakespeare Quarterly* 46 (1995), 257–76.
Belt, Debra. 'Anti-Theatricalism and Rhetoric in Marlowe's *Edward II.' English Literary Renaissance* 21 (1991), 134–60.
Bentley, Gerald Eades. *The Profession of Dramatist in Shakespeare's Time 1590–1642.* Princeton: Princeton University Press, 1971.
Berry, Ralph. *Shakespeare and the Awareness of the Audience.* London: Macmillan, 1985.
Bevington, David. *From 'Mankind' to Marlowe: Growth of Structure in the Popular Drama of Tudor England.* Cambridge, Mass.: Harvard University Press, 1962.
Bevington, David, and James Shapiro. '"What are kings, when regiment is gone?": The Decay of Ceremony in *Edward II.'* In Friedenreich et al., 263–78.
Birringer, Johannes H. 'Marlowe's Violent Stage: "Mirrors of Honor" in *Tamburlaine.' English Literary History* 51 (1984), 222–34.
Bluestone, Max. '*Libido Speculandi:* Doctrine and Dramaturgy in Contemporary Interpretations of Marlowe's *Doctor Faustus.'* In *Reinterpretations of Elizabethan Drama.* Ed. Norman Rabkin. New York: Columbia University Press, 1969, 33–88.
Boas, Frederick S. *Christopher Marlowe: A Biographical and Critical Study.* Rev. ed. Oxford: Oxford University Press, 1953.

Bolgar, R.R. *The Classical Heritage and Its Beneficiaries.* New York: Harper and Row, 1954.

Bono, Barbara J. *Literary Transvaluation: From Vergilian Epic to Shakespearean Tragicomedy.* Berkeley: University of California Press, 1984.

Boyette, Purvis E. 'Wanton Humour and Wanton Poets: Homosexuality in Marlowe's *Edward II*.' *Tulane Studies in English* 22 (1977), 33–50.

Boyle, A.J. '*His Epvlis Locvs:* The Tragic Worlds of Seneca's *Agamemnon* and *Thyestes*.' In *Seneca Tragicus: 'Ramus' Essays on Senecan Drama.* Ed. A.J. Boyle. Berwick, Victoria (Australia): Aureal, 1983.

Braden, Gordon. *The Classics and English Renaissance Poetry.* New Haven: Yale University Press, 1978.

– *Renaissance Tragedy and the Senecan Tradition: Anger's Privilege.* New Haven: Yale University Press, 1985.

Bray, Alan. 'Homosexuality and the Signs of Male Friendship in Elizabethan England.' In *Queering the Renaissance.* Ed. Jonathan Goldberg. Durham: Duke University Press, 1991, 48–77.

– *Homosexuality in Renaissance England.* London: Gay Men's Press, 1982.

Brecht, Bertolt. *Brecht on Theatre: The Development of an Aesthetic.* Ed. and trans. John Willett. London: Methuen, 1978.

– *Edward II: A Chronicle Play.* Trans. Eric Bentley. New York: Grove, 1966.

Bredbeck, Gregory W. *Sodomy and Interpretation: Marlowe to Milton.* Ithaca: Cornell University Press, 1991.

Brennan, Michael. 'Christopher Marlowe's *Dr. Faustus* and Urbanus Rhegius's *An Homelye ... of Good and Evill Angels*.' *Notes and Queries* 38 (1991), 466–9.

Briggs, William D. 'Marlowe's *Faustus*.' *Modern Language Notes* 38 (1923), 385–93.

Brinker, Ludger. 'The Art of Marlowe's Prologues: Subtle Innovations within Traditional Patterns.' *Cahiers Élisabéthains* 42 (1992), 1–15.

Bristol, Michael D. *Shakespeare's America, America's Shakespeare.* New York: Routledge, 1990.

Brooke, C.F. Tucker. 'The Reputation of Christopher Marlowe.' *Transactions of the Connecticut Academy of Arts and Sciences* 25 (1922), 347–408.

Brooke, Nicholas. 'The Ending of *King Lear*.' In *Shakespeare 1564–1964*. Ed. Edward A. Bloom. Providence: Brown University Press, 1964, 71–87.

– 'Marlowe the Dramatist.' In *Elizabethan Theatre.* Ed. John Russell Brown and Bernard Harris. Stratford Upon Avon Studies 9. London: Edward Arnold, 1961, 86–105.

Brown, William J. 'Marlowe's Debasement of Bajazet: Foxe's *Actes and Monuments* and *Tamburlaine, Part I*.' *Renaissance Quarterly* 24 (1971), 38–48.

Bruno, Giordano. *The Heroic Frenzies.* Trans. Paul Eugene Memmo, Jr. University

214   Works Cited

of North Carolina Studies in Romance Languages and Literatures 50. Chapel Hill: University of North Carolina Press, 1964.
Bruster, Douglas. '"Come to the Tent Again": "The Passionate Shepherd," Dramatic Rape and Lyric Time.' *Criticism* 33 (1991), 49–72.
Bugliani-Knox, Francesca. 'Atheist or Ironist?' *Times Literary Supplement*, 18 July 1997, 26.
Bunker, Henry Alden. 'Tantalus: A Preoedipal Figure of Myth.' *Psychoanalytical Quarterly* 22 (1953), 159–73.
Burke, Kenneth. *Counter-Statement*. Chicago: University of Chicago Press, 1957.
Burke, Seán. *The Death and Return of the Author: Criticism and Subjectivity in Barthes, Foucault, and Derrida*. Edinburgh: Edinburgh University Press, 1992.
Burnett, Mark Thornton. 'Edward II' [review of a production at the Swan Theatre]. *Marlowe Society of America Newsletter* 10:2 (1990), 3.
– 'Tamburlaine and the Body.' *Criticism* 33 (1991), 31–47.
Bush, Douglas. *Mythology and the Renaissance Tradition in English Poetry*. Rev. ed. New York: W.W. Norton, 1963.
– 'Notes on Marlowe's *Hero and Leander*.' *PMLA* 44 (1929), 760–4.
Byron, George Gordon, Lord. *The Complete Poetical Works*. Ed. Jerome J. McGann. 7 vols. Oxford: Clarendon, 1986.
Campbell, Marion. '*Desunt Nonnulla*: The Construction of Marlowe's *Hero and Leander* as an Unfinished Poem.' *English Literary History* 51 (1984), 141–68.
Camus, Albert. *The Myth of Sisyphus and Other Essays*. Trans. Justin O'Brien. New York: Vintage, 1955.
Carlson, Marvin. 'Theatre Audiences and the Reading of Performance.' In *Interpreting the Theatrical Past: Essays in the Historiography of Performance*. Ed. Thomas Postlewait. Iowa City: University of Iowa Press, 1989.
Cartelli, Thomas. 'Marlowe and the New World.' In Grantley and Roberts, 110–18.
– *Marlowe, Shakespeare, and the Economy of Theatrical Experience*. Philadelphia: University of Pennsylvania Press, 1991.
Cartwright, Kent. *Shakespearean Tragedy and Its Double*. University Park: University of Pennsylvania State Press, 1991.
Cassirer, Ernst. *The Individual and the Cosmos in Renaissance Philosophy*. Trans. Mario Domandi. Philadelphia: University of Pennsylvania Press, 1963.
Certaine Sermons or Homilies. Ed. Mary Ellen Rickey and Thomas B. Stroup. Gainesville: Scholar's Facsimiles and Reprints, 1968.
Chambers, E.K. *The Elizabethan Stage*. 4 vols. Oxford: Clarendon, 1923.
Chaucer, Geoffrey. *The Works of Geoffrey Chaucer*. Ed. F.N. Robinson. 2nd ed. Boston: Houghton Mifflin, 1957.

Cheney, Patrick. *Marlowe's Counterfeit Profession: Ovid, Spenser, Counter-Nation-hood*. Toronto: University of Toronto Press, 1997.

Clemen, Wolfgang. 'Shakespeare and Marlowe.' In *Shakespeare 1971*. Ed. Clifford Leech and J.M.R. Margeson. Toronto: University of Toronto Press, 1972, 123–32.

Cole, Douglas. *Suffering and Evil in the Plays of Christopher Marlowe*. Princeton: Princeton University Press, 1962.

Collins, S. Ann. 'Sundrie Shapes, Committing Headie Ryots, Incest, Rapes: Functions of Myth in Determining Narrative in Marlowe's *Hero and Leander*.' *Mosaic* 4 (1970), 107–22.

Comes, Natalis [Natale Conti]. *Mythologiae*. Venice, 1567; rpt. in *The Renaissance and the Gods* 11. New York: Garland, 1976.

Conrad, Peter. *The Everyman History of English Literature*. London: J.H. Dent, 1985.

Cooper, Thomas. *Thesaurus Linguae Romanae et Britannicae* (1565).

Cope, Jackson I. 'Marlowe's *Dido* and the Titillating Children.' *English Literary Renaissance* 4 (1974), 315–25.

Copley, Frank O. *Exclusus Amator: A Study in Latin Love Poetry*. Baltimore: American Philological Association, 1956.

Craik, T.W. 'The Reconstruction of Stage Action from Early Dramatic Texts.' In *The Elizabethan Theatre V*. Ed. G.R. Hibbard. Toronto: Macmillan of Canada, 1975.

Creasy, William C. 'The Shifting Landscape of Hell.' *Comitatus* 11 (1980), 40–65.

Crundell, H.W. 'Nashe and *Doctor Faustus*.' *Notes and Queries* 9 (1962), 327.

Cunningham, J.S., and Roger Warren. '*Tamburlaine the Great* Re-discovered.' *Shakespeare Survey* 31 (1978), 155–62.

Cunningham, Karen. 'Renaissance Execution and Marlovian Elocution: The Drama of Death.' *PMLA* 105 (1990), 209–22.

Curtis, Mark H. 'The Alienated Intellectuals of Early Stuart England.' In *Crisis in Europe 1560–1660*. Ed. Trevor Aston. New York: Anchor, 1967, 309–31.

Cutts, John P. *The Left Hand of God: A Critical Interpretation of the Plays of Christopher Marlowe*. Haddonfield, NJ: Haddonfield House, 1973.

Daalder, Joost. 'Bibliography, Criticism, and the Problem of *Doctor Faustus*.' *Bibliographical Society of Australia and New Zealand Bulletin* 15 (1991), 89–102.

Davis, John T. *Fictus Adulter: Poet as Actor in the 'Amores.'* Amsterdam: J.C. Gieben, 1989.

de Bosque, Andrée. *Mythologie et Maniérisme*. Paris: Albin Michel, 1985.

de Grazia, Sebastian. *Machiavelli in Hell*. New York: Vintage, 1994.

Deats, Sara Munson. 'Myth and Metamorphosis in Marlowe's *Edward II.' Texas Studies in Literature and Language* 22 (1980), 304–21.

Dessen, Alan. *Elizabethan Stage Conventions and Modern Interpretations.* Cambridge: Cambridge University Press, 1984.

Dickinson, Emily. *The Complete Poems.* Ed. Thomas H. Johnson. Boston: Little, Brown, 1960.

Diehl, Huston. 'Dazzling Theatre: Renaissance drama in the Age of Reform.' *Journal of Medieval and Renaissance Studies* 22 (1992), 211–35.

– 'The Iconography of Violence in English Renaissance Tragedy.' *Renaissance Drama* 11 (1980), 27–43.

Donne, John. *The Poems of John Donne.* Ed. Herbert J.C. Grierson. 2 vols. London: Oxford University Press, 1912.

– *The Sermons of John Donne.* Ed. George R. Potter and Evelyn M. Simpson. 10 vols. Berkeley: University of California Press, 1962.

Donno, Elizabeth Story, ed. *Elizabethan Minor Epics.* New York: Columbia University Press, 1963.

Drayton, Michael. *The Works of Michael Drayton.* Ed. J. William Hebel. 5 vols. Oxford: Blackwell, 1961.

Duane, Carol Leventen. 'Marlowe's Mixed Messages. A Model for Shakespeare?' *Medieval and Renaissance Drama in England* 3 (1986), 51–67.

Du Quesnay, I.M. Le M. 'The *Amores.*' In *Ovid.* Ed. J.W. Binns. London: Routledge and Kegan Paul, 1973, 1–48.

Duncan, Douglas. *Ben Jonson and the Lucianic Tradition.* Cambridge: Cambridge University Press, 1979.

Easthope, Anthony. *Poetry and Phantasy.* Cambridge: Cambridge University Press, 1989.

Edwards, Thomas. *Cephalus and Procris.* In Donno, 155–79.

Egan, Robert. 'Kent and the Audience: The Character as Spectator.' *Shakespeare Quarterly* 32 (1981), 146–54.

Ellis-Fermor, Una. *Christopher Marlowe.* 1927: rpt. Hamden, Conn.: Archon, 1967.

Emerson, Ralph Waldo. *Journals and Miscellaneous Notebooks.* Ed. William H. Gilman. 16 vols. Cambridge, Mass.: Harvard University Press, 1960–82.

– 'Tantalus.' In *Uncollected Writings.* 1912; rept. Port Washington, NY: Kennikat, 1971, 115–22.

Empson, William. *Faustus and the Censor.* Ed. John Henry Jones. New York: Basil Blackwell, 1987.

The English Faust Book. Ed. John Henry Jones. Cambridge: Cambridge University Press, 1994.

English Renaissance Drama and Audience Response. Special Issue of *Studies in the Literary Imagination* 26:1 (1993).

Erasmus, Desiderius. *Adages I vi 1 to I x 100*. Trans. Margaret Mann Phillips. The Collected Works of Erasmus, vol. 32. Toronto: University of Toronto Press, 1982.

– *Adages II i 1 to II vi 100*. Trans. R.A.B. Mynors. The Collected Works of Erasmus, vol. 33. Toronto: University of Toronto Press, 1991.

– *On Copy of Words and Ideas*. Trans. D.B. King and H.D. Rix. Milwaukee: Marquette University Press, 1963.

– *Spiritualia*. Ed. John W. O'Malley. The Collected Works of Erasmus, vol. 66. Toronto: University of Toronto Press, 1988.

Eriksen, Roy T. *The Forme of Faustus Fortunes: A Study of the Tragedie of Doctor Faustus*. 1616. Oslo: Solum Forlag, 1987.

Esler, Anthony. *The Aspiring Mind of the Elizabethan Younger Generation*. Durham, NC: Duke University Press, 1966.

Fehrenbach, Robert J., et al. *Concordance to the Plays, Poems, and Translations of Christopher Marlowe*. Ithaca: Cornell University Press, 1982.

Ficino, Marsilio. *The Letters of Marsilio Ficino*. Trans. Members of the Language Department of the School of Economic Science, London. 5 vols. London: Shepheard-Walwyn, 1978.

– 'Marsilio Ficino's Commentary on Plato's *Symposium*: The Text and Translation.' Trans. Sears Jayne. University of Missouri Studies 19. Columbia: University of Missouri, 1944, 121–239.

Field, Edward. *Stand Up, Friend, with Me*. New York: Grove Press, 1963.

Fieler, Frank B. *'Tamburlaine, Part One' and Its Audience*. Gainesville: University of Florida Press, 1961.

Foakes, R.A. *Hamlet Versus Lear: Cultural Politics and Shakespeare's Art*. Cambridge: Cambridge University Press, 1993.

Forsythe, R.S. '"The Passionate Shepherd" and English Poetry.' *PMLA* 40 (1925), 692–742.

Fraunce, Abraham. *The Third Part of the Countesse of Penbrokes Yvychurch*. 1592; rpt. in *The Renaissance and the Gods* 13. New York: Garland, 1976.

Freeman, Arthur. 'Marlowe, Kyd, and the Dutch Church Libel.' *English Literary Renaissance* 3 (1973), 44–52.

Freer, Coburn. 'Lies and Lying in *The Jew of Malta*.' In Friedenreich et al., 143–65.

Freud, Sigmund. 'On the Universal Tendency to Debasement in the Sphere of Love.' In *On Sexuality*. Pelican Freud Library 7. Harmondsworth: Penguin, 1977.

Fricker, Robert. 'The Dramatic Structure of *Edward II.' English Studies* 34 (1953), 128–44.

Friedenreich, Kenneth, et al. *A Poet and a Filthy Play-Maker: New Essays on Christopher Marlowe*. New York: AMS, 1988.

Fulgentius. *The Mythologies*. In *Fulgentius the Mythographer*. Trans. Leslie George Whitbread. Columbus: Ohio State University Press, 1971.

Ganz, Timothy. *Early Greek Myth: A Guide to Literary and Artistic Sources*. Baltimore: Johns Hopkins University Press, 1993.

Garber, Marjorie. '"Infinite Riches in a Little Room": Closure and Enclosure in Marlowe.' In Kernan, 3–21.

– '"Vassal Actors": The Role of the Audience in Shakespearean Tragedy.' *Renaissance Drama* 9 (1978), 71–89.

Gardner, Helen. 'The Second Part of *Tamburlaine the Great.' Modern Language Review* 37 (1942), 18–24.

Gatti, Hilary. *The Renaissance Drama of Knowledge: Giordano Bruno in England*. London: Routledge, 1989.

Geckle, George L. *'Tamburlaine' and 'Edward II.'* Text and Performance. London: Macmillan, 1988.

Geneva Bible. 1560. Intro. Lloyd E. Berry. Madison: University of Wisconsin Press, 1969.

Gent, Lucy. *Picture and Poetry*. Leamington Spa: James Hall, 1982.

Gentillet, Innocent. *A Discourse ... Against Nicholas Machiavell*. Trans. Simon Patericke. London, 1602.

Giamatti, A. Bartlett. 'Marlowe: The Arts of Illusion.' *Yale Review* 61 (1972), 530–43.

Gibbons, Brian. 'Unstable Proteus: Marlowe's *Tragedy of Dido, Queen of Carthage.'* In Morris, 27–46.

Gifford, Humfrey. *A Posie of Gilloflowers*. 1580. Ed. F.J.H. Darton. London: Hawthornden, 1933.

Gill, Roma. 'Marlowe and the Art of Translation.' In Friedenreich et al., 327–41.

– 'Snakes Leape by Verse.' In Morris, 133–50.

Ginzburg, Carlo. 'High and Low: The Theme of Forbidden Knowledge in the Sixteenth and Seventeenth Centuries.' *Past and Present* 73 (1976), 28–41.

Glenn, Edgar M. *'The Metamorphoses': Ovid's Roman Games*. Lanham, Md.: University Press of America, 1986.

Godshalk, William L. *'Hero and Leander*: The Sense of an Ending.' In Friedenreich et al., 293–314.

Goldberg, Dena. 'Sacrifice in Marlowe's *The Jew of Malta.' Studies in English Literature* 32 (1992), 233–45.

Goldberg, Jonathan. 'Textual Properties.' *Shakespeare Quarterly* 37 (1986), 213–17.

Goldman, Michael. 'Marlowe and the Histrionics of Ravishment.' In Kernan, 22–40.

Gomez, Jesus Pastor. *El Simbolismo de Tantalo: Estudio fenomenológico*. Madrid: Editorial Coloquio, 1989.

Gomme, Alice Bertha. *The Traditional Games of England, Scotland, and Ireland*. 1894–8; rpt. London: Thames and Hudson, 1984.

Goya, Francisco. *The Complete Etchings of Goya*. New York: Crown, 1943.

Grantley, Darryll, and Peter Roberts, eds. *Christopher Marlowe and English Renaissance Culture*. Aldershot: Scolar Press, 1996.

Greenblatt, Stephen. *Learning to Curse: Essays in Early Modern Culture*. New York: Routledge, 1990.

– *Renaissance Self-Fashioning: From More to Shakespeare*. Chicago: University of Chicago Press, 1981.

Greene, Thomas. *The Vulnerable Text: Essays on Renaissance Literature*. New York: Columbia University Press, 1986.

Grimal, Pierre. *The Dictionary of Classical Mythology*. Trans. A.R. Maxwell-Hyslop. New York: Blackwell, 1986.

Gross, John. *Shylock: A Legend and Its Legacy*. New York: Simon and Schuster, 1994.

Gurr, Andrew. 'The General and the Caviar: Learned Audiences in the Early Theatre.' *Studies in the Literary Imagination* 26 (1993), 7–20.

– *Playgoing in Shakespeare's London*. Cambridge: Cambridge University Press, 1987. 2nd ed. 1996.

Guy-Bray, Stephen. 'Homophobia and the Depoliticizing of *Edward II*.' *English Studies in Canada* 17 (1991), 125–33.

Haber, Judith. 'Submitting to History: Marlowe's *Edward II*.' In *Enclosure Acts: Sexuality, Property, and Culture in Early Modern England*. Ed. Richard Burt and John Michael Archer. Ithaca: Cornell University Press, 1994, 170–84.

Hall, Peter. *Peter Hall's Diaries*. Ed. John Goodwin. New York: Harper and Row, 1984.

Harris, Wendell V. *Literary Meaning: Reclaiming the Study of Literature*. New York: New York University Press, 1996.

Hattaway, Michael. 'Christopher Marlowe: Ideology and Subversion.' In Grantley and Roberts, 198–223.

– *Elizabethan Popular Theatre: Plays in Performance*. London: Routledge and Kegan Paul, 1982.

Healy, Thomas. *Christopher Marlowe*. Writers and Their Work. Plymouth: Northcote House, 1994.

Heaney, Seamus. *The Redress of Poetry: Oxford Lectures*. London: Faber and Faber, 1995.

Henderson, Diana E. *Passion Made Public: Elizabethan Lyric, Gender, and Performance*. Urbana: University of Illinois Press, 1995.

Henryson, Robert. *The Poems of Robert Henryson*. Ed. Denton Fox. Oxford: Clarendon, 1981.

Henslowe, Philip. *Henslowe's Diary*. Ed. R.A. Foakes and R.T. Rickert. Cambridge: Cambridge University Press, 1961.

Herbert, George. *The English Poems of George Herbert*. Ed. C.A. Patrides. London: Dent, 1974.

Heywood, Ellis. *'Il Moro': Ellis Heywood's Dialogue in Memory of Thomas More*. Trans. Roger Lee Deakins. Cambridge: Harvard University Press, 1972.

Himmelfarb, Martha. *Tours of Hell: An Apocalyptic Form in Jewish and Christian Literature*. Philadelphia: University of Pennsylvania Press, 1983.

Hobson, Harold. 'All This and Helen, Too.' In *Jump*, 222–4.

Hodge, Bob. 'Marlowe, Marx, and Machiavelli: Reading into the Past.' In *Literature, Language and Society in England 1580–1680*. Ed. David Aers et al. Dublin: Gill and Macmillan, 1981, 1–22.

Holinshed, Raphael. *Holinshed's Chronicles of England, Scotland, and Ireland*. 6 vols. 1807; rpt. New York: AMS Press, 1965.

Holland, Norman N. Introduction. In *Henry IV, Part Two*. Signet Shakespeare. New York: New American Library, 1965.

Homer. *Chapman's Homer*. 2 vols. Ed. Allardyce Nicoll. Princeton: Princeton University Press, 1956.

Honigmann, E.A.J. 'Ten Problems in *Dr. Faustus*.' In *The Arts of Performance in Elizabethan and Early Stuart Drama*. Ed. Murray Biggs et al. Edinburgh: Edinburgh University Press, 1991, 173–91.

Hotine, Margaret. 'The Politics of Anti-Semitism: *The Jew of Malta* and *The Merchant of Venice*.' *Notes and Queries* 38 (1991), 35–8.

Houseman, John. 'Memoir of the Federal Theatre Project Production, 1937.' In *Stages of Drama*. Ed. Carl H. Klaus et al. 3rd ed. New York: St Martin's, 1995, 198–9.

Howell, Thomas. *Howell's Devises*. 1581; rpt. Oxford: Clarendon, 1906.

Hughes, Robert. *Heaven and Hell in Western Art*. London: Weidenfeld and Nicolson, 1968.

Hulse, Clarke. *Metamorphic Verse: The Elizabethan Minor Epic*. Princeton: Princeton University Press, 1981.

Hunter, G.K. *Dramatic Identities and Cultural Tradition*. Liverpool: Liverpool University Press, 1978.

– *John Lyly: The Humanist as Courtier*. London: Routledge and Kegan Paul, 1962.

Hunter, Robert G. *Shakespeare and the Mystery of God's Judgements.* Athens: University of Georgia Press, 1976.

Hussey, Maurice. *The World of Shakespeare and His Contemporaries.* New York: Viking, 1977.

Hylén, Johan Emil. *De Tantalo.* Uppsala: Almquist and Wiksell, 1896.

Ingram, R.W. '"Pride in Learning Goeth Before a Fall": Dr. Faustus' Opening Soliloquy.' *Mosaic* 13 (1979), 73–80.

Jacobsen, Eric. *Translation: A Traditional Craft: An Introductory Sketch with a Study of Marlowe's 'Elegies.'* Copenhagen: Gyldendalske Boghandel-Nordisk Forlag, 1958.

Jardine, Lisa. 'Alien Intelligence: Mercantile Exchange and Knowledge Transactions in Marlowe's *The Jew of Malta.'* In her *Reading Shakespeare Historically.* London: Routledge, 1996, 98–113.

Jones, Robert C. *Engagement with Knavery: Point of View in 'Richard III,' 'The Jew of Malta,' 'Volpone,' and 'The Revenger's Tragedy.'* Durham: Duke University Press, 1986.

Jump, John, ed. *Marlowe's 'Doctor Faustus': A Casebook.* London: Macmillan, 1969.

Kastan, David Scott, and Peter Stallybrass, eds. *Staging the Renaissance: Reinterpretations of Elizabethan and Jacobean Drama.* New York: Routledge, 1991.

Kaufman, Peter Iver. *Prayer, Despair, and Drama: Elizabethan Introspection.* Urbana: University of Illinois Press, 1996.

Keach, William. *Elizabethan Erotic Narratives.* New Brunswick, NJ: Rutgers University Press, 1977.

Kelsall, Malcolm. *Christopher Marlowe.* Leiden: E.J. Brill, 1981.

Kernan, Alvin, ed. *Two Renaissance Mythmakers: Christopher Marlowe and Ben Johnson.* Selected Papers from the English Institute, 1975–6. Baltimore: Johns Hopkins University Press, 1977.

Kerrigan, William, and Gordon Braden. 'Milton's Coy Eve: *Paradise Lost* and Renaissance Love Poetry.' *English Literary History* 53 (1986), 27–51.

Kinney, Arthur F. *Markets of Bawdrie: The Dramatic Criticism of Stephen Gosson.* Salzburg: Institut für Englische Sprache und Literatur, 1974.

Knoll, Robert E. *Christopher Marlowe.* New York: Twayne, 1969.

Kocher, Paul. *Christopher Marlowe.* Chapel Hill: University of North Carolina Press, 1946.

– 'Nashe's Authorship of the Prose Scenes in *Faustus.'* *Modern Language Quarterly* 3 (1942), 17–40.

Kott, Jan. *The Bottom Translation: Marlowe and Shakespeare and the Carnival Tradition.* Trans. Daniela Miedzyrzecka and Lillian Vallee. Evanston: Northwestern University Press, 1987.

Kuriyama, Constance Brown. *Hammer or Anvil: Psychological Patterns in Christopher Marlowe's Plays*. New Brunswick, NJ: Rutgers University Press, 1980.

Kyd, Thomas. *The Spanish Tragedy*. In *Drama of the English Renaissance*. Ed. Russell A. Fraser and Norman Rabkin. 2 vols. New York: Macmillan, 1976.

La Primaudaye, Pierre de. *The French Academie*. Trans. T[homas] B[owes]. London, 1586.

The Lamentable Tragedy of Locrine: A Critical Edition. Ed. Jane Lytton Gooch. New York: Garland, 1981.

Lee, Sidney, ed. *Elizabethan Sonnets*. 2 vols. 1904; rpt. New York: Cooper Square, 1964.

Leech, Clifford. *Christopher Marlowe: Poet for the Stage*. Ed. Anne Lancashire. New York: AMS Press, 1986.

– 'Marlowe's *Edward II*: Power and Suffering.' *Critical Quarterly* 1 (1959), 181–96.

– 'Marlowe's Humor.' In *Marlowe: A Collection of Critical Essays*. Ed. Clifford Leech. Englewood Cliffs, NJ: Prentice-Hall, 1964, 167–78.

Leggatt, Alexander. 'The Critical Fortunes of Christopher Marlowe.' *Queen's Quarterly* 88 (1981), 93–9.

– 'Tamburlaine's Sufferings.' *Yearbook of English Studies* 3 (1973), 28–38.

Leslie, Nancy T. '*Tamburlaine* in the Theatre: Tartar, Grand Guignol, or Janus.' *Renaissance Drama* 4 (1971), 105–20.

Levin, Harry. *The Overreacher: A Study of Christopher Marlowe*. Cambridge, Mass.: Harvard University Press, 1952.

Levin, Richard. 'The Contemporary Perception of Marlowe's Tamburlaine.' *Medieval and Renaissance Drama in England* 1 (1984), 51–70.

– 'The Poetics and Politics of Bardicide.' *PMLA* 105 (1990), 491–504.

Lindley, Arthur. 'The Unbeing of the Overreacher: Proteanism and the Marlovian Hero.' *Modern Language Review* 84 (1989), 1–17.

Lucian. *Selected Satires of Lucian*. Ed. and trans. Lionel Casson. New York: Norton, 1968.

Lyly, John. *Euphues and His England*. Ed. M.W. Croll and Harry Clemons. 1916; rpt. New York: Russell and Russell, 1964.

Lynche, Richard. *The Fountaine of Ancient Fiction*. 1599; rpt. in *The Renaissance and the Gods* 13. New York: Garland, 1976.

– *Diella*. In Lee.

Manley, Lawrence. *Literature and Culture in Early Modern London*. Cambridge: Cambridge University Press, 1995.

Marcus, Leah S. 'Textual Indeterminacy and Ideological Difference: The Case of *Doctor Faustus*.' *Renaissance Drama* 20 (1989), 1–29.

Marlowe, Christopher. *The Complete Plays of Christopher Marlowe.* Ed. Irving Ribner. New York: Odyssey, 1963.

– *The Complete Poems and Translations.* Ed. Stephen Orgel. Harmondsworth: Penguin, 1971.

– *The Complete Works.* Ed. Fredson Bowers. 2 vols. Cambridge: Cambridge University Press, 1973.

– *The Complete Works of Christopher Marlowe.* Ed. Roma Gill. 4 vols. to date. Oxford: Clarendon, 1987– .

– *'Dido Queen of Carthage' and 'The Massacre at Paris.'* Ed. H.J. Oliver. Revels Plays. London: Methuen, 1968.

– *'Doctor Faustus': A- and B-Texts (1604, 1616).* Ed. David Bevington and Eric Rasmussen. Revels Plays. Manchester: Manchester University Press, 1993.

– *'Doctor Faustus': A 1604–Version Edition.* Ed. Michael Keefer. Peterborough, Ont.: Broadview, 1991.

– *Doctor Faustus.* Vol. 2 of *The Complete Works of Christopher Marlowe.* Ed. Roma Gill. Oxford: Clarendon, 1990.

– *'Doctor Faustus' 1604–1616.* Ed. W.W. Greg. Oxford: Clarendon, 1950.

– *'Doctor Faustus' and Other Plays.* Ed. David Bevington and Eric Rasmussen. World's Classics. Oxford: Oxford University Press, 1995.

– *Edward II.* Ed. William Dinsmore Briggs. London: David Nutt, 1914.

– *Edward II.* Ed. H.B. Charlton and R.B. Waller. London: Methuen, 1930.

– *Edward the Second.* Revels Plays. Ed. Charles R. Forker. Manchester: Manchester University Press, 1994.

– *Edward II.* Ed. W. Moelwyn Merchant. New Mermaid Plays. London: Ernest Benn, 1967.

– *The Jew of Malta.* Ed. N.W. Bawcutt. Revels Plays. Manchester: Manchester University Press, 1978.

– *The Jew of Malta.* Ed. H.S. Bennett. London: Methuen, 1931.

– *The Jew of Malta.* Ed. James R. Siemon. New Mermaid ed. 2nd ed, New York: Norton, 1994.

– *The Plays of Christopher Marlowe.* Ed. Leo Kirschbaum. Cleveland: Meridian, 1966.

– *The Poems.* Ed. Millar Maclure. Revels Plays. London: Methuen, 1968.

– *Tamburlaine the Great.* Ed. J.S. Cunningham. Revels Plays. Manchester: Manchester University Press, 1981.

– *Tamburlaine the Great.* Ed. U.M. Ellis-Fermor. London: Methuen, 1930.

– *Tamburlaine the Great.* Ed. Tatiana Wolff. London: Methuen, 1964.

– *'Tamburlaine the Great': An Acting Version by Tyrone Guthrie and Donald Wolfit.* Heinemann: London, 1951.

- *The Translations*. Vol. 1 of *The Complete Works of Christopher Marlowe*. Ed. Roma Gill. Oxford: Clarendon, 1987.
- *The Works of Christopher Marlowe*. Ed. C.F. Tucker Brooke. Clarendon: Oxford University Press, 1910.
- *The Works of Christopher Marlowe*. Ed. A.H. Bullen. 3 vols. London: J.C. Nimmo, 1885.
Martin, Richard A. 'Fate, Seneca, and Marlowe's *Dido, Queen of Carthage*.' *Renaissance Drama* 11 (1980), 45–66.
Masten, Jeffrey. 'Playwrighting: Authorship and Collaboration.' In *A New History of Early English Drama*. Ed. John D. Cox and David Scott Kastan. New York: Columbia University Press, 1997, 357–82.
Maus, Katharine Eisaman. *Inwardness and Theatre in the English Renaissance*. Chicago: University of Chicago Press, 1995.
McCloskey, Susan. 'The Worlds of *Edward II*.' *Renaissance Drama* 16 (1985), 35–48.
McElroy, John F. 'Repetition, Contrariety, and Individualization in *Edward II*.' *Studies in English Literature* 24 (1984), 205–24.
Meyer, Edward. *Machiavelli and the Elizabethan Drama*. 1897; rpt. New York: Burt Franklin, n.d.
Miller, David Lee. 'The Death of the Modern: Gender and Desire in Marlowe's *Hero and Leander*.' *South Atlantic Quarterly* 88 (1989), 757–87.
Minshull, Catherine. 'Marlowe's "Sound Machevill."' *Renaissance Drama* 13 (1982), 35–53.
Montaigne, Michel de. *Montaigne's Essays*. Trans. John Florio. 3 vols. London: Dent, 1965.
Montrose, Louis A. 'Spenser's Domestic Domain: Poetry, Property, and the Early Modern Subject.' In *Subject and Object in Renaissance Culture*. Ed. Margreta de Grazia et al. Cambridge: Cambridge University Press, 1996, 83–130.
Morgan, Gerald. 'Harlequin Faustus: Marlowe's Comedy of Hell.' *Humanities Association Bulletin* 18 (1967), 22–34.
Morris, Brian, ed. *Christopher Marlowe: Mermaid Critical Commentaries*. London: Ernest Benn, 1968.
- 'Comic Method in Marlowe's *Hero and Leander*.' In ibid., 113–32.
Moss, Ann. *Ovid in Renaissance France: A Survey of the Latin Editions of Ovid and Commentaries Printed in France before 1600*. Warburg Institute Surveys 8. London: Warburg, 1962.
Motto, Anna Lydia, and John R. Clark. *Senecan Tragedy*. Amsterdam: Adolf M. Hakkert, 1988.
Mulryne, J.R., and Frank Fender. 'Marlowe and the "Comic Distance."' In Morris, 49–64.

Murgatroyd, P. '*Militia amoris* and the Roman Elegists.' *Latomus* 34 (1975), 59–79.

Musaeus. *Hero and Leander*. Trans. George Chapman. In Donno, 70–84.

Nagy, Gregory. *Pindar's Homer*. Baltimore: Johns Hopkins University Press, 1990.

Nashe, Thomas. *The Works of Thomas Nashe*. Ed. Ronald B. McKerrow. 5 vols. Corrected ed. Oxford: Blackwell, 1966.

Nelson, John Charles. *The Renaissance Theory of Love*. New York: Columbia University Press, 1955.

Nicholl, Charles. *A Cup of News: The Life of Thomas Nashe*. London: Routledge and Kegan Paul, 1984.

– *The Reckoning: The Murder of Christopher Marlowe*. Chicago: University of Chicago Press, 1992.

Orgel, Stephen. *Impersonations: The Performance of Gender in Shakespeare's England*. Cambridge: Cambridge University Press, 1996.

– 'What Is a Text?' In Kastan and Stallybrass, 83–7.

Ornstein, Robert. 'The Comic Synthesis in *Doctor Faustus*.' *English Literary History* 22 (1955), 165–72.

Ovid. *Amores, Book I*. Trans. and ed. John Barsby. Oxford: Clarendon, 1973.

– *Amores II*. Trans. and ed. Joan Booth. Warminster: Aris and Phillips, 1991.

– *The Erotic Poems*. Trans. and ed. Peter Green. Harmondsworth: Penguin, 1982.

– '*Heroides*' and '*Amores*.' Trans. Grant Showerman. Loeb Classical Library, 1914; 2nd ed., rev. G.P. Goold. Cambridge, Mass.: Harvard University Press, 1977.

– *The Love Poems*. Trans. A.D. Melville, intro. E.J. Kenney. Oxford: Oxford University Press, 1990.

– *Metamorphoses*. Trans. Frank Justus Miller. 2 vols. Loeb Classical Library, 1916; 2nd ed., rev. G.P. Goold. Cambridge, Mass.: Harvard University Press, 1984.

– *Shakespeare's Ovid: Arthur Golding's Translation of 'The Metamorphoses.'* Ed. W.H.D. Rouse. New York: Norton, 1966.

Parr, Johnstone. *Tamburlaine's Malady and Other Essays on Astrology in Elizabethan Drama*. Auburn: University of Alabama Press, 1953.

Patrides, C.A. *Premises and Motifs in Renaissance Thought and Literature*. Princeton: Princeton University Press, 1982.

Patterson, Lee. *Negotiating the Past: The Historical Understanding of Medieval Literature*. Madison: University of Wisconsin Press, 1987.

Pavel, Thomas. *The Poetics of Plot: The Case of English Renaissance Drama*. Minneapolis: University of Minnesota Press, 1985.

Pearcy, Lee T. 'Marlowe's Translation of Ovid, *Amores*, III. 6, 51.' *Notes and Queries* 25 (1978), 435–6.

Pechter, Edward. 'On the Blinding of Gloucester.' *English Literary History* 45 (1978), 181–200.

Peele, George. *The Dramatic Works of George Peele.* Ed. Frank S. Hook. New Haven: Yale University Press, 1961.

– *The Life and Minor Works of George Peele.* Ed. David H. Horne. New Haven: Yale University Press, 1952.

Petowe, Henry. *The Second Part of Hero and Leander, Containing their Further Fortunes.* In Christopher Marlowe, *The Complete Poems and Translations.* Ed. Stephen Orgel. Harmondsworth: Penguin, 1971, 90–110.

Pettegree, Andrew. *Foreign Protestant Communities in Sixteenth-Century London.* Oxford: Clarendon, 1986.

Pettitt, Thomas. 'Formulaic Dramaturgy in *Doctor Faustus.*' In Friedenreich et al., 167–91.

Pigler, Andor. *Barockthemen.* 2 vols. Rev. ed. Budapest: Akadémiai Kiadó, 1974.

Poirier, Michel. *Christopher Marlowe.* London: Chatto and Windus, 1951.

Prescott, Anne Lake. 'Tantalus.' In *The Spenser Encyclopedia.* Ed. A.C. Hamilton et al. Toronto: University of Toronto Press, 1990, 676–7.

Proser, Matthew N. '*Dido Queene of Carthage* and the Evolution of Marlowe's Dramatic Style.' In Friedenreich et al., 83–99.

– *The Gift of Fire: Aggression and the Plays of Christopher Marlowe.* Renaissance and Baroque Studies and Texts 12. New York: Peter Lang, 1995.

Raab, Felix. *The English Face of Machiavelli.* Toronto: University of Toronto Press, 1964.

Raleigh, Walter. *The Poems of Sir Walter Ralegh.* Ed. Agnes M.C. Latham. London: Routledge and Kegan Paul, 1951.

– *The Works of Sir Walter Raleigh.* Ed. William Oldys and Thomas Birch. 8 vols. 1829; rpt. New York: Burt Franklin, 1960.

Rasmussen, Eric. *A Textual Companion to 'Doctor Faustus.'* Manchester: Manchester University Press, 1993.

Reid, Jane Davidson. *Oxford Guide to Classical Mythology in the Arts.* Oxford: Oxford University Press, 1993.

Rhodes, Neil. *The Power of Eloquence and English Renaissance Literature.* New York: Harvester Wheatsheaf, 1992.

Ricks, Christopher. '*Doctor Faustus* and Hell on Earth.' In his *Essays in Appreciation.* Oxford: Clarendon, 1996, 1–18.

Robertson, Toby (interview with J.R. Brown). 'Directing *Edward II.*' *Tulane Drama Review* 8 (1964), 174–83.

Rollins, Hyder Edward, ed. *Tottel's Miscellany.* 2 vols. Rev. ed. Cambridge, Mass.: Harvard University Press, 1966.

Rose, Mary Beth. *The Expense of Spirit: Love and Sexuality in Renaissance Drama.* Ithaca: Cornell University Press, 1988.

Royston, Pamela L. 'Hero and Leander and the Eavesdropping Reader.' *John Donne Journal* 2 (1983), 31–53.

Rozett, Martha Tuck. *The Doctrine of Election and the Emergence of Elizabethan Tragedy.* Princeton: Princeton University Press, 1984.

Rudd, Niall. 'Daedalus and Icarus (ii): From the Renaissance to the Present Day.' In *Ovid Renewed.* Ed. Charles Martindale. Cambridge: Cambridge University Press, 1988, 37–53.

– 'Dido's *Culpa.*' In *Oxford Readings in Vergil's 'Aeneid.'* Ed. S.J. Harrison. Oxford: Oxford University Press, 1990.

Rusche, H.G. 'Two Proverbial Images in Whitney's *A Choice of Emblemes* and Marlowe's *The Jew of Malta.*' *Notes and Queries* 209 (1964), 261.

Sales, Roger. *Christopher Marlowe.* New York: St Martin's, 1991.

Sanders, Wilbur. *The Dramatist and the Received Idea.* Cambridge: Cambridge University Press, 1968.

Sasaki, Shoji. '"If Words Will Not Serve": Marlowe's Provocative History Play.' *Shakespeare Studies* (Tokyo) 19 (1980–1), 25–53.

Schwartz, Regina M. *Remembering and Repeating: Biblical Creation in 'Paradise Lost.'* Cambridge: Cambridge University Press, 1988.

Segal, Erich. 'Marlowe's *Schadenfreude*: Barabas as Comic Hero.' In *Veins of Humor.* Ed. Harry Levin. Harvard English Studies 3. Cambridge, Mass.: Harvard University Press, 1972, 69–92.

– 'Hero and Leander: Góngora and Marlowe.' *Comparative Literature* 15 (1963), 338–56.

Seneca. *Four Tragedies and 'Octavia.'* Trans. E.F. Watling. Harmondsworth: Penguin, 1966.

– *Thyestes.* Ed. R.J. Tarrant. American Philological Association Textbook Series 11. Atlanta: Scholars Press, 1985.

Shakespeare, William. *The Riverside Shakespeare.* Ed. G. Blakemore Evans. Boston: Houghton Mifflin, 1974.

– *2 Henry IV.* Intro. Norman N. Holland. Signet Edition. New York: New American Library, 1965.

Shapiro, James. *Rival Playwrights: Marlowe, Jonson, Shakespeare.* New York: Columbia University Press, 1991.

– *Shakespeare and the Jews.* New York: Columbia University Press, 1996.

Shapiro, Michael. *Children of the Revels: The Boy Companies of Shakespeare's Time and Their Plays.* New York: Columbia University Press, 1977.

Sheidley, William B. 'The Seduction of the Reader in Marlowe's *Hero and Leander.*' *Concerning Poetry* 3 (1970), 50–6.

Shepard, Alan Clarke. 'Marlowe's Anatomy of Desire.' Diss., University of Virginia, 1990.

Shepherd, Simon. *Marlowe and the Politics of Elizabethan Theatre*. Brighton: Harvester, 1986.

Sheppeard, Sallye. 'Icarus and the Old Man: The Mythic Center of Marlowe's *Doctor Faustus*.' *Conference of College Teachers of English Studies* 57 (1992), 57–63.

Shoham, S. Giora. *Haikhe Tantalus* [*The Tantalus Ratio: A Scaffolding for an Ontological Personality Theory*]. Tel Aviv: Gommeh, 1977.

Shuger, Debora. 'Excerpts from a Panel Discussion.' In *Renaissance Discourses of Desire*. Ed. Claude J. Summers and Ted-Larry Pebworth. Columbia: University of Missouri Press, 1993, 269–76.

Sidney, Philip. *An Apology for Poetry*. Ed. Geoffrey Shepherd. Manchester: Manchester University Press, 1973.

Sinfield, Alan. *Faultlines*. Oxford: Clarendon, 1992.

Skura, Meredith. 'Is There a Shakespeare after the *New* New Bibliography?' In *Elizabethan Theatre: Essays in Honor of S. Schoenbaum*. Ed. R.B. Parker and S.P. Zitner. Newark: University of Delaware Press, 1996, 169–83.

Smith, Hallett. *Elizabethan Poetry*. Cambridge, Mass.: Harvard University Press, 1964.

Smith, James L. 'The Jew of Malta in the Theatre.' In Morris, 3–23.

Smith, Mary E. *Love Kindling Fire: A Study of Christopher Marlowe's 'Tragedy of Dido Queen of Carthage.'* Salzburg: Institut für Englische Sprache und Literatur, 1977.

Smith, William. *Chloris*. In Lee.

Snow, Edward A. 'Marlowe's *Doctor Faustus* and the Ends of Desire.' In Kernan, 70–110.

Sourvinou-Inwood, Christiane. 'Crime and Punishment: Tityos, Tantalos and Sisyphos in *Odyssey* 11.' *Bulletin of the Institute of Classical Studies* 37 (1986), 36–58.

Speaight, Robert. *William Poel and the Elizabethan Revival*. London: William Heinemann, 1954.

Spenser, Edmund. *The Faerie Queene*. Ed. A.C. Hamilton. London: Longman, 1977.

– *The Yale Edition of the Shorter Poems of Edmund Spenser*. Ed. William A. Oram et al. New Haven: Yale University Press, 1989.

Stapleton, M.L. *Harmful Eloquence: Ovid's 'Amores' from Antiquity to Shakespeare*. Ann Arbor: University of Michigan Press, 1996.

Steadman, John M. 'Tantalus and the Dead Sea Apples (*Paradise Lost*, X, 547–73).' *Journal of English and Germanic Philology* 64 (1965), 35–40.

Steane, J.B. *Christopher Marlowe: A Critical Study*. Cambridge: Cambridge
University Press, 1968.

Stein, Wilhelm. *Holbein*. Berlin: Julius Bond, 1929.

Stock, Lorraine Kochanske. 'Medieval *Gula* in Marlowe's *Doctor Faustus*.'
Bulletin of Research in the Humanities 85 (1982), 372–85.

Strauss, Walter L., ed. *Hendrik Goltzius: The Complete Engravings and Woodcuts*. 2
vols. New York: Abaris, 1977.

Stroup, Thomas B. 'Ritual in Marlowe's Plays.' In *Drama in the Renaissance*. Ed.
Clifford Davidson et al. New York: AMS Press, 1986, 21–44.

Summers, Claude J. *Christopher Marlowe and the Politics of Power*. Salzburg:
Institut für Englische Sprache und Literatur, 1974.

– 'Sex, Politics, and Self-Realization in *Edward II*.' In Friedenreich et al., 221–40.

Summers, Claude J., and Ted-Larry Pebworth, eds. *Renaissance Discourses of
Desire*. Columbia: University of Missouri Press, 1993.

Sunesen, Bent. 'Marlowe and the Dumb Show.' *English Studies* 35 (1954),
241–53.

Symonds, John Addington. *Shakespere's Predecessors in the English Drama*.
London: Smith Elder, 1884.

Tanselle, G. Thomas. 'Textual Instability and Editorial Idealism.' *Studies in
Bibliography* 49 (1996), 1–60.

Thomas, Elizabeth. 'Variations on a Military Theme in Ovid's *Amores*.' *Greece
and Rome* n.s. 11 (1964), 151–65.

Thomson, Peter. *Shakespeare's Professional Career*. Cambridge: Cambridge
University Press, 1992.

The Three Parnassus Plays. Ed. J.B. Leishman. London: Nicholson and Watson,
1949.

Thurn, David H. 'Sights of Power in *Tamburlaine*.' *English Literary Renaissance* 19
(1989), 3–21.

Tofte, Robert. *Laura*. In Lee.

The Tragical Reign of Selimus. 1594. Malone Society Reprints. Oxford, 1908.

Turberville, George. *Epitaphes, Epigrams, Songs and Sonets*. 1567; rpt. Delmar, NY:
Scholar's Facsimiles, 1977.

Turner, Alice K. *The History of Hell*. New York: Harcourt Brace, 1993.

Tydeman, William. '*Doctor Faustus*.' Text and Performance. London: Macmillan,
1984.

Tyler, Sharon. 'Bedfellows Make Strange Politics: Christopher Marlowe's
Edward II.' In *Drama, Sex, and Politics*. Ed. James Redmond. Cambridge:
Cambridge University Press, 1985, 55–68.

Urry, William. *Christopher Marlowe and Canterbury*. Ed. Andrew Butcher.
London: Faber, 1988.

von Klarwill, Victor. *Queen Elizabeth and Some Foreigners*. Trans. T.H. Nash. New York: Brentano's, 1928.

von Koppenfels, Werner. 'Dis-covering the Female Body: Erotic Exploration in Elizabethan Poetry.' *Shakespeare Survey* 47 (1994), 127–37.

Wager, W. *'The Longer Thou Livest' and 'Enough Is as Good as a Feast.'* Ed. R. Mark Benbow. Regents Plays. Lincoln: University of Nebraska Press, 1967.

Waith, Eugene M. *'Edward II*: The Shadow of Action.' *Tulane Drama Review* 8 (1964), 59–76.

– *The Herculean Hero*. New York: Columbia University Press, 1962.

– *Ideas of Greatness: Heroic Drama in England*. New York: Barnes and Noble, 1971.

Walter, John, and Keith Wrightson. 'Dearth and Social Order in Early Modern England.' *Past and Present* 71 (1976), 22–42.

Warren, Michael. *'Doctor Faustus*: The Old Man and the Text.' *English Literary Renaissance* 11 (1981), 111–47.

Watson, Thomas. *The Hekatompathia, or Passionate Centurie of Love*. 1582. Ed. S.K. Heninger, Jr. Gainesville: Scholar's Facsimiles, 1964.

Watt, Ian. *Myths of Modern Individualism*. Cambridge: Cambridge University Press, 1996.

Webster, John. *The Duchess of Malfi*. In *Drama of the English Renaissance*. Ed. Russell A. Fraser and Norman Rabkin. 2 vols. New York: Macmillan, 1976.

Weever, John. *Faunus and Melliflora*. In Donno, 253–80.

Weil, Judith. *Christopher Marlowe: Merlin's Prophet*. Cambridge: Cambridge University Press, 1977.

Wernham, R.B. 'Christopher Marlowe at Flushing in 1592.' *English Historical Review* 91 (1976), 344–5.

Whitlock, Baird. *John Hoskyns, serjeant-at-law*. Washington, DC: University Press of America, 1982.

Whitney, Geffrey. *A Choice of Emblemes*. Ed. John Manning. Facsimile of the 1586 edition. Menston: Scolar, 1989.

Williams, Carolyn. '"This Effeminate Brat": Tamburlaine's Unmanly Son.' *Medieval and Renaissance Drama in England* 9, ed. John Pitcher (1997), 56–80.

Williams, Gordon. *A Dictionary of Sexual Language and Imagery in Shakespeare and Stuart Literature*. 3 vols. London: Athlone, 1994.

Wilson, F.P. *Marlowe and the Early Shakespeare*. Oxford: Clarendon, 1953.

Wilson, Richard. 'Visible Bullets: *Tamburlaine the Great* and Ivan the Terrible.' In Grantley and Roberts, 51–69.

Wilson, Robert. *Three Ladies of London* (1584) and *Three Lords and Ladies of London* (1590). Ed. H.S.D. Mithal. New York: Garland, 1988.

Wilson, Thomas. *The Art of Rhetoric*. 1560. Ed. Peter E. Medine. University Park: Pennsylvania State University Press, 1994.

Wind, Edgar. *Pagan Mysteries in the Renaissance*. Rev. ed.; New York: Norton, 1968.

Wraight, A.D. *Christopher Marlowe and Edward Alleyn*. Chichester: Adam Hart, 1993.

Zucker, David Hard. *Stage and Image in the Plays of Christopher Marlowe*. Salzburg: Institut für Englische Sprache und Literatur, 1972.

Index